Manual of Travel Agency Practice

338.4

Dedicated to the memory of
George Syratt, Sylvia, Daisy and Frederick Plumley

Manual of Travel Agency Practice

Third edition

Gwenda Syratt FInstTT, FInstCM
with
Jane Archer

ELSEVIER
BUTTERWORTH
HEINEMANN

AMSTERDAM BOSTON HEIDELBERG LONDON NEW YORK OXFORD
PARIS SAN DIEGO SAN FRANCISCO SINGAPORE SYDNEY TOKYO

Elsevier Butterworth-Heinemann
Linacre House, Jordan Hill, Oxford OX2 8DP
200 Wheeler Road, Burlington MA 01803

First published 1992
Reprinted 1993
Second edition 1995
Reprinted 1996, 1997, 1998, 1999, 2000
Third edition 2003
Reprinted 2004

British Library Cataloguing in Publication Data
A catalogue record for this book is available from the British Library

Library of Congress Cataloguing in Publication Data
A catalogue record for this book is available from the Library of Congress

ISBN 0 7506 5689 1

For information on all Butterworth-Heinemann publications
visit our website at www.bh.com

Composition by Genesis Typesetting Limited, Rochester, Kent
Printed and bound in Great Britain

CONTENTS

Foreword

The growth of the Internet has had a huge impact on travel, with more businesses driving sales direct to consumers via the web and airlines reducing distribution costs by cutting commission to travel agents.

Ironically, though, there's never been a better time to be a travel retailer. Notwithstanding terrorist attacks, international upheaval and health scares, research proves people now see an annual holiday as a necessity, not a luxury. And the growth of the no-frills carriers has meant more people are taking more overseas trips more often.

There's no doubt the drive by airlines and tour operators to cut costs makes it an extremely challenging environment for the trade, but the best staff in the best agencies will continue to thrive.

Many high street retailers now charge service fees on air ticket sales where the airline does not pay commission, and this trend looks set to continue. But only those travel agents providing quality service will be able to persuade customers to pay a fee rather than go to an Internet café and do it themselves.

With its comprehensive guide to selling everything from coaching and cruising to car rental and air tickets, this book tells you how to stay ahead of the pack.

Martin Lane
Editor
Travel Weekly

Preface

Why are you looking at this book? Are you interested in working in the travel and tourism industry and would you like to know more about it? This book has a wide range of topics and levels of knowledge and will give you a good insight into the background of the industry and the services provided by travel agencies. If you have decided you would like to have a career within the industry and are about to choose a travel and tourism course to study, my advice is to select an internationally recognised qualification with external examinations. If studying at college, opt for one that has been officially recognised by the examining board. Some colleges produce an impressive prospectus but do not offer an internationally acceptable qualification and write the examination papers themselves. These courses can be very expensive but sadly the qualification means very little within the industry. The following addresses will help you to make the right choice, as they provide information on recognised qualifications available and where to study them.

IATA/UFTAA INTERNATIONAL TRAVEL AND TOURISM TRAINING
PROGRAMME
(See Chapter 8 for details)

Ttento (Travel, Tourism Services & Events National Training Organisation)
Suite 5, Claremont House
12–14 Claremont Road
West Byfleet
Surrey KT14 6DY
Tel: 01932 345835

The Travel Training Company
The Cornerstone
The Broadway
Woking
Surrey GU21 5AR
Tel: 01483 727321 email: ttctraining@ttctraining.co.uk

The City & Guilds of London Institute (City & Guilds)
1 Giltspur Street
London
EC1A 9DD
Tel: 020 7294 2850 Fax: 020 7294 2400

The Association of British Travel Agents Ltd
68–71 Newman Street
London W1P 4AH
Tel: 020 7637 2444 email: abta@abta.co.uk

The titles of the qualifications frequently change and the syllabus will be slightly modified, but generally they will follow the topics you need to know in the travel and tourism industry. This book concentrates on travel agency operations and travel destinations, but it also touches on most of the remaining topics from foundation to diploma (management). In particular, we will be delving into:

IATA/UFTAA
City & Guilds
SCOTVEC
VCE's UNIT & ADVANCED
HND/C

If you have completed a course and are now working within the industry you will find this an invaluable reference book – hopefully you will find it entertaining reading too.

If you are a lecturer in travel and tourism, this book will save you some preparation time. Each chapter has quizzes, case studies, discussion topics and relevant subjects for students to research. I hope this book will provide a new perspective on the travel and tourism industry, while the lesson plans, which I used in practice as a lecturer, might be useful to you.

These accompanying tutor resources can be found online at www.bh.com/ manuals. The area is password protected, so please follow the instructions on the site. In case of technical difficulties, please email j.blackford@elsevier.com.

Technology plays a large part in our industry and help is at hand in Chapters 9 and 10. This manual is designed to help travel personnel on an international level, and examples will be given on a worldwide basis.

I hope you enjoy reading this book and that you will find it useful. If you have chosen a career in the travel and tourism industry, I hope you really enjoy the exciting years to come.

Gwenda Syratt

Acknowledgements

I wish to thank those who helped me in the preparation of this book by supplying material for inclusion, and in particular:

The Association of British Travel Agents (ABTA)
Answers Direct, Essex Libraries
Butlins (Biss Lancaster Euro RSCG)
City & Guilds
Department of Trade and Industry
Europcar UK Ltd
Financial Ombudsman Service
International Air Transport Association (IATA)
Travel Training Company
Travel, Tourism Services & Events (ttento)

Graphics by Clive Benson

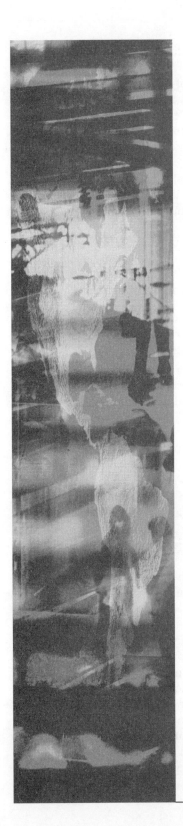

Introduction

If you are interested in being part of the travel and tourism scene you have chosen to be part of an industry with a very long history and a bright, although ever changing, future. Tourism has been defined as the movement of people away from their normal place of residence and if we delve way back into history we will realise people have always travelled.

Merchants travelled to trade with other countries or tribes, Greeks and Romans travelled extensively as their empires increased, and people were travelling for pleasure in 776 BC for the first Olympic Games! Travellers would stay in monasteries but if we move swiftly forward to the seventeenth century when sprung coaches were in use drawn by horses, this brought about the need for inns and many of them can be seen today used as public houses and restaurants, still with the original oak beams and stables. It was necessary to change the team of horses because they were driven at high speed between the inns en route. Later we have the same parallel with railways when the rail companies built small towns around depots where train locomotives were changed, because, like horses, the locomotives were unable to complete a long journey in one go.

Now let's look at just a few dates in our long history of tourism because I'm sure there will be names you will recognise to be going strong even today.

1825   The first railway opened from Stockton to Darlington – steam train.
1830   Liverpool to Manchester opened and brought about the world's first rail fatality. Mr Huskisson was a local member of parliament and was at the opening ceremony (as was the Duke of Wellington). He was run down by a locomotive at Parkside Station and later died of his injuries.
1840   Cunard built the first steamship for leisure cruises.
1841   Thomas Cook opened the first travel agency and organised tours by train.
1855   We have the all-inclusive tour business.
1879   Thomas Cook organised the first package tours to Europe and the USA.
1881   Frames Tours (now Frames Rickard) was founded.
1899   The Savoy and Claridges hotels were opened in London.

By Victorian England, wealthy citizens were travelling to Germany and Switzerland and enjoying ski holidays. At the same time we had developments in sea travel by steamship to the USA, the pioneers being Thomas Cook and Sir Henry Lunn, now Lunn Poly. Around this time American Express, founded partly by Henry Wells and William Fargo, of Wells Fargo fame, initiated money orders and traveller's cheques.

There were radical changes after the First World War (1914–1918) with the development of cars, rail, hotels, holiday centres and longer paid holidays. The Second World War (1939–1945) brought about more radical changes with aircraft and cheap package holidays. Tour operators were formed, private car ownership increased and motorways, motels and ferry services all saw increased growth. Two very good places to learn more is to visit The London Transport Museum at Covent Garden Plaza, WC2 (tel: 020 73796344) and the archives at Thomas Cook, 15 Coningsby Road, Peterborough, PE38 5B (tel: 01733 416800).

When people have more time to spare they begin to look for ways to spend those hours and usually turn to recreation. In the Western world we have second-generation senior citizens, people who retire between the ages of 50 and 60, with some aged between 70 and 90, many of whom are all eager to travel and are a growing area of the market. Recent statistics show that 29 million people travel from Britain each year, spending £15 billion. Worldwide approximately 120 million people are employed in the travel and tourism industry.

Travel and tourism is a fast-growing industry, which ebbs and flows according to circumstance, but which responds well to the changes taking place around the world. So where do you fit into this industry? This book hopes to answer some of your questions about the tourism industry. It explains the different types of agency, and the services provided. It gives background knowledge on the products, technology, skills and finance at various levels. If you are working in the travel industry, I hope this book will help to add to your product knowledge, and if you are still at the 'deciding' stage, I hope it will help to formulate your plans.

The kind of work carried out in a travel agency is enormously varied. It is nearly always satisfying, mainly because you never stop learning – the scene is always changing. A travel agency is just a link in the long chain and through this book you will get an insight into the whole picture of the travel industry.

I wish you a happy (lucrative!), exciting and satisfying career. Good luck!

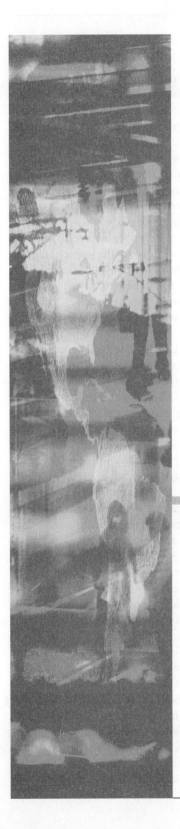

Package and group tours

In this chapter we are going to discuss:

- How package tours began
- Choosing a package tour
- Information found in brochures
- Components of a package tour
- Planning a group tour to include marketing, costing, brochure production and advertising
- Deterrents to tourism
- Association of British Travel Agents (ABTA)
- Air Travel Organiser's Licence (ATOL)
- 'Bare bones' and 'tiered pricing'
- Package tour laws
- Chain of distribution
- Horizontal integration
- Types of travel agency and sales outlets
- Changes in working conditions

Introduction

Although we have a wonderful variety of work to do within the travel agency environment, the bulk of it probably stems from airline reservations and package holidays. There are numerous holiday brochures from which to choose and many offer the same destinations. So how can you help your client to choose the right one for them?

First of all, in the UK there are actually very few independent package tour companies. One company will operate under several different names. There has been much consolidation in the past 2 or 3 years. It should also be said that many travel agencies enjoy the 'overriding commission' system, whereby, for showing loyalty to a big tour operator or their subsidiary, a higher rate of commission will be paid above an agreed total of sales. Tour operators also offer personal incentive gains to travel consultants offering free holidays or gift vouchers to be spent in large, popular department stores. These factors could well influence the travel consultant when helping the client to choose the right package tour! The customer's choice must always come first, and the traveller can also benefit from a closer working relationship between tour operator and travel agent where product knowledge is concerned.

How did package tours begin? As often happens when we dig back into history, there is doubt about who was first. There cannot be any doubt that Thomas Cook made the greatest impact on the travel and tourism industry with the packaging of group tours. In 1841, as secretary of the South Midland Temperance Association, Cook organised an excursion for his members from Leicester to Loughborough at a fare of one shilling return (approximately five pence today). Five hundred and seventy passengers took part in this successful venture and this encouraged him to continue by chartering trains for specific holidays. The business continued to grow, and by 1841 Thomas Cook had opened the first travel agency, and in 1879 organised the first package tours to Europe and the USA.

But it is really in the late 1940s and early 1950s that package tours to warm, sunny places in the Mediterranean, such as Majorca, the Spanish coastline and Italy, began. An excess of aircraft after the Second World War, longer paid holidays, more disposable income and families wanting to holiday together after (often) years of separation all contributed to the increase in package tours.

Vladimir Raitz has been credited with establishing the mass charter air movement to the sun as we know it today. In 1949, he was left £3000 by his grandmother and with this launched Horizon Holidays by organising an inclusive tour to Corsica, using tented accommodation.

At the time of writing, two tourists have travelled into space at a cost of approximately £14 million each. The travel industry has come a long way from the first adventurous overseas holiday to Benidorm in the early 1950s.

Another pioneer – for ski packages – is Erna Low, who died in 2002 aged 92 years. The former Austrian javelin champion was studying in London in 1932 when she placed an advertisement in the *Morning Post* saying 'Viennese undergraduate taking party to Austria, fortnight £15'. The plan was to fund a trip to see her parents but it marked the start of her pioneering contribution to the British travel industry. In 1948, Erna Low offered an all-inclusive fortnight skiing holiday to Murren, Switzerland, and the package ski holiday was born.

Let's think about the different elements that encourage a client to choose one package tour from another.

It is not always price. Certainly prices do vary for exactly the same holiday, and this is mainly due to one tour operator negotiating more favourable competitive rates with the principals (i.e. hoteliers and transport suppliers) than another. The more guests a tour operator is able to guarantee to a hotel week after week, the cheaper the accommodation becomes. Other factors affecting choice may be:

- Reputation of tour operator
- Previous experience of consumer
- Airline used
- Aircraft type
- Flight times
- Airport of departure

Flight times can be particularly important to families with young children not wishing to arrive at their destination late at night or be hanging around a hotel all day waiting to board a late evening departure. Many clients like to be up and away on the flight home, once their last day of the holiday arrives.

Can we trust the information supplied in the brochure? Where conditions of booking are concerned, yes, but descriptions can vary. Do read as many brochures as possible and compare descriptions of the same hotel, and the same resort. Learn to read between the lines. Often more is learnt from what is left unsaid than from what is actually explained in the brochure. 'Lively' can mean 'noisy', 'relaxing' can mean 'miles from anywhere'. Travel agents have a resort gazetteer. This publication will paint a more realistic picture, and this should be consulted if you do not have first-hand experience of the resort.

Do not trust the brochure for days of departure, flight times, etc. as often there are changes. If a tour operator is not selling as many holidays as it would like on a particular departure date it will 'consolidate', meaning cancel that departure and offer the few passengers who have booked (and paid) an alternative holiday that is guaranteed to operate. The tour operator (naturally) does not want to operate the tour at a loss. The clients (naturally) will be very upset by the change of plans. They may be in a situation where the alternative holiday being offered is unsuitable, and a full refund will be unsatisfactory because it will now be too late to book the same holiday elsewhere. This is where your problem-solving skills are required!

Do not rely on the mainstream tour operators alone. There will be many more tour operators offering what you are looking for, and they should be approached before confirming to the client that there is no alternative. This is where good service given by experienced staff can outshine the run-of-the-mill travel consultant.

Millions of people travel on package holidays each year and are very happy to do so because the benefits are enormous. As previously explained, the tour operators benefit by bulk buying and this reduction is passed on to the customer, so there is the financial advantage of travelling on a package tour. Then there is the 'no-hassle' element – everything is arranged for the traveller: flight reservations; transport between airport and hotel on arrival and again on the day of departure; accommodation at a hotel, villa or apartment confirmed; and the services of a representative.

The choice is also very wide. Package tours are available to almost every country, providing a wide range of flight services, days of operation, flight departure and arrival times, choice of type and standard of accommodation, and many other services, such as sightseeing tours, car rental, welcome packs (grocery packs for holidaymakers staying in apartments). A study of numerous tour operators' brochures will help us to appreciate the great choice available.

Components of a package tour

- Transportation – air, sea, road, rail, etc. to/from destination
- Accommodation – hotels, guest houses, lodges, etc.
- Transfers – between air/sea ports and hotel and vice versa at destination
- Sightseeing tours – to include events, trade fairs, etc.
- Insurance – and other ancillary services
- Car rental – for business and leisure purposes

Whilst working at a travel agency you may be involved in organising a group tour. This boosts the travel agent's income when originating a package tour rather than just earning commission from the tour operator. Although the travel agency would earn a larger profit, it has greater responsibilities and a higher risk factor.

Many local clubs and associations enjoy forming a group and having a common interest holiday. Your travel agency may be organising a tour for a local golf, tennis or bowls club, for example.

Planning a group tour

How would we go about organising group travel? The following steps give a very simplistic outline to tour operating:

Step 1 Market research
Step 2 Determine destinations, hotels, capacity, dates, etc.
Step 3 Set up contracts with principals
Step 4 Calculate cost of tour
Step 5 Brochure production
Step 6 Advertising campaign
Step 7 Documentation

If you were working for a tour operator each stage would be in-depth and far more involved. For the purpose of this exercise we will say you are organising a tour to Cyprus for a group of local bowlers.

Step 1: market research

- **Economic research** Study the economy of the country to be visited, exchange rates, etc.
- **Demand research** Study volume of business available for the planned product. Is there a need for your tour? Is demand growing or declining?
- **Consumer study** Age group, interests in addition to bowls, activities required. When do they wish to travel? Standard of accommodation?
- **Competitor research** Investigate what your competitors are offering and charging. Can you offer similar or better?

- **Product research** Study the components, airline, transfers, hotels, sightseeing, baggage allowance (bowls are heavy), dress code. Best time to travel (weather conditions)
- **Sales research** You would need to monitor the number of sales achieved and action any need for change if sales decrease.
- **Distribution research** Establish how this tour will be distributed. A tour operator may sell the tour via a travel agent but in this exercise you are the travel agent and this is a 'one-off' venture.
- **Promotional research** Decide how this tour is going to be advertised. How will you get the information across to the customer?
- **Effectiveness of research methods** Are you obtaining all the intelligence required? Do you need to amend the research methods to meet the ever-changing market?

The term 'marketing mix' is used when describing all the various marketing operations, and the amounts of them that will be, or have been, employed. The term 'communications mix' is used to describe the advertising, sales promotion, public and press relations, personal selling and packaging.

Assignment 2.1

Describe in detail the market research you would conduct for your bowls tour to Cyprus, following the topics discussed.

- Economy of home country
- Economy of host country
- Exchange rates
- Seasons/climate
- Transportation
- Accommodation, number of meals included
- Tours and transfers
- Who would be interested in the tour?
- Life cycle of participants
- Length of tour
- How many clients do you anticipate?
- Cost of operating tour
- Are competitors operating a similar tour?

It is important to keep up to date with current affairs. There are many deterrents to tourism and the situation can change quickly. For example, terrorism attacks, abnormal weather conditions, earth tremors, cyclones, forest fires, increase in crime, lack of law and order, disputes between countries, civil war, unfavourable currency exchange rates may all deter tourists from visiting a country or particular area.

Step 2: Determine destinations, hotels, capacity, dates, etc.

Based on the data you have obtained you would now be in a position to decide the location of the tour, the best time to travel, the standard of accommodation required, how many passengers could be expected. A balance between bowling, sightseeing and leisure days would be established.

Step 3: Set up contracts with principals

Best tariffs would be agreed with the principals and contracts completed. Make sure it is clear which date is the last available date to release any unsold components.

Step 4: Calculate cost of tour

The first example is for a specialist tour where a group air fare is negotiated. The figures are hypothetical.

Flight cost based on net group air fare, per person	£100.00
Net hotel costs per person, 14 nights twin room Cyprus pound 70.00 per room (Cyprus pound 0.85 = UK£1)	£416.50
Transfers £3.00 each way	£6.00
Gratuities, porterage	£2.00
Sight-seeing tours Cyprus pound 17.50 × 4	£59.50
	£584.00
Add 25% mark-up	£146.00
Selling price	£730.00

The mark-up percentage is flexible. Compare the tour with others similar on the market. Alternatively, a marketing strategy may be used where a very limited number of holidays will be sold at a very low price, known as the lead price to attract customers. The basic price can be used for out-of-season departure dates and a higher mark-up used during peak season such as summer, Easter and Christmas holidays.

As the originator of this tour you would expect to earn more than the 10 per cent commission when selling other tour operators' tours. From the mark-up there will be advertising and brochure production expenses and, as we have said, there is the work involved in putting the tour together and a high-risk factor.

Assignment 2.2

Tour calculation

(a) Research an area of your choice in Spain
(b) Using the method described, calculate the tour using euro rate of exchange 1.48 = £1.

Exercise 2.1

Deterrents

During the last three years, where have the following tourism deterrents that have made newspaper headlines taken place?

DETERRENT	COUNTRY
Forest fires	
Cyclones	
Earthquakes	
Civil war	
Dispute between two countries	
Foot and mouth disease	
Increase in street crime	
Floods	
Terrorism attacks	
Industrial action disputes	
Marine accidents	
Aircraft accidents	
Tidal waves	
Riots	
Revolution	
Hijacking	
Dangerous wildlife, e.g. spiders, snakes, jellyfish	

Another method of calculating the cost of an original tour used by tour operators for the mass market is to hire the aircraft. We need to understand two terms used in this method: 'Back to back' and 'empty leg'. Back to back means when an aircraft has passengers to carry to a destination and has passengers to pick up and bring back on the return journey. A mass market tour operator operating tours throughout the summer would be taking holidaymakers out one week and bringing them home one or two weeks later (see Figure 2.1).

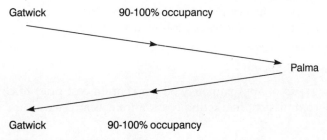

Figure 2.1 Flight Pattern – Back to Back

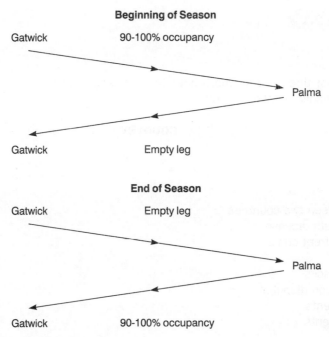

Figure 2.2 Flight pattern – empty leg

'Empty leg' refers to the beginning of the season when perhaps 350 passengers would be taken out to the resort but there are no passengers to bring back (Figure 2.2). At the end of the season, the aircraft would travel out to the destination empty and bring back, say, 350 passengers. Tour operators will sell 'seat only' on a chartered aircraft in order to utilise space and maximise profit.

Flight costs, based on 22 departures (back to back) on 350-seat aircraft. £25 000 per return flight	£550 000.00
Plus one empty leg each way at the beginning and end of the season	£25 000.00
Total flight costs	£575 000.00
Cost per flight	£26 136.00
Cost per seat at 90% occupancy (£26 136 divided by 315 seats)	£82.97
Net hotel costs per person, 14 nights half-board	£350.00
Resort agent's handling fees and transfers per person	£10.00
Gratuities, porterage	£3.00
Total cost per person	£445.97
Add mark-up of approximately 30 per cent on cost price to cover agency commission, marketing costs, administrative costs and profit	£133.79
Selling price	£580.00

Once again, adjustments can be made with a lead price, low, mid and high season, mark-up percentage within the profit margin.

Step 5: Brochure production

For the 'one-off' group tour perhaps a simple leaflet will suffice giving details of date, destination, what is included in the price, itinerary, booking conditions, and one or two pictures to attract attention. For the mass market, brochure production will be on a large scale offering a variety of destinations.

Assignment 2.3

Collect six different tour operators' brochures and study the information carefully.

The type of questions your client could ask, or indeed, you should advise them on, are as follows. Bear in mind that all the answers will be found in the brochure.

Price

What does the price include: flights, in-flight meals, half-board, full-board, baggage allowance, airport taxes, hotel service charge and taxes, representatives at airports and resorts, transfers between airport and hotel?

Welcome party

Will anyone be there to explain the procedures to us? When will the representative visit our hotel? What happens if we arrive at the apartment on a day when shops are closed: will a welcome pack of groceries be supplied?

Excursions

Will they be available? How much will they cost? What are the car rental rates? Any special festivities for Christmas and New Year? Can I take a two- centre holiday? Are there holidays catering for guests travelling alone?

Special offers

Are there any great reductions? What is the charge for an infant? What is the reduction for children? Is there a single-room supplement? Will the cost of the holiday be guaranteed not to increase once the deposit has been paid? What is the cancellation charge?

Health and visa requirements

Are vaccinations or visas required?

The only way to answer these questions and many more is to read the brochure thoroughly and be confident of knowing where to find the answer.

Assignment 2.4

Association of British Travel Agents (ABTA)

ABTA
68–71 Newman Street
London W1P 4AH
Tel: 020 7637 2444
Telefax: 020 7637 0713
Email: abta@abta.co.uk

Contact ABTA and obtain an information pack explaining the role of ABTA and a guide for organisers and retailers called 'Looking into the Package Travel Regulations'.

Air Travel Organisers' Licencing (ATOL)

Civil Aviation Authority
ATOL Section
CAA House
45–49 Kingsway
London WC2B 6TE
Tel: 020 7379 7311

Contact the Civil Aviation Authority and obtain an information pack explaining the role ATOL plays in tour operating.

Step 6: Advertising campaign

How might a tour be promoted? Try adding to the list by brainstorming.

- Brochures circulated to tour operators and door-to-door distribution
- Videos
- National newspapers for specialist tours
- Local newspapers
- Magazines
- Restaurants
- Posters on buses, trains and transport terminals
- Clubs and associations
- Radio
- Television (expensive)
- Open evenings at travel office
- Trade fairs and exhibitions
- Internet, teletext

Step 7: Documentation

This will include: tickets, vouchers, itinerary, luggage labels, useful information and so on – placed in a wallet See Figure 2.3.

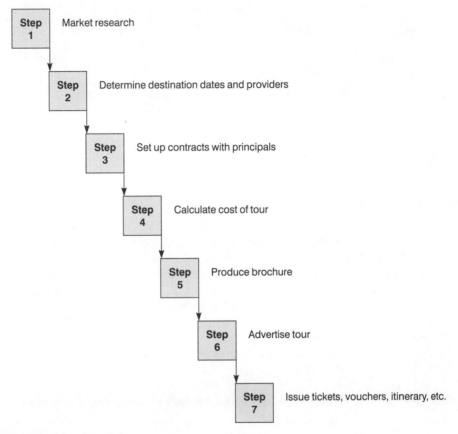

Figure 2.3 Tour operating

Discussion

Are we seeing the end of the package tour? Many tour operators have started to charge a basic price with supplements for services that used to be included in the packaged price. There has always been the opportunity to pay more to upgrade, mainly in connection with accommodation, but now there are further choices. For example:

- New surcharge / services previously included
- Pre-bookable seats to guarantee family and friends sit together
- Pre-bookable window or aisle seat
  Premium seats with wider seats and extra leg room

- Extra leg room next to emergency exit
  Extra baggage allowance
- In-flight meals
- Coach transfer
  Taxi transfer
  Late check-out
- Last minute check-in
  Accommodation options
  Balconies
- Extra airport security
- Ticket on departure (when departure is less than 10 days)

Assignment 2.5

Discounted holiday

Mrs Edmonds saw a bargain holiday to Ibiza advertised in the travel agency window, a week for £129.00 per person. When she tried to book it, she was told that in addition to this she would have to pay £15 per person for transfers, £7 for extra airport security, £10 for in-flight meals, and £10 for ticket on departure because departure was in less than ten days. The total cost for two was therefore £342, and not £258 as expected. Recent newspaper headlines flashed through the travel consultant's mind:

'Travellers tricked by false discounts!'
'Holiday bargains that are too good to be true!'
'Don't count on discounts!'

Research what is happening with discounted holidays and analyse the outcome.

Assignment 2.6

Tour operating law

Using your ABTA and ATOL reference material, research and analyse the following package holiday laws:

1 Misleading the consumer
2 Circumstances in which particulars in the brochure are binding
3 Contents and form of contract
4 Transfer of bookings
5 Bonding
6 Changing prices
7 Overbooking

8 What happens if a tour operator or travel agent goes out of business unexpectedly – will clients be stranded?
9 The role of ATOL
10 Are scheduled fares covered?

It has been said that one reason for prices of exactly the same holiday varying so much is due to negotiating competitive rates with suppliers and volume of business. Another is vertical integration in the chain of distribution (Figure 2.4).

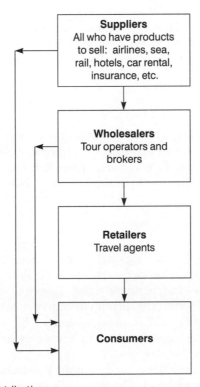

Figure 2.4 The chain of distribution

Airlines, cruise ships, tour operators and travel agents are one company. This gives the company a large slice of the cake, more buying power and control over prices and availability. Horizontal integration means companies on the same level of the chain of distribution that have merged.

TUI UK

As an example of integration, travel agents Lunn Poly, Skydeals, Team Lincoln, Callers Pegasus, Sibbald Travel and Travel House are part of the same company as tour operators Thomson Holidays, Austravel, Club Freestyle, Crystal, Headwater

Holidays, Jetsave, Just, Magic Travel Group, OSL Villas, Portland Direct, Simply Travel, Skytours, Something Special Holidays, Spanish Harbour Holidays, Thomson Ski, Thomson Cities, Thomson Lakes & Mountains, Tropical Places, Thomson Cruises and Budgetholidays.com.

MyTravel

Agents Going Places, Travelworld and Holidayworld belong to the same company as tour operators Airtours, Aspro, Bridge, Cresta, Direct Holidays, Jetset, Escapades, Manos, Panorama, Tradewinds and Airtours Sun Cruises.

Thomas Cook UK

Thomas Cook travel agents are part of the same company as tour operators Thomas Cook, JMC, Club 18–30, Neilson, Style Holidays, Sunset, Time Off and Thomas Cook Tours. Thomas Cook owns both Thomas Cook and Thomas Cook Signature tour operators.

First Choice

Agents Travel Choice, Bakers Dolphin and Holiday Hypermarket are part of the same company as tour operators First Choice Holidays, First Choice Ski, Citalia, Eclipse, Flexiski, Exodus, Waymark, Hayes & Jarvis, Longshot Golf Holidays, Meon Villas, Sovereign, Sunquest, Sunsail, Unijet, 2wentys and Island Cruises (joint venture with RCI).

Types of travel agency

These multiples will have regional offices where they try to build up a personal service with the local residents but lack flexibility in selling conditions due to vertical integration. Independent travel agencies and tour operators, although in competition, often form a consortium to help each other increase business by sharing marketing, technology and booking systems. The truly independent travel agency (up to six branches) has freedom to sell every travel and tourism service and represent any provider (Figure 2.5).

Great changes are taking place within the industry. High street agencies are becoming very streamlined. Thomas Cook is a good example. They often have a receptionist, sections for destinations and type of holiday, and a telephone-free area for undisturbed holiday planning. Occasionally a clinic is attached for vaccinations.

Many of the multiples now also have warehouse-style agencies that offer something quite different from the usual high street outlets. They occupy a large area and are sectioned off into travel categories. Many will have a play area for children, café, driving simulator for clients to adjust to driving on the right-hand side of the road, a skiing simulator and a small cinema to show travel films. Often travel consultants do not take telephone calls so allowing the visitor to receive uninterrupted attention.

With sales outlets such as the Internet (at home and the high street, all types of providers have websites), Ceefax/Teletext, newspaper competitions, calls direct, computer brochures, holiday clubs where the client makes a 'one-off' payment and

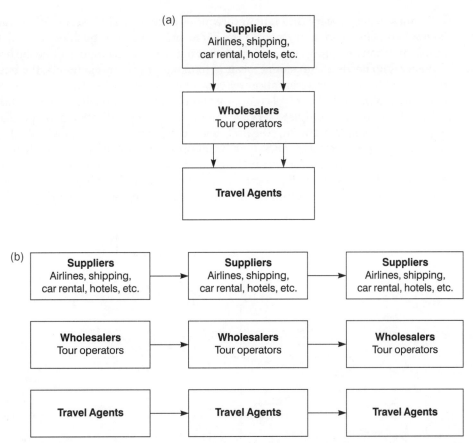

Figure 2.5 (a) Vertical integration (companies merge up ↑ and down ↓ in the chain of distribution); (b) Horizontal integration

is promised discounted holidays, and so on, great changes have taken place with working conditions. These include home workers, call centres, working on a self-employed basis, and 'paperless' working conditions. Another innovation is to rent a travel desk at a travel agency making a payment each month to include administration fees.

Along with changes in sales outlets, travel industry training has also moved forward. An increase of in-house training, many companies use the National Vocational Qualification route. The Association of British Travel Agents has increased its distance learning programme and there are many computer/workbook packages from which to choose.

There have also been changes in the travelling public's perception of holidays. Many people are informed, experienced travellers, and access to reservations is usually readily available.

When a travel agency offers retail and business travel services, they will be kept separate. With retail, holidaymakers will need to go to a location that is conveniently situated and take time discussing the travel arrangements.

Business travel is very different and requires different skills. Reservations have to be made quickly, and confirmed to the client promptly. The business traveller will often have many meetings in various parts of the world to arrange. Unlike the holiday traveller who needs a convenient location to make travel arrangements, the business traveller will make the reservation by computer or telephone. Business companies have an account with the travel company and pay for travel services each month.

In order to offer a complete service, the travel agency will often arrange sea, rail, air, coach, hotel, restaurant, theatre, insurance, car rental, travellers' cheques, interpreters, guide services, and so on, from providers not offered to retail clients. It is often more beneficial for a travel agency to have many small companies with accounts rather than a few big companies. Should a large business house account go out of business a large portion of the travel agency's income is lost (Figure 2.6).

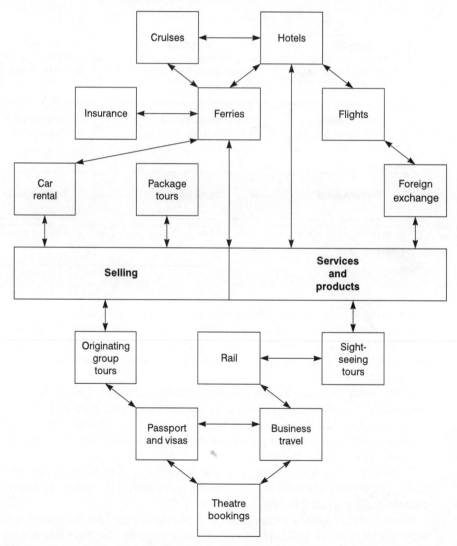

Figure 2.6 The work of a travel agency

Assignment 2.7

The future for travel agencies

Research and discuss the following:

1 Describe how you see the future for travel agencies.
2 Will travel agencies be asked to do only work that the traveller is unable to do for themselves?
3 Describe the advantages and disadvantages for the customer making travel arrangements with a multiple organisation.
4 Describe the advantages and disadvantages for the customer making travel arrangements with a truly independent travel agency.

Case study

Early bird booking

Using the Package Travel Regulations book from ABTA, help Mr and Mrs Addison with their problem.

In April, Mr & Mrs Addison booked a package tour to Portugal for the following October at £559 each. In July, the tour operator published a brochure advertising the holiday, same date, same hotel but £100 per person cheaper.

Is this illegal? Can Mr and Mrs Addison receive a refund of the £100 per person?

Dilemma

Aurora Borealis

You have clients who wish to see the Northern Lights.

Action

Advise when is the best time to travel. Where can they be seen?

Discussion

Great Wall of China

Tourism is putting the Great Wall of China at risk. A development boom in the land surrounding the world's largest cultural relic has been instigated by an increase in tourists and preparations for the 2008 Olympic Games. Sites full of archaeological relics are being built on by tourism developers and will be lost forever. Competition among tourist businesses has led to 'inappropriate sideshows', including bungee-jumping and sledge rides.

Research and discuss what can and is being done to control the negative effects of mass tourism in this region. Your discussion should include World Heritage laws and the World Monuments Fund.

Where in the world?

1 A Spanish Island in the Mediterranean Sea. George Sand, the French novelist, lived there at one time. The capital city of this island is overlooked by the Castillo de Beliver (a castle high on a hill).
   Name the island.

2 This place is in London and can be reached by boat from Westminster, the Embankment and the Tower of London. Explore the history of time and astronomy. See the Astronomer Royal's apartments. Watch the time ball fall. Admire John Harrison's amazing timekeepers.
   Name the attraction.

Short breaks, special interest holidays, theme parks, holiday centres, accommodation and theatre reservations

In this chapter we are going to discuss:

- Short breaks and their benefits
- Different types of holidays available
- What a holiday centre has to offer
- A family day out – theme parks
- Different types of accommodation
- Making theatre bookings

Short breaks

It has been said that short breaks is the fastest growing sector of the travel industry. Why? There are several factors that have brought about these changes to our holiday travel:

- Pressure of work – many people feel a full week or two or three weeks is too long to be away from the workplace
- Low-cost airline flights makes travelling further afield for shorter periods of time financially viable
- Family commitments make only short trips possible (animals to look after; children or grandma)
- Greater choice of destinations and accommodation available
- Many new and interesting or exciting activities on offer
- Some holidaymakers feel several short breaks each year benefit them more than one long holiday, and can help to break up a long winter. Short breaks during half-term school holidays are ideal for families to get away.

Assignment 3.1

Collect brochures giving information on:

Short breaks by car
Short breaks by sea
Short breaks by rail
Short breaks by coach
Short breaks by air

From each brochure choose one destination

For example: Center Parcs in Belgium by car; Le Touquet in France by sea; Paris by rail, perhaps to include Disneyland Paris; Amsterdam by coach; and Florence by air – the choice is yours.

Look up and write down the following information for each journey:

1 Departure point (there may be several choices)
2 Arrival point (this may differ from the actual destination point: follow the journey through)
3 Length of time for journey
4 Frequency of service
5 Facilities en route
6 What the destination has to offer the holidaymaker (what there is to do and see)
7 Expected climate for the dates you have chosen, and an explanation why the anticipated climate could influence the client's decision to travel
8 Different types of accommodation on offer
9 The cost for two adults travelling on each short break, and describe what the holiday includes.

There is a strong link between short break holidays and holidays with special interests, and I would like to discuss the many different types of holiday available.

Special interest holidays

Special interest holidays can be divided into certain groups by:

- **Age:** for example, there are many holidays available for the over-55s, 18–30s, and adventure holidays for children.
- **Destination interests:** for example, Iceland may appeal to some people as a very special interest destination because it offers something quite different from the usual type of holiday choice.
- **Venue:** for example, many universities are available to holidaymakers during the summer months when not being used by students, and hotel groups offer weekend or midweek special interest breaks.

Special interest holidays provide a good source of revenue for the travel agency, as often the clients will be travelling as a group.

Consider the clubs and associations in your area, make contact: there could be a lot of untapped business there. It could open up a new world. You will find holidays available that you never knew existed, and who knows, you may get involved in a different, very special interest yourself.

Here are a few different types of special interest holidays to consider:

- **Antiques** A fascinating hobby, delving back into our past, actually touching elegant pieces of history.
- **Archaeology** 'Dig' further back into our past, in fascinating surroundings in countries such as Greece, France, Germany, Peru.
- **Athletics** World Wide Marathon on Barbados, and in London. Train for the event at La Santa on Lanzarote, Canary Islands, which has Olympic training facilities.
- **Bird watching** Virtually all countries offer this peaceful and fascinating hobby, but imagine bird watching in Kenya, Ecuador, the Scottish Hebrides or the Seychelles Bird Island. What beautiful birds there are to be seen.
- **Botany/flowers** Most countries offer the beauty of flowers but perhaps Holland with the spring bulbs or the Jersey flower festival also come to mind.
- **Castles** Have you clients who are interested in castles? They can be found in most countries especially in Europe, but perhaps we think of Germany and Austria for this type of special interest holiday.
- **City breaks** City breaks are of great interest and are the biggest in terms of sales.
- **Cookery/food** Something we do every day, but perhaps we have clients who would like to learn how to make entertaining easy, or gain more knowledge of vegetarian cooking. Or perhaps explore something completely different for them – Italian, or Chinese, or Indian cooking. Perhaps they would enjoy a 'Gourmet Delights' holiday where guests do not do the cooking but just enjoy eating! Perhaps a visit to a food festival in Hong Kong would appeal, combining discovering a new destination with a hobby.

- **Cycling** Cycling is very popular at home and abroad, and not only for the very young. Many cyclists who began this hobby at 16 are still cycling strong at 60 years!
- **Dinghy sailing** Learn to sail a small boat, or improve on this skill. Where better than around the islands of Greece and Turkey?
- **Fishing** Many countries offer fishing holidays whether in the sea or lakes and rivers, where peace, excitement, solitude or companionship can be found.
- **Gambling** Las Vegas! Monte Carlo?
- **Golf** So many countries offer golf holidays either to learn or improve or just to enjoy beautiful courses or follow 'the stars'. We think of countries like the United States, the Caribbean, the United Kingdom, Hong Kong, Singapore, Thailand, Spain, Portugal, Austria, and many more.
- **Health/keep fit/beauty** Most of us probably fit in there somewhere in terms of our need for this type of holiday! Many countries offer health farms or spas with healing waters. Many clients like just to set aside a week or even a few days to concentrate on trying to get fit or improve their fitness condition. Lovely for the ladies to spend a few days feeling 'treasured' at a health and beauty farm. Many of them are converted stately homes and stand in magnificent grounds offering peace, luxury, and an opportunity for self-improvement that time does not permit in our everyday routine.
- **Horse riding/pony trekking** Again, offered by most countries, perhaps to learn or improve or just to enjoy being close to these sensitive animals. For clients not wanting to ride, there are horse-drawn caravan holidays – travel at a slow pace enjoying the countryside.
- **Motor racing** Holidays to the worldwide Grand Prix circuits. This special interest has a great following.
- **Music** What a tremendous range worldwide! The type of music can determine the venue – jazz, classical, country and western, 1950s and 1960s music, the Glenn Miller sound, opera, ballet – the variety is endless. There are many festivals throughout the year, and we think of Vienna and Milan in particular.
- **Painting** On canvas, paper, china, cloth, indoors, outdoors – in every country the choice is endless. Whether to study by attending lectures, or to try a new experience where beginners are welcome, or to improve or perfect a recognised gift.
- **Parachuting/jumping** Do you have a client with the courage and adventurous spirit looking for this special interest holiday? Be sure to collect full payment before they go! Also make sure they have adequate travel insurance.
- **Skiing** An exhilarating holiday for active holidaymakers. We think of the ski resorts in Europe, but of course many countries with mountains offer this special type of holiday. A few lessons on dry ski slopes at home can speed up learning to ski during the holiday. We will discuss skiing holidays in more detail in the next few pages.
- **Survival** Adventure holidays for children and adults. 'Robinson Crusoe' holiday on an uninhabited Greek island, and survival training on an uninhabited Scottish island – something different.
- **Walking** A great favourite for all ages and can be organised by walking clubs and tour operators or just an informal gathering of family and friends. There are a wealth of destinations with beautiful scenery and easy footpaths to follow.

Only 22 different types of special interest holidays have been mentioned. There are at least 150. Can you think of the remaining 128?

Assignment 3.2

Research some of the special interest holidays available by contacting the tour operators or companies direct. Check the website for information. Also *Travel Weekly*, the travel trade paper, which has several pages of ideas plus addresses and telephone numbers. The travel section of weekend newspapers is also a good source of information.

Exercise 3.1

Write down the special interest holiday of your choice, the destination, and match it with the type of tourist who might be suitable for that particular type of holiday.
Give ten examples.

	SPECIAL INTEREST HOLIDAY	DESTINATION	TYPE OF TOURIST
1			
2			
3			
4			
5			
6			
7			
8			
9			
10			

Useful addresses

Walking holidays

Walking Through Europe and the Mediterranean
Headwater Holidays
Tel: 01606 720166
www.headwater.co.uk

HF Holidays
Tel: 020 8905 9558
www.hfholidays.co.uk

Walks Worldwide
Tel: 01524 262255
www.walksworldwide.com

Health and beauty spas

Capri Beauty Farm, Palace Hotel, Capri
Tel: 00 39 081 8373800

Merv Griffin's Resort Hotel and Givenchy Spa, Palm Springs, California
Tel: 00 1 760 770 5000

Sandy Lane Hotel, Barbados
Tel: 00 1 246 444 2000

The Regent Hotel and Spa, Kowloon, Hong Kong
Tel: 00 852 2721 1211

Crowne Plaza Resort Madeira, Funchal, Madeira
Tel: 00 351 291 717 700

Holidays for singles

Travelsphere Just You Single Travellers
Tel: 01858 410 818
www.travelsphere.co.uk

Solo's
Tel: 0870 0746 453
www.solosholidays.co.uk

Travel One
Tel: 020 7721 8484
www.travelone.co.uk

Saga Special Interest Holidays for Singles (age 50 plus)
Tel: 0800 414 4444
www.saga.co.uk

Culture Tours
Travel Club of Upminster (Discovery Holidays Brochure)
Tel: 01708 225000
www.travelclub.org.uk

JMB Opera Holidays
Tel: 01905 830099
www.jmb-travel.co.uk

Cox and Kings
Tel: 020 7873 5006
www.coxandkings.co.uk

Prospect
Tel: 020 7486 5704
www.prospecttours.com

Page & Moy
Tel: 08700 106 400
www.pagemoy.com

Nature holidays

Many people love nature holidays – to see animals, birds and flowers in the wild.
(See Figure 3.1 UK National Parks.)

Explore Worldwide
Tel: 01252 319448
www.exploreworldwide.com

Discover the World
Tel: 01737 218802
www.discover-the-world.co.uk

Wildlife Worldwide
Tel: 020 8867 9158
www.wildlifeworldwide.com

Worldwide Journeys and Expeditions
Tel: 020 7386 4646
www.worldwidejourneys.co.uk

South Africa Travel
Tel: 01904 692469
www.southernafricatravel.co.uk

Kuoni World Class
Tel: 01306 747001
www.kuoni.co.uk

1	Northumberland
2	Lake District
3	North Yorkshire Moors
4	Snowdonia
5	Peak District
6	Norfolk Broads
7	Pembrokeshire Coast
8	Brecon Beacons
9	Exmoor
10	Dartmoor

Figure 3.1 Map of UK showing national parks

National parks

A wide variety of wildlife is found at all the national parks and some species are more plentiful in specific national parks. It is a wonderful experience never to be forgotten to enjoy a close-up view of animals in the wild. The surroundings can be very peaceful and natural. It is well worth getting up at 4.30 am to view the animals coming together around a drinking hole.

Here are just a few of the national parks and beauty spots around the world (see Figure 3.2):

1 Churchill, on Hudson Bay, Canada for polar bears
2 Banff and Jasper National Parks, Canada
3 North Bimini, Bahamas to swim with dolphins
4 Yosemite National Park – a few hours' drive from San Francisco, USA
5 Community Baboon Sanctuary, Belize
6 The Amazon, Brazil. Has 15 000 animal species, thousands of birds, fish and hundreds of mammals not yet classified. The jungle has over 1800 species of butterfly.

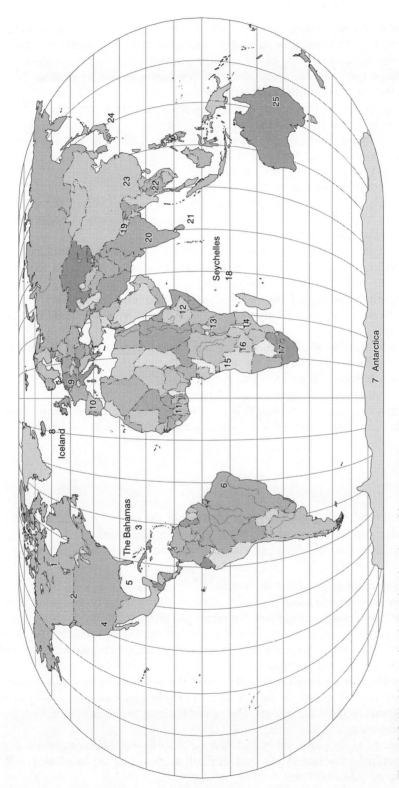

Figure 3.2 World map showing national parks and beauty spots

7 Antarctica for seals, whales, albatrosses and hundreds and thousands of penguins. The best time to visit is December to March. Antarctic cruises are not cheap but provide one of the world's greatest wildlife adventures.

8 Iceland for seals, the arctic fox and it's a bird watcher's paradise.

9 Carpathian Mountains, Romania for wolves.

10 Gibralta for the Barbary ape, the only wild primate in Europe.

11 Mole National Park, Ghana

12 The National Parks of Treetops, Masai Mara, Amboseli, Tsavo in Kenya

13 Luangwa National Park, Zambia

14 Mana Pools National Park, Zimbabwe

15 Damaraland and Etosha National Park, Namibia

16 Victoria Falls, Chobe National Park and Okavango Delta in Botswana

17 South Africa has eleven National Parks, to name just three: Kruger, Kirsten Bosch and Hluhluwe (for white rhino).

18 Seychelles – Cousin Island, home of thousands of seabirds; Bird Island, hundreds of thousands of sooty terns nest and breed between April and November.

19 Nepal – Royal Bardia National Park

20 Nagarhole National Park and Periyar Tiger Sanctuary in India

21 Pinnawela Elephant Orphanage, Yala and Uda Walawe National Parks in Sri Lanka

22 Thailand – Khao Sok National Park on Phuket. Lovely to learn about the lifestyle of elephants and you will fall in love with the baby ones!

23 South-western China for giant panda

24 The hot springs of Jigokudani – Japan

25 Hamilton Island – gateway to the Great Barrier Reef, Queensland, Australia. See migrating humpback whales between mid July and late September.

Skiing

You will need in-depth knowledge of many of the special interest holidays in order to advise your clients correctly. What sort of information?

Well, let's take ski holidays as an example. You would need to know:

- **Skiing areas** throughout the world
- **Travelling time** to reach the resort. Bear in mind that airports cannot be built close to or halfway up a mountain! Therefore the transfer times between airport and ski resort can be rather long. Also, the various modes of transport to reach the ski resort, travelling independently by car, or by rail, coach, sea, air or a combination of these modes of transport.
- **Mountain and snow conditions** Study the symbols in brochures. Height of ski resort is often given in feet or metres. There can be a considerable difference between the height of resorts. The upper limit or 'top station' is not necessarily the mountain top.
- **Types of skiing and ski runs** Most ski resorts will offer beginners slopes, easy slopes, intermediate slopes and difficult slopes. The ski brochures will indicate these by coloured lines:

Green or blue lines	Easy runs
Red lines	Medium runs
Black lines	Difficult runs

Altitude is important to consider because at the end of the season in Europe, as the days grow longer, the sun rises higher in the sky to melt the lower slopes.

Aspect is the outlook of a mountain. The sunniest aspect will be on south-facing slopes, looking towards the sun. North-facing slopes may not see the sun at all during the winter months (because the sun is too low).

- **Types of ski lift** How to ascend a mountain:

Drag lift – A bar is held between the legs and a continuously moving chain pulls the T-bar up the slope. It's not really a seated ride.

Chair lift – A continuously moving cable with chairs attached. Each chair holds two or three persons and has a safety bar clamped across the front. Skiers board the chair whilst it is still moving slowly.

Gondola – A much warmer method because the chair is enclosed, like a bubble with windows. The skis are strapped to a rack on the outside of the gondola.

Cable car – Used for long difficult mountain terrains. Skiers stand inside with their skis.

Funicular – Mountain railway. The carriages are set at a permanent slant so that the seats inside are always upright.

- **Ski equipment**

Skis and bindings

Ski boots

Ski sticks

Essential clothing

Ski packs – lift pass, ski equipment and ski school, can be purchased in advance or at the ski centre.

- **Ski school** Available at all levels. As mentioned earlier, before a client goes on their first ski holiday they may like to take a few lessons on a dry ski slope near where they live. Alternatively, most items may be hired.
- **Type of ski resort** There are various types of resorts. Some where skiing is away from the village, and here the lift system often becomes congested. The traditional ski resort with chocolate box type of scenery and quaint villages and hotels. Or the purpose-built ski resort offering ideal conditions for experienced skiers.
- **Après-ski** What to do when not skiing. Here are just a few of the non-skiing facilities on offer at most resorts: parties, trips to restaurants, disco, tobogganing parties, night-clubs, fondue parties, sleigh rides, skating, snowboarding, curling, ski walking, swimming, sauna, bowling, squash, tennis, sun-bathing.
- **Accommodation** A wide choice – check the brochures for location, facilities and cost for the following:
  - Hotels with all amenities
  - Simple guest houses
  - Chalets (often serviced, with meals provided)
  - Snowhouses (a room in a private house)
  - Apartments (offer freedom)

- **The best time to go** Look at brochures giving information of ski resorts worldwide. Remember, high season will be when snow is most likely to be at its best: it could mean more tourists and higher prices. We are talking in millions rather than in thousands of skiers every year during a relatively short period of time.

Accidents are plentiful and we will cover the risks in Chapter 11 on travel insurance.

What happens if there is not enough snow? It's true there is usually a battery of snow cannons firing 24 hours a day if no snow falls but what is the tour operator's policy for compensating the client should there be insufficient snow? Do they transfer their clients to a resort where natural snow is available, making this resort even more crowded?

Skiing holidays are not cheap holidays. Look at all your information outlets to find the best value. Look further than the Alps.

Despite the costs, crowds and muscle pains, some will say it is the best special interest holiday you can possibly have!

Assignment 3.3

Mr and Mrs Gordon and their two sons aged 18 years and 15 years are looking for a skiing holiday for one week. They live in London. They all have leave available during February, and would like to travel by air. They would like to stay in a picturesque resort with plenty to do other than skiing as one member of the family is fearful of having a skiing accident. Mrs Gordon definitely does not want to cook, and hotel accommodation has been requested.

Where would you suggest? Give reasons for your choice. Advise Mr and Mrs Gordon on the following:

- Name of ski resort
- Day and date of departure
- Return day and date
- Flight times
- Journey time between airport and resort
- Name of hotel
- Facilities of hotel
- Facilities of ski resort

Holiday centres/hotels

Moving away from special interest holidays, I would like to discuss different types of holiday centres and all-inclusive holiday hotels.

Gather some brochures giving details of all-inclusive hotel holidays – Sandals, Airtours (My Travel) and holiday villages (Butlins, Pontins and so on). Study what is included in the price for each type of holiday.

Most holiday villages have a host of indoor and outdoor facilities of which many are available at an extra charge. All-inclusive hotels vary between hotels that include meals and drinks in the price and those that include all activities as well. A spidergraph of a holiday village could be as shown in Figure 3.3.

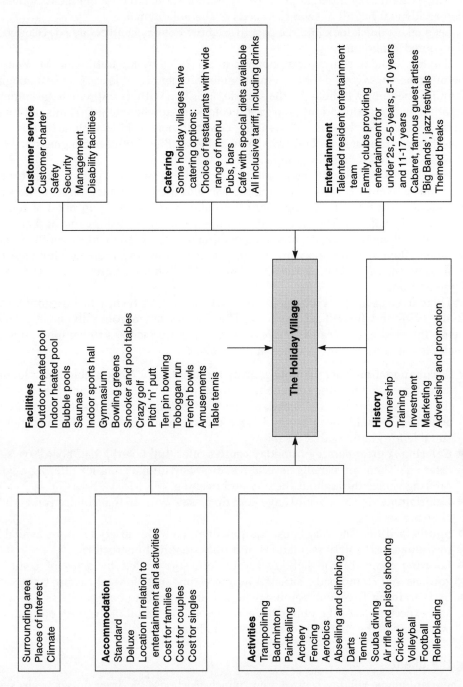

Figure 3.3 Spidergraph of a holiday village

Customer service
Customer charter
Safety
Security
Management
Disability facilities

Catering
Some holiday villages have
catering options:
Choice of restaurants with wide
range of menu
Pubs, bars
Café with special diets available
All inclusive tariff, including drinks

Entertainment
Talented resident entertainment
team
Family clubs providing
entertainment for
under 2s, 2-5 years, 5-10 years
and 11-17 years
Cabaret, famous guest artistes
'Big Bands', jazz festivals
Themed breaks

Facilities
Outdoor heated pool
Indoor heated pool
Bubble pools
Saunas
Indoor sports hall
Gymnasium
Bowling greens
Snooker and pool tables
Crazy golf
Pitch 'n' putt
Ten pin bowling
Toboggan run
French bowls
Amusements
Table tennis

The Holiday Village

History
Ownership
Training
Investment
Marketing
Advertising and promotion

Surrounding area
Places of interest
Climate

Accommodation
Standard
Deluxe
Location in relation to
entertainment and activities
Cost for families
Cost for couples
Cost for singles

Activities
Trampolining
Badminton
Paintballing
Archery
Fencing
Aerobics
Abseiling and climbing
Darts
Tennis
Scuba diving
Air rifle and pistol shooting
Cricket
Volleyball
Football
Rollerblading

There are many different types of holiday centre in almost every corner of the world, each offering different kinds of accommodation and entertainment. Some are non-residential but all answer the needs of the holidaymaker.

Let's take a quick look into the past to see how holiday centres have developed in the United Kingdom.

The first holiday centres were opened in the 1930s by Mr Butlin and Mr Warner because there was a need for all-weather entertainment complexes. Can you imagine families spending a holiday by the seaside in Britain with its unpredictable summer weather, walking around in the wet and cold with nowhere to go? That's not much of a holiday! So the first all-weather entertainment centre with activities and entertainment indoors and out was opened by Mr Billy Butlin in Skegness in 1936. It was known as a 'holiday camp'.

The Second World War interrupted the growth of holiday centres. In fact, they were taken over by the troops during the war and used as training centres. After the war, families wanted to be together on holiday and this is when holiday centres became very popular. They reflected the life-style of the British people at that time. They offered good value for money, something to interest all members of the family whatever their ages, and no worries – the price included meals and accommodation and some activities. During the 1950s and 1960s holiday centres were very basic, large and organised.

There have been vast changes to holiday centres since then, which mainly began in the 1970s and are still going strong! The changes range from millions of pounds being invested every year to improve holiday centre facilities to banning large all male/female groups and 'Mother in Law' jokes!

- **Accommodation** There is now a great choice of very comfortable and pleasant accommodation ranging from deluxe caravans to suites. A point to watch is where the accommodation is situated in relation to the entertainment/dining room activities. It could mean a very long walk for some guests and this may not be suitable for guests with a disability.
- **Catering** A great choice of holiday centres offer 'full board', 'half board' or 'self-catering'. There are usually several restaurants within a complex offering a wide catering choice throughout the day and evening.
- **Entertainments** These really have kept up to date with all that children and adults alike are seeking.
- **Sports facilities** The very latest equipment and a wide variety of sports available. Including strict safety regulations and fully qualified instructors.
- **Location** Many of the holiday centres are surrounded by acres of beautiful gardens and countryside, situated in interesting areas for sightseeing trips.
- **Staff training** Excellent training schemes are offered to employees as demands and expectations of the public have increased. The result of the in-depth training is evident as the centres become increasingly sophisticated.

Helping the client

There are many holiday centres from which to choose. So how do you help your client to choose the right one?

It means finding out exactly your client's needs and expectations of the holiday, and getting as many different types of brochures as possible and really reading them well so that you are familiar with each product. Information on holiday centres can be obtained from tourist offices throughout the world, the website, *Travel Weekly*, tour operators' brochures, and many companies will send their own manual to a travel agency.

Contact several companies to request a student pack which will give you invaluable information such as history, information on the product, advertising and promotion, customer service and some interesting fun facts.

If selling holiday centre holidays does not appeal, would you like to work at one? Many famous people started their career as a Butlins redcoat!

To find out more, contact Biss Lancaster PLC, 69 Monmouth Street, London WC2H 9JW (Tel) +44 (0) 20 7497 3001 (Fax) +44 (0) 20 7497 8915 (Web) www.bisslancaster.com. Good luck!

What are the considerations?

The size of the centre

Some centres hold just a few hundred guests and are managed by a family (such as Hoseasons holidays), others are enormous, accommodating 16 000 plus guests, making a village seem more like a town. The larger the holiday centre, the more facilities are offered. More choice, more people, more noise pollution! Therefore check to see what your clients are really seeking – a large lively centre, or a small quiet location.

Age group

Are your clients travelling without children and would like to stay at an adults-only centre? This is possible as there are several catering for adults only (such as Warners, and during certain weeks, Potters in Norfolk which is not booked by the trade).

Are your clients young and looking for lots of night-life and sports facilities? It is easy to accommodate them.

Location

Is the location important? As mentioned earlier, there are many holiday centres throughout the world. Perhaps a tropical climate is important, perhaps a country with interesting areas to visit.

Special reduction

Is the cost important to your client? Compare prices and the many special reductions available. Are they applicable to your client's circumstances?

All-inclusive hotels

If you have collected a Sandals brochure you will see that these holidays are for couples, and their Beaches resorts are for couples, singles, families and friends. At selected resorts the price includes:

- Accommodation in deluxe rooms
- Gourmet dining at up to 11 speciality restaurants per resort
- Unlimited premium brand drinks
- All land sports including tennis and golf
- All water sports including scuba diving and water-skiing
- Sports tuition
- Use of spa facilities (treatments are payable locally)
- Entertainment and night-life
- All children's facilities and entertainment
- All tips and extras

Theme parks

Does a family visiting a theme park help the travel agent? Not if they are travelling by car and taking their own packed lunch! But the visit may well include travel arrangements, entry package tariffs, and be included in an itinerary you are planning for your client.

Exercise 3.2

Compile a spidergraph of a well-known theme park situated in a country of your choice. Some of the headings you should include are:

1 Location: accessibility to include parking for coaches and cars, rail, travel, climate, seasons, tariff.
2 Attractions: there must be many! Age range.
3 Facilities: to include shops, restaurants, fast-food outlets, provision for people with walking difficulties.

These are just a few ideas. It is your spidergraph – I am sure you can give really detailed information.

Some helpful addresses

Disneyland Paris
Bâtiments Administratifs
Route Nationale 34
Chessy, 77144 Motevrain
Tel: 0870 5030303
www.disneylandparis.com

Chessington World of Adventures
Leatherhead Road
Chessington, Surrey KT9 2NE
Tel: 0870 4447777
www.chessington.com

Blackpool Pleasure Beach
Ocean Boulevard
Blackpool FY4 1EZ
Tel: 0870 4445566
www.blackpoolpleasurebeach.com.uk

Vulcania (opened 2002)
Rte de Mazayes
63230 Saint Ours
Auvergne, France
Tel: 00 33 4 7319 7000
www.vulcania.com

Vulcania is situated ten miles from the city of Clermont-Ferrand and is built on 140 acres of land. Visitors descend through a massive crater before enjoying a variety of simulations and presentations. There is a volcanic garden and a vibrating cinema with one of the world's largest projectors. Guides accompany tours of the interior and exterior of the building.

Thorpe Park
Staines Road
Chertsey
Surrey KT16 8PN
Tel: 0870 444 4466
www.thorpepark.co.uk

Alton Towers
Alton
Staffordshire ST10 4DB
Tel: 08705 204060
www.altontowers.com

Legoland Windsor Park Ltd
Winkfield Road
Windsor
Berkshire SL4 4AY
Tel: 08705 04 0404
www.lego.com

Accommodation

Hotel accommodation – what a choice! And what a disaster it can be if we make the wrong choice!

Is the location important? Close to the sea, or near the city centre? Perhaps the hotel must be near a conference centre, or factory site. Are the facilities important? Large enough to have swimming pool and health centre, or perhaps conference rooms. Are our clients looking for accommodation that is small and friendly, perhaps family-owned and managed?

The choice is enormous and many manuals have been published to assist the travel consultant in gaining the product knowledge. First of all, we will discuss some of the different types of accommodation available. As you listen to your client, a picture will soon form as to which type of accommodation is required.

Holiday resort hotels

Usually the location is very important. If the resort is a beach resort, tourists usually prefer to be very close to the beach front. The hotel can be located in a beautiful scenic area, or close to special facilities – a golf course or skiing area, for example.

Many of these resort hotels have an excellent entertainment programme and sport facilities for all the family.

Motels

Motels have enjoyed an increase in their business in recent years as the increase in private car owners has materialised. A motel is a hotel mainly for motorists and located conveniently near a major motorway.

City hotel

City hotels are used by business travellers and tourists alike. Often the tourists require a hotel in the centre of the city, convenient for sightseeing, not necessarily expensive, whereas the business traveller will also need the convenient location but may need a hotel with relevant facilities.

Pension or guest house

These are very popular with tourists not wanting the large hotel with many facilities they may never use, but are looking for a more personal place to stay which will cost less and have a 'home from home' feeling.

We are not restricted to booking hotels, motels and pensions for our clients. Other interesting accommodation can include castles and stately homes. There are many, particularly in Europe, where guests can experience the homes of kings. Game lodges can be very peaceful venues, often designed and built to merge with the game reserve, offering a tranquil watering hole for humans! A 'cabana' is a room adjacent to the pool area, with or without sleeping facilities, often separate from the hotel's main building. We have floating hotels, camping, mobile homes and caravan sites, a room in a taverna, and for some guests, a room with a lovely view is very important.

Staying in a lighthouse cottage is different. Contact Rural Retreats Tel: 01386 701177. You can choose from 34 cottages throughout the UK and residents can visit the automated lighthouses by arrangement with the warden.

Fancy living like royalty? There are many castles now to rent:

Amberley Castle in West Sussex Tel: 01798 831992
Culzean Castle at Ayreshire (clifftop) Tel: 01655 884455
Inverlochy, set among the foothills of Ben Nevis Tel: 01397 702177

The Landmark Trust Tel: 01628 825925 is a charity that restores endangered buildings and rents them out to holidaymakers.

Unfortunately there is no international agreement on the grading of hotels. Often the star system is used, but a 3-star award in one country can mean a very different standard in another. Many countries do not employ hotel inspectors to enforce any standards, making service and facilities offered poor.

It will always be difficult for the travel consultant actually to recommend a particular hotel as the industry is constantly changing. Perhaps a very reliable chef has left, making the quality of meals in the restaurant disappointing. Perhaps management has changed, causing the discipline of staff and comfort of the guests to decline. We rely on our hotel manuals and computers to provide factual information and listen to our clients who have just returned and keep our own record on the feedback received from clients. Many travel consultants have the opportunity to visit hotels on educational visits and this can help to build the product knowledge. Many clients prefer to stay at the hotels belonging to large chains or organisations, where, although the service may be impersonal, the standards are high and stability is usually guaranteed.

Making hotel reservations

There are many outlets for the travel agent to make hotel reservations:

- Direct with the hotel: through a central reservation office. Large hotel chains such as Hilton Hotels, Holiday Inn, etc. have a central booking office which means by making one contact the travel consultant can book more than one hotel in the chain, often in several different countries.
- Hotel representatives: A hotel representative or agent will represent many hotels in many different countries and, again, by the travel consultant making just one contact, it is possible to book hotels around the world – not with just one particular group but with many different hotel companies.

All these reservation outlets can be contacted through your computer. When we make a reservation we need to be crystal clear with our requests and the information passed to the client. The points we need to be particularly aware of are as follows.

Time of arrival and time of departure

This is important. Guests may need a room any time – 24 hours a day. Should the client expect to arrive at, say, 2.00 am – in the early hours of the morning – the room would have to be booked for the preceding night. We need to establish what time our client may check-in to the hotel, and if there is 24-hour check-in. Unless the accommodation has been secured by paying a deposit (a credit card may be used, and is especially useful in securing last-minute bookings) the accommodation will be released by 6.00 pm and re-sold. So we would need to advise the hotel if our client is planning to be a 'late arrival'.

Type of room and dates

We need to be sure we are reserving the type of room required. How many bedrooms when reserving a suite? Room with a balcony or patio? Is a bath required by a client who will not accept a shower? Are we trying to squeeze four guests into a room that will accommodate only three? Is a view important to our clients? Must the room be located on a lower floor because our client is nervous of heights, or disabled? There are hundreds of special requests that need attention – rooms for non-smokers, for example.

A clear way of stating the dates required is to say '24 June for 3 nights', or 'in 24 June out 27 June', leaving no doubt.

The tariff

What does it include? Meals? Taxes? Service charge? We need to ask those questions when making the booking.

Cancellation charges

We need to advise our client about cancellation charges at the time of making the booking. Waiting until the event happens is too late.

So now we have made the reservation, we are happy about the details being correct, what happens next? Your client will need written confirmation – a print-out from your computer.

Here is a reminder of the main points to note when making a hotel reservation:

- Check name, address, contact number of hotel
- Check tariff – is the rate quoted per room or per person?
- What does the tariff include – tax? service charge?
- Are there any supplements for a sea view, balcony, etc.?
- Are there any cancellation charges?
- Are the dates correct?
- What meal basis is included – breakfast (Continental?), lunch or dinner?
- Have there been any changes in the itinerary? If so, have we changed the hotel reservation?
- How is payment to be made?
- When and how much commission is to be paid to the travel agent?
- Has the voucher been made out correctly and, if a long itinerary is involved, has a separate voucher been issued for each hotel?

Going through this checklist will become automatic after a while and will help to avoid the silly mistakes that can easily happen.

Theatre reservations

Why book with a travel agency? From the client's point of view it is a very convenient service that travel agents provide. If a client decides to book with the theatre direct, they have a choice of either visiting the theatre's box office during business hours which could involve a long and expensive journey, or telephoning the box office and giving their credit card details, and the theatre will either post the tickets to the card holder or hold them until the client collects on the day. If the client does not have a credit card a cheque may be sent with a covering note to pay for the tickets. Many theatres charge an agency fee for telephone and postal bookings, and a lot of patience is required by the client trying to make contact by telephone to the box office. If the show is fully booked for the date required, a quick decision needs to be made regarding an alternative date or theatre. If it is to be an alternative theatre, the process begins again: trying to get through to the next box office on the list. Not everyone has access to theatre bookings via computer.

By contrast, when a client books theatre tickets through a travel agent, a seat in pleasant surroundings can be provided whilst the travel consultant does the job in a fraction of the time.

There are two types of theatre ticket agents:

1 Principal agent who holds large allocations of theatre seats and may have direct reservation lines with many theatres.
2 Sub-agent (the travel agent) who holds an account with one or more principal agents, and contacts the principal agent when requested to make a booking.

The principal agent will keep the travel agent up to date with lists of shows, special events, posters to help advertise theatres, prices of seats, theatre plans and books of theatre tickets. Reservations can be made by the travel agent using a computer to view availability and to make a booking.

Position of seat

Most theatres have seats on the ground floor – called the stalls – and the dress circle and upper circle – in tiers. This is a matter of preference, but think of the type of performance. If most of the show takes place 'in the air' (a circus act perhaps), then circle seats would be the best choice. Many clients do not enjoy sitting in the front row of the stalls as it means 'looking up' at the stage, which can be uncomfortable. Many lovely ornate Victorian theatres do not have lifts – how many steps lead to the dress circle, and can your customer manage to climb them?

Cost of seats

The cost of the seats you quote to the customer includes the agency fee. Ask the customer for a price range in case you are unable to obtain the first choice. It is very easy to make a photocopy of the theatre plan and present this to your customer with the theatre tickets. It will help them find their seats more easily, and gives an extra touch of personal service.

'Theatre breaks' are very popular, and include one or two nights in London (or another major city) and the evening at the theatre. Some also include an evening meal. They are financially rewarding for the travel agent.

Exercise 3.3

Using a Brittany Ferries brochure

1 Advise the daytime crossing time between Portsmouth and Caen.
2 The number of which road takes you from Caen to Paris?
3 Name two theme parks in the region of Ile-de-France.
4 Name the famous art museum in Paris.
5 Name the new attraction for Disneyland Paris in 2002.

Using a Butlins brochure

6 Butlins has three holiday centres. Where are they located?
7 Name three activities for children under five years of age.
8 Name three themed breaks.
9 Your clients are due to travel to Butlins on 28 June, but cancel their holiday on 16 June. What percentage cancellation fee will be charged?

Discussion

1 Once man feared the mountains, now the mountains fear man! Discuss what is and can be done about the destruction that follows overcrowding at ski resorts.
2 Investigate an all-inclusive holiday village in the Caribbean and discuss the impact that the all-inclusive location has on the island as a whole. Your discussion should include:

(a) Benefits for local residents
(b) Amount of foreign investment
(c) Amount of foreign labour used
(d) Opportunities for tourists and local residents to mix
(e) Does an all-inclusive village have any effect on an increase in crime?
(f) Discuss security measures being taken
(g) Describe the benefits for the tourist.

Dilemma

Walking holiday in France

Miss Handley would like to enjoy a walking holiday in France where bags are transported between hotels.

Action

Can you suggest any operators?

Where in the world?

1 This is in one of the Benelux countries. It is a vast Victorian red-brick building facing the outermost of the city's concentric ring of canals and the country's most prestigious and important museum. In addition to a superb collection of sixteenth- and seventeenth-century paintings, it houses over 35 000 books on art, and has over 30 galleries of eighteenth-century furniture, glass, porcelain, gold and silver, making it the largest collection of its kind in Europe.
   Name the building.

2 This country has the slogan 'A World in One Country'. It has eleven National Parks and 3000 km of coastline. It has a mountain view that dominates the city. It has a luxury train service operating from north to south (taking 27 hours) called The Blue Train. Travel along 'The Garden Route' and visit an ostrich farm.
   Name the country.

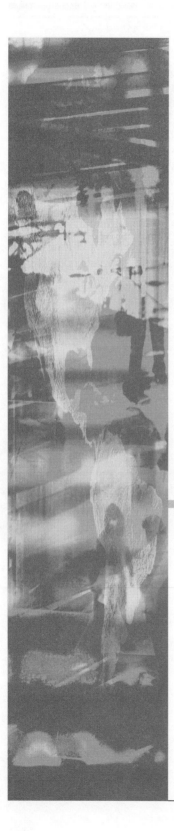

Coaching and incoming tourism

In this chapter we are going to:

- Discuss the benefits of travelling by coach
- 'Brainstorm' the things we need to know about travelling by coach
- Plan an itinerary for a coach tour in Australia
- Make a reservation
- Assignment on helping the client
- Solve a problem
- Brief outline of tourist attractions in Australia
- Incoming tourism services
- The positive and negative aspects of tourism
- Why tourists come to the United Kingdom
- Case study – devising a one-month itinerary for the UK
- Assignment on a location that has turned to tourism due to industrial changes

Coaching

Why sell coach travel?

Coach travel can offer a versatile form of transport, providing the travel agent and client with convenient links between 'A' and 'B', simple reservation procedures and excellent commission earnings. Let's think about the opportunity to sell coach travel: for transfers between airport and hotel, for half-day or full-day sightseeing tours, for hire – perhaps you have organised a group tour for a local club or association. Coach travel can be used for travelling from one city to another – a similar service to rail, coach tours can be enjoyed when an escort is provided.

Coaches can be very luxurious, offering comfortable facilities – reclining seats, toilets, air-conditioning, entertainment and a buffet. They can be very basic – uncomfortable for long journeys or have a 'vintage' charm! They come in all sizes with seating capacity ranging from 10 to 50, although the average seating capacity is 40.

There are many interesting routes. Greyhound International offer a complete network across the USA and Canada. European railways created Europabus to complete their already extensive rail network, providing luxury coaches for their 50 000 km scenic routes across Europe. Eurolines also offers travel from the UK to Europe.

Where can you find the information you need?

Look in the trade directories under the heading 'Coach Tours', and study special interest overseas touring holidays, giving details of hundreds of touring holidays involving coach travel to almost every part of the world – with fascinating themes.

Why are coach tours so popular?

- **Fun together** It is a fact that people enjoy doing things together. Friendships blossom and the unescorted person can enjoy the companionship of a coach tour.
- **Convenience** Many elderly clients can enjoy the 'door-to-door' service. Often the coach will pick up passengers from their home town or even at a central location near their home. Clients without their own transport find a coach tour an excellent way to sightsee.
- **Low cost** Students find a coach tour a cheap way of seeing a country. Travelling with a pre-planned group is like buying merchandise wholesale, there is greater economy in the tour package which an individual traveller could not obtain. This applies to sightseeing, entertainment, transfers, meals and hotel reservations.
- **Fixed outlay** As the coach tour is usually a completely packaged trip the traveller is able to know the total cost in advance. There are no hidden or surprise expenses.
- **Worries gone** We sometimes overlook the importance of travel worries. Travellers are concerned about the many things that could go wrong. When the coach tour has a trained escort onboard, the worries are removed! In the event of illness or

other emergencies, travellers can be assured of their escort's personal interest in their welfare. There may be difficulties with a foreign language or currency. The presence of an experienced and congenial escort assures a carefree trip.

Have you ever thought about the Greyhound coach network through the USA and Canada? If you are booking flights for your clients to travel to the USA the chances are that they intend to sightsee and will travel by coach or car.

In Chapter 2 we examined booking conditions in detail. So at this stage please think about a few general points to keep in mind for all coach travel.

If you were booking a coach tour for a client, what would you need to know? Try brainstorming – write down everything you can think of in connection with coach travel. It may look as follows:

Discussion

Coach tours

Pick-up points and timings	Itinerary
Feeder coaches	Places to visit
Seat rotation	Length of time spent at each attraction
Non-smoking	Any night-time travel?
Experience of drivers and couriers	
	Journey time to first destination
	Amount of free time
Air/coach tour	What is included in tour?
Airline used	Accommodation – food basis
Flight times	Insurance – cancellation cover
Baggage allowance	Entrance fees
	Excursions
	Special events
	Airport taxes
	Channel crossing
	Porterage of luggage
	Extra supplements
	Special offers on specific dates
Booking conditions	
Can tour be extended?	
Special requests	
Complaints procedure	
Travel documentation	
Cancellation conditions	
Facilities for disabled people	
Reputation of coach company	

Let's take some of those discussion points in more detail.

Feeder coaches

Quite often the coach that picks up passengers from their home town is not the coach that will take them on the coach tour. It is just taking them to a central point in the country where a big changeover of coaches is made. There could be sixty coaches at one time, each with forty or so passengers needing to find the correct numbered coach going to their destination, and having their suitcase to carry during the search. This really does need to be studied carefully because passengers often travel miles/hours out of their way to accommodate everyone going to the same destination but from different directions.

Reputation of coach company

The reputation of the coach company should also be studied. Are routes often changed during the holiday, and without notice, for the benefit of the company and not the passengers? How good is their safety record?

Extra supplements

Study all that the cost of the coach tour includes. There are many benefits from travelling as a group when it comes to entrance fees, accommodation and so on. As this type of holiday is often ideal for people travelling alone, are there single-room supplements to pay?

Journey time

The length of time spent on the coach is also important. Does it include overnight travel? Some people find sitting in a coach for very long periods of time uncomfortable and an air/coach holiday would be better for their circumstances.

Itinerary

Study the itinerary carefully. Are there any special events on specific dates, such as carnivals, festivals or sights that just must not be missed?

Bookings

Get your facts straight about cancellation charges and all booking conditions. Follow the itinerary and check whether your client will require a visa.

Climate changes and time zones

Be aware of climatic changes and time zones (especially in the USA and Australia). There are four time zones in the USA – Eastern, Central, Mountain and Pacific with one hour difference between each zone, one hour earlier if travelling East to West, and one hour later if travelling West to East.

Department/return dates

If the coach tour is just part of your client's holiday, make sure that the departure and return dates fit in with the remainder of your client's itinerary.

Seating plan

Study the seating plan of the coach and the seat numbers. Does the coach operator work on a 'first come first served' system for seating, or will the passengers rotate during the coach tour? Or is seating fixed for the whole trip?

Non-smoking

Is the rule 'no smoking' for the entire coach or is part of the coach sectioned off – smoking and non-smoking? Most companies have a no-smoking rule, in which case, how often are 'comfort' stops made?

European coach holidays

Because coach holidays are so popular there is a great variety of tour operators, routes and destinations. For the holidaymaker who does not own a car, the coach holiday is a boon and many tours have local pick-up points or free or reduced rail travel to London enabling a trouble-free start to the holiday. Despite my earlier warnings, most of the coach companies operating tours to Europe have been in the business for many years and have a wealth of experience in planning the routes with care and a long success story of satisfied customers. Considerable cash savings are made by travelling through Europe by coach, and it provides the opportunity of seeing the countryside. For clients who feel the travelling time is too long, there are a great selection of short holidays, centre holidays (travel by coach to a centre and stay awhile), and a combination of transport such as coach cruising, air coach, and rail coach to chose from. With the euro in place, the need to constantly change money to various currencies has fallen away, making that side of the holiday a lot easier.

Coach holiday brochures are usually well presented and easy to read (aren't you pleased to hear that?). In the contents page the type of tour, destination and tour number is clearly listed. Excellent photographs of the places to be visited with maps indicating the route chosen for each itinerary is helpful. The cost of the holiday for each departure date, again, is usually clear and the many questions you will be asked by an interested client can be answered quickly and confidently after a little practice as most of the points are covered in the brochure.

Making a reservation

Once again, we need to obtain all the necessary information from the client before going ahead with the reservation. Apart from personal details we need to know where they intend to join the coach, any special requests, if they require visas, and have alternative dates at hand in case the tour is not available.

The reservation can be made by contacting the coach operator by telephone, fax, telex or by use of the office computer. Once the reservation has been made, it will be secured by collecting a deposit from your client, and you will then assist your client to complete the booking form. Usually within two weeks a written confirmation from the coach company will be received confirming the exact details (which you must check against your original request) and showing the date of when the balance of payment is due.

Assignment 4.1

You have two clients who are planning to travel on a Continental coach holiday and have a shopping list of questions to ask before making a booking.

Choose any well-known established coach holiday company, study their brochure and try to find the answers to the following queries. Please give reasons for your reply – a 'yes' or 'no' will not do – these customers like to know the details!

1 Can we be sure the couriers are experienced?
2 Is the cost of the holiday subject to any surcharges?
3 Are there any 'special offers'? If so, are we eligible?
4 Can we join the coach in our home town? (Clients reside in the same town as you, the reader.)
5 How can we be sure the route is scenic and not motorway travel most of the way?
6 Will there be onboard entertainment? If so, will it be suitable for everyone on the coach? One of the ladies recalls a film being shown on a coach that she found embarrassing due to the content of the story and bad language. It was true that the courier had asked if anyone would mind if the film was shown, but, as this client did not know what the film was about, she did not object. It was only after a short time into the film that she realised how unsuitable it was, especially as there was a young family onboard, but lacked the courage to say anything and decided to 'grin and bear it' – or rather, try to read her book!
7 Can we be sure not to travel by coach during the night?
8 What grade of hotels are used on the tours?

Imagine you are that lady who found herself in the embarrassing situation on the coach and on returning home decided to complain to the coach operator. Describe your feelings and the points you would be making in the complaint.

Imagine you are the marketing director of the coach operator and describe your point of view and how you will respond to the lady making the complaint.

We did say there would be a strong flavour of geography in this edition because it is very necessary to know the tourist attractions and, if possible, some history of most tourist spots worldwide. Product knowledge is very much valued.

Assignment 4.2

Coach tour in Australia

Read the general information given on Australia and then compile an itinerary as follows.

The journey begins in Brisbane, is for eleven days/ten nights and travels to Cairns. You will need to find a good detailed map of this area, and study your information guides on Australia. Advise on the places of interest the itinerary should include en route.

Day 1   Brisbane, Hervey Bay, Fraser Island
Day 2   Fraser Island
Day 3   Fraser Island, Rockhampton

Day 4	Rockhampton, Hamilton Island
Day 5	Hamilton Island
Day 6	Hamilton Island, Townsville
Day 7	Townsville, Port Douglas (two nights)
Day 8	Great Barrier Reef
Day 9	Port Cairns, Douglas
Day 10	Tjapukai
Day 11	Morning at leisure. Afternoon connect with onward flight

Some very brief general tourist information on Australia, just to get you started. Read as much as you can about this lovely country.

Queensland

Capital city – Brisbane. 'The Sunshine State'. The Gold Coast. The Great Barrier Reef is 2000 kilometres parallel with the coast. Cairns is the main gateway to the Great Barrier Reef. Surfer's Paradise. The Northernmost tip – the Cape York peninsula – is an area of scrubland and has some of Australia's largest national parks with caves and rock paintings revealing Aboriginal history. This area is virtually inaccessible during the monsoon months between November and March.

Western Australia

Capital city – Perth. Mining area, iron, diamonds, gold. Perth is actually geographically closer to Singapore than Sydney. It is a clean, modern, attractive city, where parks, gardens, galleries and museums abound. The beaches are superb and skies are unpolluted. The Swan River flows through the city offering scenic cruises and peaceful river beach resorts. Freemantle is 19 kilometres from Perth, situated at the mouth of the Swan River. Many sheep stations here.

Northern territory

Capital city – Darwin. Aborigines have gained title to land. Kakadu National Park – cave paintings. Ayers Rock is in an area known as the Red Centre. Alice Springs is an important centre for departure point for excursions of all kinds into the mysterious Australian outback, including Ayers Rock.

Victoria

Capital city – Melbourne. The Garden State – has 30 National Parks, over 100 wineries. Murray River borders Victoria and New South Wales. In winter the snow-covered dividing range of mountains attracts many skiers. The quality of the sandy beaches has earned the south-eastern coastal region the name of the Victorian Riviera. Melbourne cricket ground and the Melbourne Cup horse race are famous.

South Australia

Capital city – Adelaide. The Murray River is important to South Australia as it provides the fresh water. Lake Eyre is muddy salt flats and seldom has any water in it. Adelaide is sophisticated and cosmopolitan with many parks and wide streets. The huge Festival Centre is built on the banks of the River Torrens which runs through the city. River cruises operate on the Murray River.

New South Wales

Capital city – Sydney (the capital city of Australia is Canberra). Snowy mountains (source of Murray River), skiing takes place June to September. Sydney Opera House, Sydney Harbour Bridge, Manly Beach, 48 Floor Centre Point Building, King's Cross, Bondi Beach, Blue Mountains, Aquarium and much, much more.

Exercise 4.1

Place the following places on a map of Australia:

1 Canberra
2 Blue Mountains
3 Sydney
4 Perth
5 80-mile beach
6 Brisbane
7 Darwin
8 Adelaide
9 Alice Springs
10 Ayer's Rock

Incoming tourism

Some travel agencies earn part of their income from providing services to incoming visitors. If, for example, you are organising a tour yourself for your clients (not booking a ready-made package tour) to, let's say, Australia, you would need the services of an incoming tourism agent. The sort of services they could offer in that country are as follows:

• Meeting and greeting at airport or seaport
• Transfers between airports/hotels and vice versa
• Sightseeing tours and guides
• Courier services

- Secretarial services
- Interpreters
- Arranging conferences
- Obtaining tickets for special events, theatre bookings and concerts
- Special interest holidays
- Restaurant reservations
- Reconfirmation of flight reservations
- Any changes required to travel documents

The travel agent receives commission on the various elements of the services provided, or by adding charges in the form of service fees. There are companies dealing solely with this side of the industry and the job is, in fact, very specialised. Whether or not you would be dealing with incoming tourists would depend mainly on the location of your office, and whether many overseas visitors were received.

When dealing with incoming tourists, whether on a large or small scale, you will need detailed information on the area, historical knowledge, new venues, maps, brochures, organisation and careful planning. Size of group and nationality will also be important, and, if involved in a sightseeing tour, an alternative route should an unexpected traffic diversion arise! You will develop a close working relationship with coach operators and understand the problems they try to avoid. The incoming tourism business is taking place throughout the world 24 hours a day, so there are many aspects to consider with ships to meet at ports, an influx of tourists during peak seasons, and availability of transport or length of sightseeing tour. The safety and satisfaction of the incoming visitor is paramount.

If arranging travel by coach in the UK it is good to choose a friendly local coach firm who is a member of the newly formed Consortium of Independent Tour Operators (CITO), when you can be sure of a good standard of service. For more information call 0117 916 1080 or visit www.cito.uk.com

There are many benefits for a country with incoming tourists. Tourism is one of Britain's leading industries worth more than £61 billion to the UK economy. Tourists spend money on accommodation, food, drink, entertainment, transportation, gifts and souvenirs, tours and so on. The profit created is used to generate more business. It is often known as the tourism income multiplier. The government benefits from incoming tourism as overseas visitors pay VAT and other taxes on services including liquor, tobacco, petrol, accommodation and souvenirs. It creates employment – approximately 7 per cent of the nation's jobs. The income can improve the local environment and help to preserve historic buildings. The industry's direct economic contribution is equivalent to over 5 per cent of gross domestic product (GDP). Indirect contributions such as car hire, financial services and insurance could be as high as 12 per cent.

We have said that tourism has decreased by 7 per cent between the year 2000 and 2001, due partly to the terrorist attack on the World Trade Center in New York on 11 September 2001. Including both UK and overseas visitors, London had 28.8 million visitors in 2001. In the year 2000, London received 36.6 million visitors. It is estimated that in the year 2002 there will be an increase of 3 per cent to 29.7 million.

The Association of British Travel Agents (ABTA) estimates that 16 tour operators and 20 travel agents went out of business in 2001 due to the terrorist

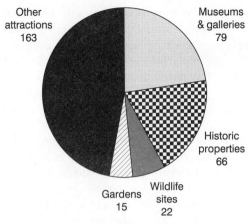

1992 - 345 Million

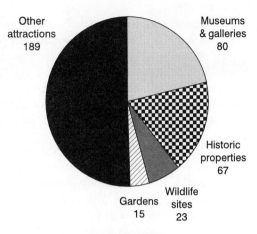

1994 - 375 Million

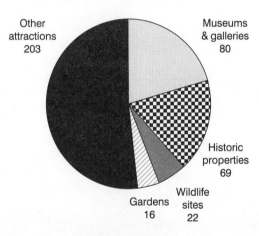

1996 - 390 Million

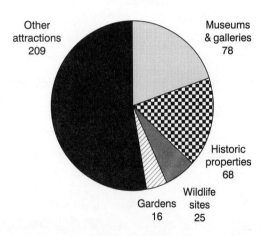

1998 - 396 Million

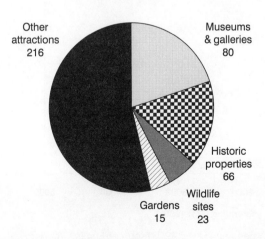

2000 - 400 Million

Figure 4.1 Market share by type of attraction 1992–2000. Attraction by volume (million admissions.) (Source: English Tourism Council)

attack and the snowball effect, compared with 6 tour operators and 19 travel agents in 2000. Well-known companies such as Thomas Cook, Thomson and Airtours have made cutbacks leading to thousands of job losses, but the industry is fighting back.

What are the negative impacts of tourism? Overcrowding, overdevelopment of land, loss of culture, erosion of ancient buildings, litter, pollution, increase in crime, transport congestion, noise pollution, overstretched facilities and services, to name a few!

What would deter tourists from visiting a country? Exchange rates may not be favourable, making the visit a very expensive one. Terrorism – the feelings of terror and fear can certainly subdue the demand for tourism. Political unrest within a country. Perhaps the country of origin has restrictions for people leaving their country by way of permits or currency control. Disease – Britain had an outbreak of foot and mouth disease in 2001 which made a large part of the countryside out of bounds. More recently, in 2003, the SARS virus. Increased crime – a feeling of unease. Family commitments, lack of money or poor health can also be a deterrent to travel.

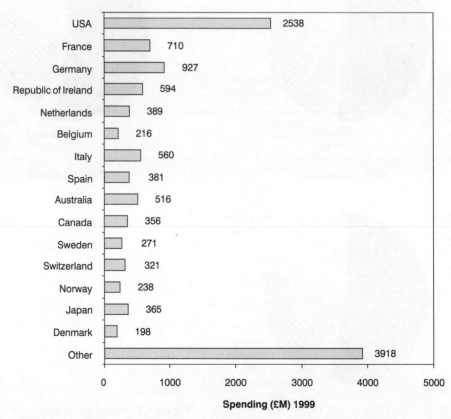

Figure 4.2 Countries of origin of incoming tourist – spending (£M) 1999. (source: English Tourism Council)

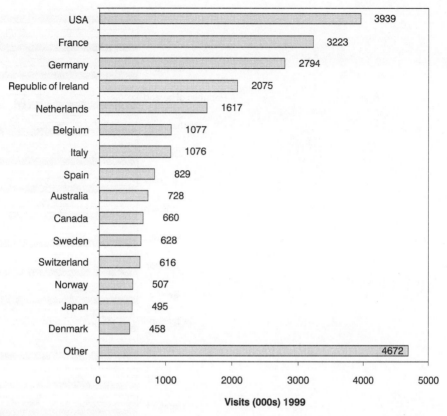

Figure 4.3 Countries of origin of incoming tourist – visits (000s) 1999. (source: English Tourism Council)

Exercise 4.2

Incoming tourism – the impacts

Describe the impacts of tourism – positive and negative – under the following headings:

	POSITIVE	NEGATIVE
Environmental		
Economic		
Cultural		

Let's look on the bright side and think about why tourists would wish to visit the United Kingdom. It has a wealth of interest for everyone and so only a fleeting visit can be made through this book.

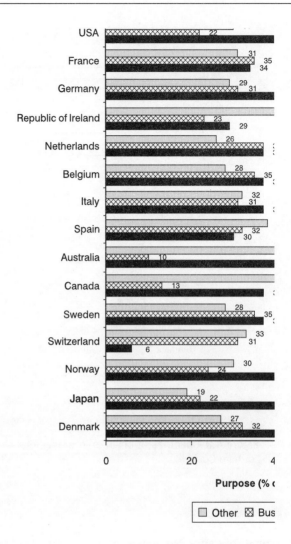

Figure 4.4 Countries of origin of incoming tourist – purpose (% of visits) 1999. (Source: Tourism Council)

Attractions

Tourists tend to visit:

- The British Museum, Great Russell Street, London WC1 (tel: 020 7323 8000; www.thebritishmuseum.ac.uk), it was founded in 1753, and is one of the greatest museums in the world, showing the works of humans from prehistoric to present time.
- Somerset House, Strand, London WC2 (tel: 020 7845 4600; www.somerset-house.org.uk), home of the Courtauld Institute Gallery, the magnificent Gilbert Collection and Hermitage Rooms.

- Science Museum, Exhibition Road, London SW7 (tel: 0870 870 4868; www.science-museum.org.uk). See, touch and experience the major scientific advances of the last 300 years at the largest museum of its kind in the world. Over 40 galleries and 2000 hands-on exhibits to inspire all. Six new interactive galleries focusing on contemporary science, including a large screen IMAX cinema and motion-ride simulator.
- Tower of London, Tower Hill, London EC3 (tel: 020 7709 0765; www.hrp.org.uk). Guarded by the famous 'Beefeaters' (the Yeoman Warders) the Tower spans 900 years of British history and has served as a palace, prison and execution site. See the Crown Jewels, Traitor's Gate, the Royal Armouries and the famous ravens.

The London Tourist Board produces a very comprehensive book called the *Official Guide to London Capital Breaks* (tel: 020 7932 2000; www.londontouristboard.com), and it is well worth obtaining.

Music may interest the incoming tourist and many famous opera and ballet companies can be seen in the UK. All types of music around the country can be enjoyed especially in parks during the summer months. The Royal Festival Hall, Barbican, Royal Albert Hall and Sadler's Wells are popular venues.

Looking for drama? London is the home of more live theatres than any other city in the world. All types of theatre – tragedy, comedy, musical, farce and, in the Christmas season, pantomime (a peculiarly English tradition). Many are around the Piccadilly area. Covent Garden Piazza offers a variety of street entertainers.

Shakespeare's Globe Theatre, New Globe Walk, Bankside, London SE1 (tel: 020 7902 1500; www.shakespeares-globe.org) is well worth a visit and offers guided tours.

The Theatre Museum, Russell Street, London WC2 (tel: 020 7943 4700; www.theatremuseum.org). The Theatre Museum illustrates the history of the performing arts in the UK. The collection includes theatre, ballet, dance, circus, opera and musicals.

Getting away from London, a journey along the River Thames to Oxford, Stratford-upon-Avon and the Cotswold hills, known as Shakespeare country, is popular with tourists.

There are special events that attract many visitors such as the Oxford and Cambridge Boat Race, the Chelsea Flower Show, the Biggin Hill International Air Show (Biggin Hill was a famous fighter airfield during the Battle of Britain), London to Brighton Veteran and Vintage Car Run, Royal Ascot, Wimbledon Lawn Tennis Championships, to mention a few. If you look at the 'Special Interest' section of this book, most of those special interests hold an exhibition during the year. It may be flowers, antiques, embroidery, art, sailing (Boat Show), model railways. .. the subjects are endless.

The United Kingdom is very easily accessible by air and sea link, and within the country by rail and road. It is possible to travel around the United Kingdom completely by the use of canals, but most tourists choose a faster route! The most popular mode of transport around London is by Underground tube trains, with a network of lines stretching fifteen miles on either side of the city.

Tourists usually visit Britain for a combination of reasons but no doubt enjoy the scenery along with every other attraction. The Lake District in the north-west of England is a spectacular area of mountains and lakes.

In the south-west are the beautiful counties of Devon and Cornwall with quaint fishing villages and the wild beauty of Dartmoor. In Scotland, the Highlands stretch across more than half of northern Scotland with its mountains and lakes, and the beauty of Snowdonia in Wales with its National Park are just some of the scenic attractions.

The traditions of Britain are interesting for many tourists who like to visit historic properties. Places such as the Roman Baths and the Pump Room at Bath, Windsor Castle, Stonehenge (Wiltshire), Warwick Castle, Leeds Castle (Kent), Hampton Court Palace, Houses of Parliament, Downing Street, St Paul's Cathedral. Visitors often like to see Trooping the Colour on the Queen's Birthday and the Changing of the Guard. Every summer, Edinburgh has a Military Tattoo which has been thrilling audiences since 1950. Over 200 000 visitors a year enjoy at first-hand the colour, pomp and pageantry of this magical event.

Colchester in Essex is Britain's oldest recorded town, dating from Roman times. Visit Colchester Castle, museum, excellent shops and, being a military town, also has a tattoo each year.

Climate

Many tourists might say they do not visit the United Kingdom for the sun, the sea and the sand. Certainly the weather is unpredictable but, between the months of June to September, the temperature can increase to be very hot and, between the showers, the sunshine can be lovely. Certainly visitors from far-off tropical countries really do enjoy the long days of light, when in summertime dawn breaks around 5.30 am and remains light until 10.30 pm. There just may be time to relax on a beach and many are clean, attractive and not crowded. Ecams, the environmental charity that runs the Seaside Award, has given its prestigious blue and yellow flag award to 317 beaches.

Resort beaches are assessed on strict criteria of beach management, including the provision of first-aid facilities, clean toilets and access for disabled visitors. For a full list of the UK's award-winning beaches call 01603 766076 or www.seasideawards.co.uk.

Cuisine

When thinking about English food there is a joke that says 'If you like the climate – you will *love* the food!' But really it is not that bad. Pub meals are popular as most public houses have a good reputation for quality food at reasonable prices and the atmosphere and characteristics of the surrounding can be unique. There are many regional dishes to try and, of course, fish and chips! Every country has its national dish and I am sure it can be found in Britain. Italian, French, Chinese, Greek – there is a wonderful variety of ethnic cuisine. Try Brick Lane in the East End of London for curry.

Shopping

Some people love it! Well-known shopping venues are:

- Austin Reed, 103–113 Regent Street, London W1R (tel: 020 7534 7777; www.austinreed.co.uk). Launched in 1926, offers classy clothes for men and women.
- Camden Lock Market, Camden Lock Place, Chalk Farm Road, London NW1 8AF (tel: 020 7284 2084; www.camdenlockmarket.com). Located in a beautiful and historic canal-side setting well known for arts, crafts and curiosities.
- Foyle's, Bookshop, 113–119 Charing Cross Road, London WC2H 0EB (tel: 020 7437 5660; www.foyles.co.uk). Established 100 years ago Foyles has been a magnet attracting booklovers from all over the world. Many of the thousands of books in stock are very rare.
- Harrods, Knightsbridge, London SW1X 7XL (tel: 020 7730 1234; www.harrods.com). A well-known departmental store which has over 300 departments arranged over seven floors. There are also 20 restaurants, bars and cafés.
- The Disney Store, 360–366 Oxford Street, London W1 (tel: 020 7491 9136). With over 1500 gift ideas featuring all the favourite Disney characters. Visitors are bound to find the perfect present. Branches also in Regent Street and Covent Garden Piazza.
- Still for children up to the age of 103 years and more: Hamleys, 188–196 Regent Street, London W1V 2AA (tel: 020 7494 2000; www.hamleys.com). Has seven floors filled with everything from the latest crazes, computer games, traditional teddies and specialist collector areas.

Afternoon tea

After shopping, how about a nice cup of tea? Any of the old elegant hotels, a reminder of the times gone by when people had time to enjoy a traditional English tea, can be recommended.

The Ritz, 150 Piccadilly, London W1 (tel: 020 7493 8181) needs to be booked well in advance. Tasteful elegance – tea times are 1.30–3.30 pm and at 5.30 pm daily. Excellent selection of sandwiches and cakes that just keep coming! Silver teapots and discreet live background music, harp or piano, a lovely experience for a special occasion.

The Lanesborough Hotel, Hyde Park Corner, London SW1 (tel: 020 7259 5599). Tea time: 3.30–6 pm Monday to Saturday and 4–6 pm on Sundays. Tea is served in the serene pastel splendour of the Conservatory restaurant, also with pianist and silver teapot!

Most of the old-established hotels have a quiet elegant lounge with deep sofas to enjoy a cup of tea.

One good way of seeing London and learning about the history is to take a London walk. Walks with titles such as Shakespeare's London, Old Mayfair, Legal and Illegal London, Along the Thames Pub Walk, Jack the Ripper Haunts. The Original London Walks (tel: 020 7624 3978; www.walks.com) provides 120 walks a week given by qualified historians and actors – can make Jack the Ripper and Ghost Walks creepy!

Mystery Walks (tel: 020 8558 9446; www.mysterywalks.com.uk). Paul Mansfield will be pleased to help and provide extensive knowledge of historic London in an entertaining way that helps to remember the facts.

Guided Walks in London (tel: 020 7243 1097; www.walkslondon.co.uk). Walks include Belgravia, the City and Hampstead as part of 30 pre-booked tours.

For those of you who may be getting interested in rail and air transportation (Chapters 7 and 8) a visit to the National Railway Museum in York (tel: 01904 621261); Duxford Air Museum (part of the Imperial War Museum) (tel: 01223 835000), and the Royal Air Force Museum, Cosford (tel: 01902 376211) would be worth while.

Case study

Incoming American tourists

Mr and Mrs Sale, who are in their mid-thirties, are making their first visit to the United Kingdom. They will arrive on 1 June and will be staying for one month. They have many interests such as history, gardening, art, theatre, books, tennis. They are eager to learn about the traditions and culture of the United Kingdom, travel to see the countryside and have asked you to check up on the dates of Royal Ascot and the Wimbledon Lawn Tennis Championships. What would you suggest they do and see for the one month? Use your travel guides to plan an exciting itinerary that will be a little different from the usual tour of the UK. Offer some highlights that will be interesting. Plan a day-to-day itinerary allowing some 'at leisure' time when they may wish to have some breathing space, some time to 'stand and stare'. Investigate suitable accommodation, choosing medium price-range hotels, preferably with some history and character. As an incoming tour operator, what services could you offer Mr and Mrs Sale?

Assignment 4.3

Rehabilitation

Many towns, locations and countries have had to rethink their economies owing to industrial or social changes, and have turned to tourism. Choose a destination that has increased its appeal to tourists and write a report covering the following topics. (Just in case you need an idea – perhaps The Marina on the Waterfront in Cape Town, or Ironbridge Gorge, Shropshire or Alcatraz, San Francisco may appeal.)

1 Why the original industry has declined
2 What attractions the destination has encouraged for tourists
3 What facilities are suitable for incoming tourists and incentive travellers
4 How accessible the destination has become
5 Describe the marketing strategy
6 Supply a brief history of the destination or country.

1 Name the company that offers a coach network across the USA and Canada
2 List three benefits of travelling by coach
3 List six information points you should know about a coach tour
4 What is a feeder coach?
5 Your passenger is travelling to Belgium by coach. Which currency would he use?
6 Name the main gateway to the Great Barrier Reef
7 Which area would you go to for tours to Ayer's Rock?
8 Name the capital city of South Australia
9 Name the river that flows through the city of Perth
10 List six services an incoming tourist agency could provide

Dilemma

Clean beach

You have been asked to organise a three-week holiday in the United Kingdom for three overseas visitors. They wish to spend two days of their holiday relaxing on a nice clean beach.

Action

Explain the Blue Flag system. Where are they in Britain?

Where in the world?

This city has many buildings made of pink sandstone and looks spectacular in the sunlight. The best-known building in this city is the Maharajah's Palace which stands in well-kept gardens in the city centre. Eleven kilometres away is a place called Amber, often reached by travelling by elephant.
   Name the city and country.

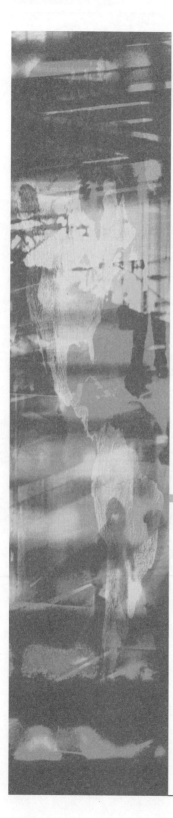

CHAPTER · · · · 5

Cruising

In this chapter we are going to discuss:

- Brief history of cruising
- Types of cruising
- Life on board ship
- Passenger density
- Factors affecting cruise costs
- Nautical terms
- River cruising
- Some ports of call
- Main cruising areas
- Flotilla sailing
- Passenger/cargo routes
- *The World* – residential cruise ship
- Some typical queries answered

Introduction

The golden age of cruising was at the end of the nineteenth century into the twentieth century when only the wealthy could afford to travel in this luxurious, privileged and elegant way. There was steerage class available for basic accommodation in the bowels of the ship for immigrants intending to start a new life in countries such as America, Canada, South Africa, Australia and new Zealand. Ships became bigger and grander as American, British, German and French companies competed to build the fastest and most luxurious liners. Royalty, heads of state and film stars would arrive at Southampton docks surrounded by glitz, glamour and photographers, on the *Queen Mary*, having sailed from New York. Today film stars often slip into London Heathrow behind dark glasses, barely recognised! It is interesting to learn the origin of the word 'posh'. On the days before air-conditioning the voyage through the Suez Canal and the Red Sea was unbearably hot, on the outward voyage from the United Kingdom the cabins on the port side had the early morning sun, but had the remainder of the day in the shade. On the return journey the reverse was true. P&O would allocate cooler cabins to government officials and dignitaries whose papers were marked 'Port Outward–Starboard Homeward', which was shortened to POSH. Memorabilia from this time during the 1920s and 1930s can be seen at the Thomas Cook Archives in Peterborough (tel 01733 563200).

Today a conventional cruise is a specially planned return voyage, with entertainment on board and organised shore excursions. Travellers normally return to their port of origin on the same vessel. During the cruise, the ship calls at many ports and islands, giving the passenger an opportunity to see a variety of new places of interest, and to venture beyond the confines of the ship. Many cruises leave from UK ports but there is also a good choice for clients wishing to take Flycruises – where the passenger first takes a flight to a large cruising area such as the Mediterranean or Caribbean to begin the cruising holiday, instead of using valuable days travelling to these places to begin the main attraction of their holiday. Note though, that whilst US/Caribbean cruises operate all year round, Mediterranean cruises mainly operate in the summer only.

There are many different types of cruises – large ships, small ships, cruises with themes, upmarket expensive cruises, budget-priced cruises, cruises for the over-50s, family-orientated cruises, river cruising, sailing on tall ships, clipper sailing, flotilla sailing and cargo boats to mention a few. We will explore the facilities of the various types of cruising holiday in a moment. First let's discuss what life is like onboard a conventional cruise – it is wonderful! There is something to please everyone. There is a wide choice of cabins (sleeping accommodation) which varies in quality depending on the deck (floor) it is on – the lower the deck, the cheaper the cabin. Cabins range in size from a small number of single cabins, through to cabins that are able to sleep 2–6 passengers, to cabins with separate sitting rooms.

The majority of cruise ships are all one class, each passenger having the full run of the ship. However, passengers can enjoy different classes of accommodation and dine in different dining rooms where most of the time the food will be excellent, equal to a very good class hotel ashore. There could be complaints about eating too much!

The entertainment will be varied. When the ship is not in port there will be deck games, swimming pools, keep-fit classes, navigational bridge visits, lectures, film shows, talks on places to be visited and many more.

For clients wishing to take a restful holiday, there are quiet lounges, sheltered decks and libraries where peace and quiet can be found. Many ships have good facilities for children and trained staff on duty to care for them. The morning may begin with keen passengers walking several times around the ship, and it will be calculated how many circumambulations to a mile so that keen joggers and walkers can keep check on their exercise! In the evening walking the promenade deck can be a great experience, with the moon shining and just the gentle swish of the waves to break the peaceful cool night air – even better if with a romantic soul! Actually cruising is ideal for passengers travelling alone – many do and thoroughly enjoy themselves. Lone women feel safe and as there is so much going on, the opportunity to make new friends is excellent. Some shipping companies do not exactly employ the mature gentlemen to dance with the ladies, but they offer free or greatly discounted cruises to gentlemen who are willing to circulate for this purpose.

For most cruises each morning a programme of the day's events and ship's newspaper will be delivered to the cabin, so the passenger will be well informed. The evening will bring the difficult decision of which entertainment to choose. There will be dancing to a choice of music – disco, ballroom, Scottish, Old Tyme – all kinds of music in various lounges. There will be bingo, theatre, films, cabaret, casino, and a variety of other attractions and entertainments available too. Many cruises also have a special interest theme such as cricket, astronomy, sequence dancing, classical music and many more in addition to the planned programme.

Perhaps your clients would like to spend more than a day in a picturesque resort – if so, the 'cruise and stay' programme would be ideal. Perhaps a two-week cruise could be combined with a week in a hotel – there are so many combinations to choose from.

Passengers and passenger density

People on cruises come from all walks of life, and represent a complete cross-section of the population. Because of the wide variety of cruises available, it is very important for you, the travel agent, to find the right cruise for your clients. The size of the ship and number of passengers on board is an important point to consider. Ships come in all sizes and we assess the size in *gross registered tonnes* (GRT). This does not refer to the weight of the ship, but to available volume capacity. Centuries ago when wine was shipped from France to England, it was in casks of a standard size. A ship carrying 20 casks would be said to measure 20 tonnes. One tonne equals 2.83 cubic metres, i.e. 100 cubic feet.

To keep the cost of the cruise down, it is necessary for a ship to carry as many passengers as is comfortably possible. This is known as a *high-density* ship. It means less space, cheaper fares and the crew member per passenger ratio is lower. A *low-density ship* means fewer passengers per gross registered tonne, and more space, better cabins and the crew/passenger ratio would be higher (perhaps one crew member to look after only two passengers). The way to establish the passenger space ratio is to divide the GRT by the number of passengers. A ship that is 67 140 GRT and has 1600 passengers would be low density – 67, 140 divided by 1600 = 41.96. A ship that is 67 140 GRT and has 3400 passengers would be high density – 67 140 divided by 3400 = 19.74. There is no official 'cut-off' line between high and low density. The majority of cruises are high density, but the crew/passenger ratio must always be considered, plus the fact that a high density ship may sail with only 75 per cent occupancy.

The larger the ship, the more facilities, and some 'superliners' or 'megaships' can carry over 2500 passengers. Some disadvantages of a large ship can be long queues to disembark or embark, and self-service buffets rather than waiter service. Also some passengers may get easily disorientated or lost in larger boats and as this has serious safety issues involved, it is vital that this is considered when discussing the cruise with your client. However, cruises with 2500 passengers dispels any myths or misconceptions of being 'cooped up with the same people' as it is likely that friends made in the bar one night may never be seen again the next! Another positive point is that these larger ships often have cabins with balconies and many other enjoyable niceties.

Medium-sized ships carry between 500 and 1500 passengers and tend to be older, although would have undergone perhaps several refurbishments and refits since originally built. They tend to be used for the mass budget market and offer great value. Many medium-sized ships are new and purpose-built for the fast-growing cruising market, able to visit smaller ports and islands. The small ships carrying fewer than 500 passengers will have far fewer facilities, a smaller entertainment programme and may not be so stable in rough seas. Nonetheless they are very popular with passengers who enjoy being at sea in a more intimate atmosphere, getting to know the captain and crew whilst experiencing 'life on the ocean waves'.

Exercise 5.1

Royal Caribbean International: Ship, *Adventure of the Sea*, GRT 142 000: passengers, 3838: crew: 1181 = 36.99 passenger space and 3.24 passengers to one crew member.

Use the example above to calculate the crew/passenger ratio of the following:

1 Royal Caribbean: Ship: *Enchantment of the Seas*: GRT 74 000 tonnes, passengers 2342, crew 760.
2 Island Cruises (First Choice RCI): Ship: *Island Escape*, GRT 40 132, passengers 1680, crew 500
3 Saga: Ship: *Saga Rose*: GRT 24 474, passengers 587, crew 350

Factors in cruise costs

As we can see so far, the choice is tremendous, so the range of fares will also be very wide. The following factors will affect the fare:

- Length of the cruise
- Type of cabin and size
- Position of cabin
- Date (season) of travel
- Number of persons in cabin
- Density of the ship

There are some amazing bargains for passengers prepared to book very early or very late, or to go on standby arrangement. Discounts available include reduced fares on flights and hotels, consecutive cruise discounts, and newcomers' discounts, special cruise promotions and onboard vouchers to spend to name just a few. They are constantly changing and so as a travel consultant you will need to keep up to date with them.

Some nautical terms

At this stage we should learn some nautical terms, as they will be needed when making the reservation.

Aft	Towards the rear of the vessel
(A)Midships	In the middle of the vessel
Berth	Nautical term for both the bed in the cabin as well as where the ship docks in port
Bow	The foremost part of the ship
Cabin	The bedroom, onboard ship, also called a stateroom
Course	The ship's route during the voyage
Deck	Each floor of a ship
Disembark	To leave the ship
Drill	Any exercise ordered by the captain (a lifeboat drill is usually held on the first day of boarding the ship).
Embark	To board a ship
Forrard	The front part of a ship
Free port	A port not included in customs territory
Funnel	The chimney of the ship
Hold	The area below deck where cargo is stored
Lifeboat	A small launch designed to carry passengers, and in the event of an emergency, crew
Manifest	List of ship's passengers, crew and cargo
Port	Left hand side of ship looking forward (indicated by red navigational lights)
Starboard	Right-hand side of ship looking forward (indicated by green navigational lights)

In the dead of night when two ships are passing, think of the following rule: 'Green to green, red to red, perfect safety, go ahead!'

Assignment 5.1

Collect at least six different types of cruise brochures and study each one. Compare price and what the price includes, facilities onboard, itineraries, and the 'small print'. Write down the main points you would wish to remember.

International river cruise destinations

River cruising or canal cruising (artificial waterways) use smaller ships travelling along rivers that are banked by beautiful scenery and can flow through interesting cities. As with the cruise ships, which normally dock in the morning allowing passengers to disembark to see the sights and sail away in the evening, river cruising offers the same opportunity to sightsee en route. Often river cruises are packaged by suppliers with flights, coach travel, ferries and Eurotunnel and hotel accommodation should the client wish to extend their stay. Some river or canal trips you may like to investigate further are sailing through France with varied peaceful scenery, or through Holland with tree-shaded canals, old interesting architecture, world-renowned museums, flower stalls and, if travelling in springtime, acres of highly perfumed bulb fields. Every ten years the Floriade World Horticultural Exhibition is held – a magnificent sight, and the next one is 2012.

The river Rhine is the biggest river cruise destination excluding the Nile. It is 1320 km long (820 miles) and with the source in Switzerland it flows through to Holland, the busiest cruising part being through Southern Germany. The boats are comfortable with friendly passengers and crew and beautiful scenery of vineyards and castles.

Assignment 5.2

Study a map of Germany and find the following places: Cologne, Andernach, Alken, Cochem, Boppard, Koblenz, Rudesheim, Speyer.

The waterways of the Tsars give an opportunity to see the treasures of Russia. In St Petersburg the passenger can visit the Hermitage State Museum and the Catharine Palace in Pushkin, the former residence of the imperial family.

Assignment 5.3

1 Study a map of Russia and find the following places in order to reach Moscow from St Petersburg, travelling on the waterways: Lake Ladoga, Kizhi Island, White Lake, Irma, Kostroma, River Volga, Uglich, Yaroslavl.
2 'Brainstorm' Moscow – write down all that you associate with the city and Russia in general, and follow up by reading about the places of interest or culture and traditions that you have thought of.

Another interesting river cruise is on the Yangtze in China. This cruise is usually combined with a brief two-week tour of China taking in the main tourist attractions. It is not a restful holiday by any means, but exhilarating and educational and a wonderful experience.

In Beijing a visit to the Temple of Heaven, the Forbidden City and the Great Wall of China is a must. A flight to Xian to see the terracotta army where over 8000 warriors (excavation is still in progress) can be observed from a platform surrounding them for a close unhurried view. Discovered in 1974, each face has a different life-like expression modelled on live soldiers. They were made to protect the first Qin emperor's tomb, which Qin Shi Huangdi arranged before his death in 210 BC. There are beautiful gorges with spectacular scenery to enjoy on the Yangtze. At Three Gorges Dam, the largest hydroelectric project in the world is in progress when a massive artificial lake will be created in 2009. It is thought that by 2007, this part of the Yangtze will not be navigable by boat.

Another famous river is the River Nile travelling from Luxor to Aswan, seeing Egyptian life along the way, together with ancient monuments and burial sites. Hop off the boat to see places such as the Valley of the Kings, Esna, Edfu and Kom Ombu and Karnak at Luxor. A qualified Egyptologist guide is essential.

Assignment 5.4

On a world map, locate the following rivers and obtain information on the area and tourist attractions: Amazon, (South America), Mississippi–Missouri (North America), Murray-Darling (Australia), Rio Grande (North America), Ganges (Asia), Negro (South America), Zambezi (Africa), River Shannon (Ireland)

Ocean, river and canal cruising

There are many inland waterways, canals and rivers in the United Kingdom where cruising can be enjoyed. The lakes and canals of Scotland with breathtaking scenery, and the Norfolk Broads where many inland waterways can be travelled in peaceful surroundings mainly using hired boats, are just two examples.

The British Waterways Board maintains about 2000 miles of inland waterways, and other bodies preserve a further 1500 miles of navigable waterways. Over 300 miles of formerly derelict canals have been returned to use and are an attraction for both foreign and British tourists.

Assignment 5.5

1 Study a map of the United Kingdom and locate the following waterways: Grand Union Canal, River Wey, River Severn, Leeds and Liverpool Canal, River Parrett.
2 Investigate and write down the main tourist attractions of the following places:

Kennet and Avon Canal	a visit to	**Bath**
Oxford Canal	a visit to	**Oxford**
River Trent	a visit to	**Nottingham**
River Thames	a visit to	**Southend-on-Sea**
Caledonian Canal	a visit to	**Loch Ness**

Many rivers and canals around the world have locks, which are a great feat of engineering and interesting to watch or participate in manipulating.

We have said that there are many different types of cruising holidays from which to choose. Many passengers enjoy a themed cruise when celebrities and experts join the ship to share their expertise. Have a look again at the special interest chapter of this book. A cruise for most of those interests can probably be found at some time. We also said there are cruises that cater for specific age groups such as Saga (www.saga.co.uk) for the mature passenger, and at the other end of the spectrum for children of all ages, we have the Disney Cruise Line. There are two ships, *Disney Magic* and *Disney Wonder,* both offering first-class standards of service and entertainment. The choice is between three- and four-night itineraries sailing from Port Canaveral to Nassau in the Bahamas and Disney's private island Castaway Cay. Also offered are seven-night itineraries including the Bahamas and combinations with onshore stays with an opportunity to visit the Walt Disney World Resort. Onboard ship, all the Disney characters can be found and the Disney theatre stages spectacular shows, classics such as *Beauty and the Beast* and *Hercules,* while the Buena Vista cinema shows new Disney movies. The Disney Cruise Line, like most cruise ships, operates a cash-free system. After taking note of the passenger's credit or charge card details, the client has charging privileges and will be able to sign for every purchase onboard ship, settling the bill at the end of the trip. Cash will be required for purchases made onshore. To learn more about Disney Cruises tel 0870 2424900 or see www.airtours.co.uk or British Airways Holidays tel 0870 442 3800.

Exercise 5.2

Walt Disney World

Your client has decided to book the Disney Cruise and combine it with a visit to Walt Disney World and has one or two questions to ask you. Use available brochures, web sites etc to answer their questions:

1 How do we get around Walt Disney World?
2 Are pushchairs, wheelchairs and lockers available?
3 What about special language needs?
4 What if I need medical assistance whilst visiting a Theme Park?
5 How large is Walt Disney World?
6 Are guests allowed to smoke?
7 What does it cost to enter the Walt Disney World?
8 Does Disney offer childcare?

Clipper class

Another type of cruise is true sailing on a clipper class boat. The *Star Flyer* accommodates 140 passengers plus 72 crew, has four masts and is 110 metres (360 feet) long. The itineraries vary considerably according to demand. From Athens to Goa the journey takes approximately 24 days. Another sailing boat in the fleet is *Star*

Clipper, which accommodates 170 passengers, has four masts and carries more than 36 000 square feet of canvas, spread among 16 separate sails, propelling the ship with the prevailing wind. *Royal Clipper* offers the ultimate sea-going experience, balancing grandeur, adventure and tradition with superb service and amenities. It's a larger sailing ship with 56 000 square feet of sail and 112 cabins. Sailing around the Mediterranean, Caribbean and Far East is offered. Useful contact: Fred Olsen Tranquil, tel 01473 292229, www.starclippers.co.uk.

Flotilla sailing

Sailing in a flotilla is another popular type of holiday when a small group of friends or family may like to sail around the Mediterranean, Caribbean or Greek islands. Some companies will accept complete novices but it is better to have some sailing experience. However, it is possible to hire a boat complete with a skipper and the client can do as much or as little as they wish towards the sailing of the boat. The lead boat's role can be compared to that of a sheepdog; it is their role to herd the flotilla to the next port of call. The evenings are spent together enjoying each other's company often in a local bar or taverna. The lead boat crew will often organise barbeques or fancy dress parties, which are great fun and enjoyed by the 'flotilla sailors' (accompanied by Greek wine!). The lead boat usually has a crew of three, the skipper, an engineer and a hostess to look after the domestic requirements. The skipper is responsible for the whole flotilla.

Each morning the lead boat crew will hold a briefing with the flotilla explaining the day's activities, the destination, what to look out for and instructions about mooring on arrival. Boats are linked with two-way radio. Here are some useful numbers for this type of holiday:

Sunsail (023 92222224), www.sunsail.com
Sailing Holidays (020 8459 8787) www.sailingholidays.com
Top Yachts (0143 520950) www.top-yacht.com
FourWinds Sailing (01 635 43 800) www.four-winds.co.uk

Cargo cruise ships

Something different could be travelling on a cargo cruise ship, which caters for between 400 to 1000 passengers and 50 cars. They are relatively small ships at between 2600 and 12 000 tonnes, calling at Norwegian ports that many large cruise liners are unable to reach. As the passenger boards the Norwegian coastal vessel, they become part of a tradition that has spanned three centuries, a service created as a vital link to the remote coastal communities, carrying supplies and passengers. There are thirteen ships in the fleet the latest being entered in April 2003.

Many of the stopping-off points along the way are little more than tranquil hamlets on tiny islands, whose inhabitants rely on the Coastal Voyage ships to bring them essential supplies, or to take them to the nearest town. Other ports of call are long-established, bustling towns, owing their prosperity to the fishing, mining or shipbuilding industries. There is little entertainment onboard, which so often is a large part of the traditional cruise ship programme, just the occasional film, lecture or pianist. The service links 35 ports from Bergen to Kirkenes in the far north of

Norway. This is a very beautiful part of the world. For details see Norwegian Coastal Voyages at www.coastalvoyages.com, tel: 020 8846 2666.

Do not forget your local or nearest day-cruise operators. Organising common-interest groups to charter a ship for a day can gain a lot of business. Or educational trips such as a nature watch – birds and seals, or special celebrations – parties, wedding anniversaries or the actual wedding ceremony.

The World

And now a big leap to *The World*: the world's first residential cruise ship – 644 feet and 43 000 tons with 320 crew. Apartments can be purchased for between £2 million and £5 million – there are 110 on board. It cost £182 million to build and began its inaugural circumnavigation from Norway in February 2002. This is for the very wealthy and, as you would expect, the passenger list is top secret. Within eleven months it travels to 120 ports in 40 countries.

Assignment 5.6

Getting back to earth – brainstorm the questions your client is most likely to ask.

Be ready to answer your client's questions. The answers can be found in the shipping company's manual; a copy should be at your travel agency and often in the cruise lines brochure. Although your client can read up on the information in the brochure himself or herself, it is good to be able to volunteer information and useful hints. When studying the brochures make a note of whether it is the actual shipping company brochure – for example, Norwegian Cruise Line, Royal Caribbean, P&O, Fred Olsen Cruises and so on. Or tour operators brochures such as Travelsphere, Travelbag, Thomas Cook etc. operating agents for the shipping company or tour operators who are also ship owners such as MyTravel (formerly Airtours) and Thomson Cruises.

Client information on cruising

A few of the topics your clients will wish to know about will probably be as follows.

Shore excursions: need I book in advance?

Yes, if there is something the client has set his or her heart on seeing. The popular cruises can become fully booked bearing in mind the number of passengers and the transport limitations of some smaller ports and islands. They can, however, be booked onboard after the passenger has had the excursions described. These are a big money-spinner for the shipping companies and are often overpriced. Check the cruise brochure for pre-excursion booking requirements.

Independent tour companies will often have staff standing at the quayside waiting to fill a minibus and will give guided tours at a much cheaper tariff. Prices with cab drivers can be negotiated and for a party of three or four, this could be a much cheaper option.

What happens if I am ill?

Most cruise ships will have a well-equipped hospital in the charge of registered doctors and qualified nursing staff.

What about my laundry?

The ships will have laundry and pressing services onboard available through the cabin steward, at extra charge. However, some ships also have laundry rooms fitted with sinks, drying cupboards, ironing boards and irons for passengers wishing to do their own laundry.

Health and beauty facilities

Most cruise ships have spa and fitness centres with exercise equipment, sauna and massage facilities. Some passengers may feel a visit to the fitness centre a must with all the fine food in which to indulge! There will be hair salons offering beauty treatments and there will be facilities for passengers to use their own hair dryers if they prefer.

Will your clients be cut off from the rest of the world while abroad?

No, the ships are fitted with modern worldwide telecommunications systems including telephone, telex, facsimile and Internet. Most cabins have telephones, but it is worth mentioning that telephone links are via satellite and if a number is called, payment begins when the telephone begins to ring, not when the receiver is picked up. Therefore payment still has to be made even if the phone at the other end is not answered. This therefore can be very expensive.

What should I wear?

This depends on the cruise. Some companies are more 'upmarket' than others, so check with the shipping companies, as you do not want your clients to feel uncomfortable. By day the dress is casual and sports or leisurewear is appropriate. In the evenings most passengers like to dress up a little and there could be two or three formal evenings depending on the length of the cruise, generally a dark lounge suit and tie for the men and smart cocktail dresses for the women. There are also some family and young-person cruises on offer where the dress code reflects the relaxed atmosphere. There may be only one formal evening during the cruise when wearing a suit will be optional, otherwise the evening dress code is smart casual. This is a matter of choice – some clients hate the thought of getting dressed up each evening and the smart casual approach will be a great relief to them, others will want to choose a cruise that has a more formal dress code. It's good to have the choice! Should an evening suit be necessary and your client does not wish to have the expense of buying one, it can be hired for the duration of the cruise.

Tipping

This can be a worry to some passengers, so put their minds at rest! It is a very personal way of expressing satisfaction for the way you have been looked after during the cruise. The shipping company sends each passenger a leaflet for guidance as to who, how much and when you might tip. Generally, the restaurant and cabin personnel will receive a gratuity and at your client's discretion, perhaps the maître'd and bar staff. With some cruises tipping is included in the price of the holiday, with others a 15 per cent charge may be made at the end of the voyage.

What currency is used onboard?

Most ships are cashless, which is lovely. However, the bill has to be settled at the end of the cruise and so the passenger needs to know the currency in which the shipping company operates. Also which credit/debit cards are acceptable and the currency used in ports of call.

Will I get seasick?

Doctors and nurses will be at hand to administer help. Before leaving home a visit to the doctor or pharmacist may be wise for seasickness-prevention tablets, or the purchase of wristbands from the pharmacy may work very well. The wristbands are a simple drug-free invention and seem to work for most passengers who do suffer in this way. The majority of cruise ships are stabilised to prevent excessive rolling on rough seas.

Consult your brainstorming assignment number 5.6 and find the answers to the many questions the client may ask. Add the following questions if they are not already on your list. When travelling on a fly/cruise:

(a) What is the free baggage allowance?
(b) Can we pay a supplement to increase the allowance?
(c) Can we choose the meals on the aircraft?
(d) Can we pay for priority check-in?
(e) Will our family sit together?
(f) How long does the flight take and how close is the destination airport to the seaport?

About the ship:

(a) Can I select the cabin when making the booking?
(b) Can special diets be catered for?
(c) What disability facilities are available?
(d) Will our children eat with us?
(e) Is childcare available?
(f) Are there children's clubs onboard?
(g) What extra costs must I consider?
(h) Are there any 'special offers' for the date and destination I wish to travel?
(i) Are there any single cabins available?
(j) Does the ship obtain 'blanket visas' or do I require individual ones?

Cruising areas

The main cruising areas are Scandinavia during the summertime for the midnight sun, the Mediterranean, the Caribbean islands, the Far East and Australia, but by now you will have studied the brochures and found many more interesting and exciting itineraries.

Let's look at one or two special ports of call. Madeira and the Canary Islands in the north Atlantic will often be included in a Mediterranean cruise itinerary. Madeira is 35 miles long and 13 miles wide but the volcanic island is so mountainous that distances are magnified in practice. Many people enjoy walking by the Levadas (irrigation canals).

Study the attractions of Madeira under the following headings:

- Banana plantations
- Botanic gardens
- Flower festival
- Ancient buildings and squares
- Harbour and old town
- Wine lodges
- Museums
- Embroidery factories
- Monte – toboggan to Funchal
- Camacha – for wicker industry
- Reid Hotel – first on the island

Christmas and New Year are a very special time to visit Madeira. The streets are beautifully ablaze with coloured lights and many decorations. Traditional skills and dances are demonstrated in the streets and the whole island has a magical atmosphere of years gone by. Several cruise ships with coloured bunting call into Funchal at this time and brass bands play in the streets, adding a wonderful atmosphere. They leave the harbour around 11.30 pm to see the magnificent firework display at midnight from the sea – it is spectacular.

It is a Madeiran custom to leave just one light on in the house on New Year's night and the whole island is 'twinkling with diamonds'. The islanders love the legend that after God had created the world he was so pleased he kissed it, and where He placed the kiss, Madeira was born – that says it all!

There are so many Caribbean islands to visit, each one with its own charm and piece of history. Under the following headings make a study of Jamaica:

- Fire Fly – the home of the late Noel Coward
- Montego Bay
- Rose Hall and Annie Palmer
- Dunn's River Falls
- Martha Brae
- Kingston

Make a study of some of the other Caribbean islands such as:

- Cayman Islands
- Cuba
- Haiti
- Granada

Let's look at Scandinavian summers and the Land of the Midnight Sun, the rugged North Cape and beyond the islands of Spitsbergen where the sun never sets between mid-May and late July. Make a study of the following locations:

- Denmark and the Jutland peninsular
- Copenhagen on the island of Zealand (one of the largest cruise departure points in Northern Europe)
- The 'Little Mermaid'
- Christiansburg and Amelienborg palaces
- Tivoli Gardens
- Sweden – Stockholm
- Gothenburg
- Malmo
- Norway – Oslo
- Viking ships
- Fjords
- Spitsbergen lying deep in the Arctic Circle.

Scandinavia has spectacular glaciers, fjords, snow-crowned peaks and an abundance of wildlife – seabirds, whales, seals, walrus, reindeer, Arctic fox, polar bear, to mention a few.

Assignment 5.7

Investigate three ports of call from each of the following cruise areas. Describe what the cruise passenger might like to do and see in and around each port of call.

1 Africa and the Indian Ocean
2 The Mediterranean
3 Scandinavia and the Baltic
4 The Caribbean and South America
5 Far East
6 Australia and New Zealand
7 Alaska

Dilemmas

Use the brochures and information sources available to you to solve the following client dilemmas.

1 America by sea

Mr Cobb, having spent many years in the Royal Navy and with 11 September 2001 still fresh in his mind, would like to travel from the UK to the USA by sea. Research the frequencies and cost of travel to America by sea from the UK.

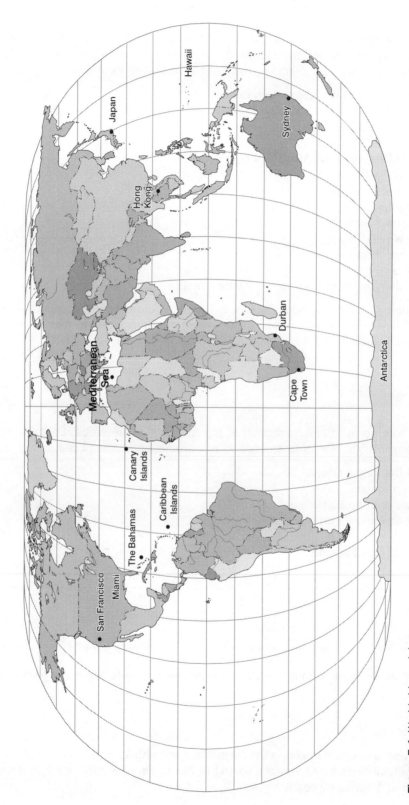

Figure 5.1 Worldwide cruising areas

2 Upper deck refund

You booked Mr and Mrs Vickery on a Rhine Cruise on an upper deck at the surcharge of £100 per person. Due to a double booking, on boarding the ship your clients were allocated a cabin on the main deck. Mr and Mrs Vickery enjoyed the cruise but have returned to your office with a letter from the hotel manager on the ship confirming what has happened, and requesting a refund of the difference between the two cabins. The cruise operator has not responded to your application for a refund over the past four weeks despite a reminder. The company is a member of the Association of British Travel Agents (ABTA). Research the terms of the European Union's Package Travel Regulations. Decide upon what action you should take.

3 Around the world without a plane

You have clients wishing to travel from the United Kingdom to New Zealand by sea or land as one member of the party has a fear of flying. Research whether it is possible to travel from the UK to New Zealand without travelling by air. Give details of the route.

Where in the world?

1 Pizza is a traditional food from this Mediterranean country. It was invented in the seventeenth century during a bad period of famine – formerly it was only flat bread with tomatoes.

 Other food associated with this country includes risotto, parma and San Daniele ham, pasta and ice cream.

 Name the country.

2 This state was purchased in 1867 for the sum of $7 200 000 (about 2 cents per acre). In the early 1900s gold was discovered here and thousands of prospectors arrived for the Goldrush. Cruise ships often visit the fjords and glaciers of the west coast. This state has very modern cities but it also has more aircraft per head of population than anywhere else in the world. To travel through uninhabited parts of the country aircraft are used instead of cars.

 Name this country/state.

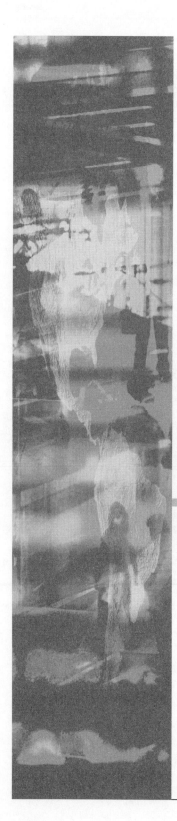

Car rental

In this chapter we are going to discuss:

- Benefits of car rental
- Growth of car rental
- Tariffs
- Car rental insurance
- Car groups
- Fuel consumption
- Organising car rental
- Selling skills
- Itinerary planning

Benefits of car rental

Let's think of some good reasons why a customer would wish to hire a car:

- The rented car may be used during a business promotion
- Perhaps to drive between airport and hotel
- It can be used to travel between cities perhaps as a replacement during car maintenance or during rail/air cancellations
- It could be used for touring by holidaymakers

Car rental provides flexibility, the freedom to go almost anywhere at any time and the pleasure to stop as one pleases. It also provides convenience to transfer between airport and hotel, to travel around a city with all baggage safely in the boot of the car. It makes the journey comfortable. The 'rent it here, leave it there' (one-way car rental) system enables a client to travel between two major points of his or her choice and then continue the trip using another form of transport if desired. Car rental provides cheap transportation compared with many other forms of transport, bearing in mind four or five persons may be travelling in the vehicle. The accessibility of car rental stations is enormous. There are approximately 1300 airports throughout the world where car rental is available and just one car rental company, Europcar for example, has 2650 rental stations in 118 countries with a fleet of over 203 000 vehicles worldwide.

Growth of car rental

The growth of car rental over the last ten years has been mainly due to the many partnerships formed with principals such as hotels, shipping companies, tour operators, travel agents and airlines, and lower all-inclusive rates. By offering additional services such as computerised booking and communication systems, a wide variety of tariffs, chauffeur-driven cars and so on, together with better agent training, car rental has appealed to an ever-increasing adventurous client.

There are approximately 230 car rental operators in the United Kingdom and most of them work along similar lines (see Tables 6.1 and 6.2). Let's have a look now at general information on car rental.

Table 6.1 Customer segmentation of short-term vehicle rental sector, % revenue 1998

UK corporate	42
UK leisure	40
Inbound corporate	6
Inbound leisure	12
Total	100

Source: British Vehicle Rental & Leasing Association

Table 6.2 Overseas visitors to the UK and total overseas visitors spending, million and £bn, 1998

Visitors (million)	26.0
Spend (£bn)	12.2

Source: Office for National Statistics

Tariffs

Rates are usually calculated on a daily basis which is 24 hours, or a weekly basis which is seven days. There is normally a time charge and a kilometre/mileage charge. So the cost of hiring a car would be quoted as so much per day plus so much per kilometre/mile.

Alternatively, there is the popular 'unlimited mileage' rate. With this a greater time charge is made and no mileage charges are made at all. For clients intending to travel long distances this is very economical.

In addition to these rates, most car rental companies have 'special offers' and brochures are available explaining the great reductions. It is also well worth contacting the car rental companies for any special rates that are unpublished but available.

No car rental company likes to have cars standing idle over a weekend, and will usually be pleased to negotiate competitive rates. There are schemes offering discounts for frequent travellers (loyalty cards), pre-paid tariffs booking 14 days in advance, or even greater discounts for booking and paying 60 days in advance providing an all-inclusive rate and even better value for money. An inclusive rate can cover:

- Unlimited mileage
- Third-party liability
- Collision damage waiver (CDW)
- Theft waiver (TW)
- Local tax
- Airport surcharge
- Licence fees

Additional services, such as 'one-way' rental, dropping the car off at a different location, ordering a baby seat, adding an additional driver, or having the car delivered and collected from the client's hotel, can also be pre-paid.

The tariff can also be seasonal in some countries. In Europe, for example, winter would be low season and summer months – June to September – would be high season.

Car rental services can be purchased through the car rental company direct, often offering travel agents higher rates of commission for increased sales. There are also car rental brokers who offer the cheapest rates and will represent many car rental companies. In order to counteract this, however, most car rental companies and brokers will have a 'price promise' to match the lower price quoted. This applies to identical cars available for hire with another international car hire company through high street agents.

Car groups

Cars are divided into groups of similar models normally ranging from 'A' the smaller cars to 'J' the largest cars. It is important when assisting your client to choose a car to consider not only the number of passengers but also the amount of luggage to be carried. Although a small car will have seating capacity for four people the luggage capacity will be two large suitcases and possibly two smaller ones.

Another point to consider is manual or automatic transmission. Your client may only be able to drive a car that has automatic transmission.

Car rental companies produce brochures clearly showing the cars they use, giving details of number of passengers and pieces of baggage each car is able to comfortably carry, and other specifications such as roof rack, airbags, air conditioning and so on.

Does your client require a three-door (two passenger doors plus the boot) or four-door car? A three-door car may mean difficulty for a passenger to reach the back seat.

Fuel consumption

A small car will travel approximately 10–12 kilometres per litre (28–31 miles per gallon), a medium-sized car approximately 8–10 kilometres per litre (22–28 miles per gallon), and a large car approximately 6–8 kilometres per litre (18–20 miles per gallon). This information, and the price of petrol in countries to be visited, is important to know, as you can then advise your clients enabling them to budget for their holidays. The client may also like to consider diesel fuel which enables cars to do approximately 20 kilometres per litre (50 miles per gallon) although the car will be noisier.

Petrol

The rates quoted do not include petrol. The client will normally rent a car with a full tank and return it also with a full tank. Oil and maintenance will usually be included in the cost – no charge for water!

Age restrictions

Both a minimum and maximum age restriction can apply depending on the company, the country where car rental is being received and the group. The minimum age is often between 23 years and 25 years, and the maximum age between 65 years and 70 years. In some countries a young driver surcharge may apply.

Driver's licence

A valid and clean driving licence is required. Does that mean someone with endorsements would be unable to rent a car? Not necessarily, this could be acceptable at the discretion of the rental company. The driver's licence for every driver needs to be from their country of residence, and may have to be valid for at least one year or longer – it varies from country to country. If the licence is of non-Roman alphabet (e.g. Arabic) then an international driver's licence will be required. Whenever driving abroad an international licence may be preferred and is obtainable from the car rental company and motor associations.

Deposits

Car rental companies will require a deposit as security. This is to cover a non-waivable excess charge in the event of damage or theft and refuelling if the car is returned with an empty tank. Charges for optional insurance and any special additional equipment will be made at collection. Deposits are normally paid in local currency by a major credit card at the time of rental. This procedure can be speeded up as most major car rental companies have a system where personal and credit card details are given to the car rental company in advance.

We now come to a very important part of selling car rental that must be fully understood.

Car rental insurance

All reputable car rental companies include third-party insurance within their rates. You should check the amount of cover provided to ensure that it is adequate and that it includes cover in the event of death or injury to third parties or damage to cars and other property belonging to third parties caused in the accident. This can be particularly important in the USA where the basic cover provided is not always sufficient to meet the amounts awarded in legal action arising from an accident. In this case, extended cover is always available as an 'optional extra' to clients. Rules relevant to the car rental company being used should always be studied carefully.

Collision Damage Waiver (CDW)

If the rental car is damaged this will cover the cost of repairs. The client will, however, have to pay a fixed amount towards this called an 'excess'. The excess will vary by country, so check at the time of reservation. An optional payment for excess waiver, sometimes termed Super Collision Damage Waiver (Super CDW) is available to reduce or eliminate the excess that the client will have to pay in the event of damage to the car.

Theft Protection (TP)

This covers the cost of replacing the rental car (or parts of it) if it gets stolen. The client may have to pay excess which will vary by country. Check at the time of reservation. Most car rental companies offer clients a chance to upgrade theft protection to cover contents and reduce the excess.

Personal Accident Insurance (PAI)

Should the client have an accident during rental, as a driver or passenger, this will cover some medical expenses, accidental death payment and assistance/rescue. Clients taking a holiday package insurance may not need this but, once again, check in advance. For additional payment, Super Personal Accident Insurance (Super PAI) covers more than the PAI plus effects/baggage and contingency expenses.

For renting a car in the USA these insurances should be included in the rental agreement:

- Public and Property Damage Protection and Third Party Liability
- Additional Liability Insurance
- Loss Damage Waiver. This is not available in the state of New York where an excess has to be paid.

Do check what is and what is not covered by the policy. Europcar, along with other car rental companies, has fully inclusive cover. The cover provided includes:

- Reduces excess to zero
- Super Personal Accident and Effects Cover
- Third Party Plus
- One Free Additional Driver

There is also the Peace of Mind (POM) programme. The cover includes:

- Reduces excess to zero
- Super Personal Accident and Effects Cover
- Third Party Plus
- Damage Waiver
- Theft Waiver
- One Free Additional Driver

What happens if the client wishes to use their credit/charge card cover? Some credit/charge card companies provide limited cover against liability. Most car rental companies are unable to advise customers on the cover provided in these schemes. Should the client choose to utilise this type of cover, they will be responsible for compensating the car rental company in full for any damage and reclaiming from their credit/charge card company. Customers declining to take the damage waiver and theft waiver cover from a car rental company will be required to complete a declaration.

For corporate customers wishing to provide their own insurance, full details of their insurance policy must be submitted for approval to Europcar's insurance department. Customer's own insurance must be on a fully inclusive basis and cover all vehicles that Europcar are contracted to supply.

Taxes

Taxes are over and above the rental charges and vary in each country. When booking a special holiday package rate check whether taxes are included.

Assignment 6.1

Car rental

Collect three major car rental brochures.

1 Compare:
  - Package tariffs
  - What is included
  - What is not included
  - Daily rate
2 Explain in your own words the following rental terms and conditions for each car rental company:
  - Reservations
  - Car models
  - Rental extension
  - Rental collection
  - Amendments
  - Cancellations

Model

Car rental companies will try to provide a specified model when confirming the reservation but they will only guarantee a particular group. If none of the vehicles from the specified group is available when the hirer collects the car, a larger model will be available at no extra cost to the client.

Rates of exchange

The rates of exchange shown in the directories are meant purely as a guide. Always check the rate of exchange at the time of making the reservation with the car rental company. Some clients may prefer to pre-purchase for guaranteed rates in pounds sterling.

Organising car rental

Working in a travel agency, you would be responsible for making the reservation. The larger companies have a Central Reservation Office – one telephone call and you will be able to reserve a car for your client in several countries. Small firms are, however, also easily located in the *Travel Trade Directory* under the appropriate separate towns, but will probably not pay commission.

Car rental can also be reserved, amended or cancelled by using your company's computer system. The information at your fingertips can include all relevant accounting data such as volume, commission earned, payments and so on, as well as car rental details such as average duration, average cost per rental, total number of rentals, method of payment, type of vehicle rented, average cost per day, average miles driven, average rental length and insurance options.

It is important to obtain all the information required before making the reservation such as:

- City and country of rental and airport where applicable. Remember, many cities have more than one airport
- Date and time of rental and flight number where applicable
- Group of car required
- City where car will be returned
- Date and time of return
- Name, address and telephone number of customer
- Tariff name (Unlimited Mileage, Business Rate, Holiday Special)
- Your company name and address
- Your company IATA code or car rental assigned number where applicable. (For easy identification for rental company to pay your agency the commission for the business)
- Any additional equipment required – roof rack, baby seat, etc.
- Age of driver, licence details, insurance required
- How payment will be made – credit card details, deposit or full payment, corporate account

The method of payment is important. Your agency may hold car hire vouchers of the principal companies. These vouchers will be numbered, completed by you and, when collecting the car, the voucher then presented by the client to the car rental company. Your client may have already paid for the hire through your travel agency, or he or she may wish to pay a deposit to your agency and the balance to the rental office. Perhaps your client would find it more convenient to pay the whole amount direct to the car rental company using his credit card. Either way, the commission earned by you for making that booking is passed to your travel agency.

Completing the car rental voucher is simple. The format for all car rental vouchers is very similar and you would be relaying the information obtained before making the reservation onto the voucher.

The voucher will have several copies so remember to press hard when writing! The copies are usually different colours for easy distribution.

Exercise 6.1

Car rental abroad

Mr and Mrs Ebanks have decided to take advantage of the cheap air fares on offer to Canada and plan to fly to Calgary where they will rent a car. They would like to drive to Yellowstone Park in the USA but need some information on the following points before making the reservation:

1 Is there a problem taking a Canadian rental car across the border?
2 They know it is a 200-mile journey from Calgary on Route 2 to cross the border at Coutts. Is there anything special to see along the way?
3 Is any documentation required at the border?
4 Can you suggest where they might stay near Yellowstone Park?

Suggested research material: Alamo, North American car rental company.

How can car rental clients learn about which routes to choose? In addition to obtaining help from car rental companies, reading maps and guide books of the area and contacting motoring associations before and during the journey, many cars are fitted with satellite navigation. Over 3600 Automobile Association (AA) patrols are fitted with state-of-the-art Blaupunkt satellite navigation systems.

Input the destination and the computer will confirm how to get there, calculate arrival time, give advance warning of each turning and reroute should the driver get lost. A choice is given between minor roads or motorways. Mapping is contained on CD and the latest DVD-based units show every motorway, major road and most country lanes in Europe. There is a choice of scales from 256 miles to the inch – enough to put Edinburgh and Rome on the same map, or 50 yards to the inch – close enough to see how far round a roundabout a driver has travelled.

One step beyond is a system called telematics. This is so far advanced that should a crash occur severe enough to set off the airbags, the car will inform the emergency services of the exact location.

Many of the services we take for granted at home will be available in the car. The most significant is the Internet, enabling us to be constantly informed about current information and make online reservations.

Assignment 6.2

Car rental

1 Collect a selection of brochures giving details of car rental packages. Then write a report on each company explaining:
  • The type of package
  • The country destinations
  • Calculate the cost of three different types of car rental package holidays based on two adults travelling together in June
2 Describe six services offered by car rental companies
3 Explain four advantages of car rental for the client
4 Discover how many car rental companies that sell through travel agencies are operating within your own country

Assignment 6.3

Car rental

Plan a detailed itinerary for Mr and Mrs Cox who will arrive in Sydney in November and would like to have an independent tour of Australia using train, domestic flights and car rental. They will stay five weeks. Your itinerary should include a description of 'must see' destinations.

How can we improve our selling skills? Here are a few finer points to keep in mind. First of all, we must think of the benefits to the client:

Mobility
Flexibility
Convenience
Cost
Speed
Suitability
24-hour emergency service

You may be able to think of additional benefits.

Secondly, get to know the many car rental companies and their services available, fully understand the car rental directory, become familiar with the booking conditions, practise costing car rental so that you will be quick and accurate when faced with a real live client. Always write clearly on the car rental travel voucher – double check the information given.

Thirdly, keep up to date with all the many special offers. Remember, we have airlines, hotels and tour operators worldwide working with car rental companies, offering excellent competitive rates, so we need to be aware of these in order to assist our clients to have the best deal available for his or her needs. We are very fortunate in the travel business to have a wealth of information at our fingertips. Keep a good supply of maps giving distances between cities. Be aware of places of interest along the way. Helping your client plan an individual itinerary can be very interesting.

When selling car rental, travel agents can enjoy one of the highest commissions earned – does that seem mercenary to you? We wish to offer a full and professional service to our customers and we are assisting the car rental companies to keep their vehicles on the road – so everyone is pleased!

Good luck with selling car rental.

Dilemmas

1 Car rental

Mrs Williamson has a son who is disabled and can only drive using hand controls. Will he be able to rent a car abroad?

Action

Find out which countries have car rental with special facilities

2 Swiss motorway pass

Your client will be driving through Switzerland on her way to Italy and has asked you the following questions:

1 Is it possible to buy a pass in the United Kingdom to travel on Swiss motorways to avoid having to queue at border crossings?
2 If your client entered Switzerland on a non-motorway road, where would she buy a pass before using a motorway?
3 Can your client pay with Euros as she is just passing through on her way to Italy?

Action

Find the answers to these questions.

3 Car rental upper age limit

You have been advised that a gentleman of 81 years will arrive in Britain from Portugal and wishes to rent a car for the duration of his holiday in the United Kingdom.

Action

Research whether a driver of 81 years will be allowed to rent a car.

4 Taking a car abroad

Mr and Mrs Bedford are having a self-drive holiday taking their car abroad this year. They have the EU/UK number plate with 'GB' surrounded by yellow stars on a blue background.

Action

Find out if they will be exempt from showing a traditional GB plate when travelling in EU countries.

Where in the world?

1 This is the largest of a group of six islands in the Central Pacific Ocean and which are spread over about 2000 miles of ocean. This island is noted for its beaches. It is volcanic and it has a very long drop waterfall – 420 feet – called Akaka Falls.

   Name the island and the five other remaining islands.

2 This is a relatively young country, having been colonised by people from all over the world since the seventeenth century. It has an area of 9 970 610 kilometres and is the second largest country in the world. The official languages are English and French. Their sporting interests are ice hockey, football, baseball and soccer. Their industrial interests are fishing, forestry, farming and mining. One city is famous for its tower which at 553 metres high makes it the world's tallest free-standing structure.

   The Inuit people were some of the first inhabitants of this country, along with the Indians. They came from Asia 4000 years ago in sealskin boats.

   Name the country and the city with the landmark tower.

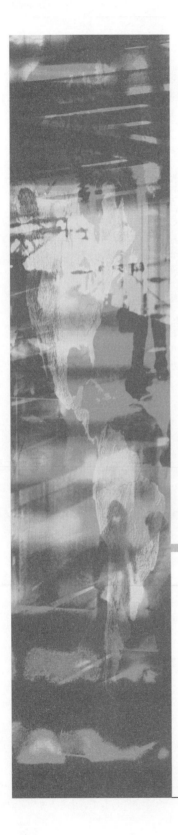

Ferry services and railways

In this chapter we are going to discuss:

- Different types of ferries
- Routings
- Taking a car to Europe
- Brochure work
- Making a reservation
- Various rail services worldwide
- Benefits of rail travel
- Eurotunnel
- Eurostar
- Motor-rail
- Tourist destinations
- Steam railways

Ferry services

Since the nineteenth century tourists have been regularly crossing the English Channel between Britain and France, but the growth of ferry services really escalated in the 1950s with the increase in private car ownership. Routes developed quickly between Scandinavia and Germany, and Britain and the Continent. The 1980s saw increased trade between Britain and Europe and with advancement in technology and a wide range of services, it is estimated that the number of cross-Channel passengers has increased to approximately 90 million each year. Ferry services have come a long way from the original sea crossings and now offer a wide range of routes, sailing schedules, fares, comfort, sleeping accommodation, entertainment and speed and are often advertised as 'mini cruises'. Travelling by ferry can be an enjoyable part of the holiday, and makes travelling by car ferry attractive.

Many ferry companies offer package holidays. These include the ferry crossing with passenger's car and hotel, camping, farmhouse or caravan site accommodation, or tours using coach and rail transportation.

Ferry services operate throughout the world. Look at a world map and study the shipping routes between the ports in different countries, especially in the Mediterranean, the North Sea and the Baltic.

Once again there are many information sources to help us find the information required for ferry services throughout the world. We have shipping guides, car ferry guides, websites and the shipping companies themselves.

What information would we need for every route (not just the English channel)?

- *About the ship*: Name of the ship and the facilities onboard. The size – the capacity for how many cars and passengers can travel onboard, whether the ship is air-conditioned and stabilised, type of craft – perhaps it is a hovercraft (part ship part aircraft, that rides on a cushion of air just above the surface of the sea). Although sensitive to bad weather these are used around the world and can be seen operating between Portsmouth and the Isle of Wight. Or perhaps it is a catamaran – these are twin-hulled vessels large enough to accommodate cars. Hoverspeed operate a service on the Superseacat and Seacat.
- *Routings*: we need to study maps and discuss the best routings. Some clients prefer a longer car journey and a shorter sea journey. Other clients enjoy the ferry crossing – it can be part of the enjoyment of the holiday and so they are happy to travel the shortest part of the journey by road and enjoy a longer sea trip. It can depend on how good a sailor the client is and so we will also need information on mileages and sailing times.
- *Car and caravan lengths*: we need to know this because they affect the fare. The tariffs are published taking the length of the client's vehicle into consideration.
- *Motorist information*: for each country to be visited, once disembarking from the ferry, each motorist will continue the journey by car and regulations vary from country to country. The sort of requirements we would be checking are shown in Table 7.1.

There are various types of vessels crossing the English Channel. 'Roll-on, roll-off' ferries are so named because drivers board the ferry at the back and drive their vehicle off at the front of the ferry on arrival. Roll-on, roll-off ferries tend to operate

Table 7.1 Requirements for travel by ferry

Passports	Validity and whether visas are required
Driving licence	All valid UK driving licences should be accepted throughout the EU. However, the old-style green licences do not conform to the EU model, and so updating to a photocard licence may be a good precautionary measure. An international driving permit may be required when travelling outside of EU/EEA.
Identification plate	These are stickers to be placed on the rear of the car or caravan and are supplied by the shipping companies. UK registration plates displaying the GB Euro-symbol (Euro-plates) make the display of a conventional sticker unnecessary when driving in the EU, provided they comply with the new British Standards (BS AU 145d). The use of a GB sticker is advisable outside the EU as the authorities in some countries still expect to see a conventional sticker.
Headlights	Drivers will need a headlamp conversion kit to avoid dazzling oncoming vehicles which can happen if headlights are dipped or full beam because they are set for right-hand-drive vehicles.
Seatbelts	Often compulsory for front and back seats
Warning triangle	In the event of breakdown a red warning triangle must be displayed behind the vehicle. In some countries (e.g. Spain), you are required to carry two triangles.

Insurance	Very important
	   Insurance for the car against breakdowns, loss or damage, and so on. Insurance companies differ in the level of cover offered when taking a car out of the country. Some insurance companies offer policies that take the place of a 'Green Card' (International Motor Insurance Card).
	   Within Western Europe, motor vehicle insurance is compulsory for minimum third-party risks. Most UK motor insurance policies provide this for all EU countries and certain other Western European countries. If your client has comprehensive insurance they may find that the overseas cover automatically reduces to minimum third-party cover unless the insurer will charge an additional premium and issue an international Green Card of insurance which is the usual evidence of motor insurance recognised in most Western European countries.
	   Motor vehicle insurance offered by insurance companies protects against accidents and damage to the car whereas breakdown insurance offered by travel agents protects only in the case of breakdown.
	   Although it is not a legal requirement, drivers are strongly recommended to carry the Green Card because it may prove more effective than a UK insurance certificate in establishing with the overseas authorities that the driver has adequate motor insurance.

Personal travel insurance	Against medical expenses, cancellation, loss of baggage, and so on. We will discuss travel insurance in more detail in Chapter 11.
Bail bond insurance	Is required by some countries should the driving offence warrant legal action.
Vehicle registration documents	The traveller must have these with them when travelling abroad with a car. If the vehicle is hired or leased the registration documents will not normally be available and a Vehicle Hire Certificate (VE103A) will be required.
First aid kit	Often compulsory in many countries, and a good idea to keep handy.
Fire extinguisher	Sensible to take one on the journey even if not compulsory.
Spare headlamp bulbs	Again, in many countries compulsory, but it makes sense to carry them even if not. Automobile associations have emergency spares kits containing items most likely to be needed in the event of a breakdown. Due to the differences between right-hand drive and left-hand drive, replacement spare parts may not be readily available from European dealers.
Speed limits	It is a legal requirement when driving abroad to know and to obey the speed limits.

short crossings (up to 24 hours long) with as many as 35 sailings a day (e.g. P&O Portsmouth and Brittany Ferries) and drivers can turn up at the last minute and hope to get aboard. The shipping company usually offers big early booking discounts to encourage the passenger to pre-book.

There are extra-fast modern ships (fast ferry) and cruise ferries which offer facilities similar to a cruise ship, and on most of these ships passengers can pay extra to have Club Class treatment – priority boarding and unloading, first class lounge, light meals and drinks. As the opportunity to buy duty-free goods has been abolished between Britain and Europe, the shipping companies have enhanced their shopping malls in order to attract the onboard shopper.

Assignment 7.1

Collect the following brochures:

Hoverspeed
P&O Ferries
SeaFrance
Stena Line
Brittany Ferries

Study each brochure carefully, taking note of the ship description, routings, journey time, facilities onboard, frequency of service, full fares, fare discounts and supplements.

When you feel 'in tune' with the various services, find the answers to the following:

Exercise 7.1

Brochure work

1 Brittany Ferries
  Complete the destination port:
  (a) Caen to _____ (b) Roscoff to _____ (c) Santander to _____
2 (a) How many sailings are there a day on the Portsmouth to St Malo route?
  (b) How long does the sailing take?
3 (a) What is the fastcraft journey time between Poole and Cherbourg?
  (b) Name the fastcraft (or fast ferry)
  (c) Give the journey time between Poole and Cherbourg on a cruise ferry.
4 Your clients are travelling to Marbella in Spain, and would prefer to have a pleasant sea trip and fewer hours driving. They live in London. Compare the driving miles between:
  London/Plymouth   London/Dover
  Santander/Marbella Calais/Marbella

5 Hoverspeed

Give sailing frequency and journey time for the following:

(a) Dover–Calais

(b) Newhaven–Dieppe

6 Stena Line

(a) The HSS *Stena Discovery* sails to the Hook of Holland in 3 hours 40 minutes. What does HSS stand for?

(b) Describe the facilities aboard HSS *Stena Discovery*.

(c) In which countries are the ports of Fishguard and Rosslare?

7 P&O Ferries

(a) Describe the facilities aboard *Pride of Bilbao*

(b) There are many themed cruises available. How can you obtain the entertainment guide?

(c) Are there facilities for taking a pet aboard?

(d) On the Portsmouth to Cherbourg route on the fastcraft service give:

(i) The number of sailings per day

(ii) The duration time of the crossing

8 SeaFrance

(a) The ships are named after famous artists. Which ship was introduced in 2002?

(b) Describe the facilities onboard *SeaFrance Manet*.

(c) How many sailings per day are there to Calais?

9 Locate the following ports on a map:

Dunkirk, Calais, Dieppe, Le Havre, Caen, Cherbourg, St Malo, Roscoff.

Discussion

Study the brochures once again to calculate fares, noting upgrading opportunities and discounts. Work as travel consultant and customer to act out real-life situations.

Many tour operators compile short-break tours based on travelling by fast ferries and cruise ferries and travelling by coach. The short-break itineraries may include lovely sightseeing trips when ashore, themed cruises, and luxurious facilities to enjoy when aboard.

Assignment 7.2

Collect a selection of brochures giving details of inclusive tours to France, Holland and Germany using the fastcraft and cruise ferry services. Study the itineraries and attractions of each destination.

Assignment 7.3

Collect a selection of brochures giving information on holidays travelling by car and ferry crossing to include hotel accommodation. Take note of all that the holiday price includes, and flexibility of itinerary.

Some ports of entry and departure in Britain

Warne
Belfast
Dun Laoghaire
Rosslare
Oban
Stranraer
Holyhead
Liverpool
Fishguard
Plymouth
Weymouth
Poole
Portsmouth
Newhaven
Dover
Harwich
Hull
Aberdeen

Exercise 7.2

Tourist destinations for The Netherlands, France and Germany

THE NETHERLANDS

1 The Netherlands is one of the Benelux countries. Name the other two.
2 Just outside Rotterdam there is a famous group of eighteenth century windmills that tourists love to photograph. Name where they are located.
3 Madurodam is famous for _____?
4 Keukenhof is famous for _____?
5 At Alkmaar – an ancient seventeenth century city – between April and September there is a famous _____ which is a great tourist attraction.

FRANCE

6 Name two former palaces.
7 The beautiful white-domed Basilica of Sacre-Coeur is on a hill overlooking which district?

8 This district is also famous for _____

9 Monet's garden can be found in _____

GERMANY

10 Hamburg stands on the river _____

11 A river famous for cruises and beautiful scenery is the _____

12 Departing from Harwich, give:
   (a) The name of the German port used by DFDS
   (b) Sailing times, departure and arrival in both directions

Some ferry services have become tourist attractions. Famous ferries include Hong Kong's Star ferry, and the Staten Island ferry in New York which links Manhattan with Staten Island. Ferries are used to island hop between Greek islands. Whilst on holiday, tourists may need to make short ferry journeys. For example, if visiting Luxor in Egypt it will be necessary to cross the river Nile to see the Valley of the Kings.

Making the reservation

We follow the same format of investigating our client's needs, obtaining all the relevant information regarding the client's personal details and requests. We have a choice when making the reservation – either to contact the shipping company direct if they have an office in our country, or to contact the agent acting on their behalf for general sales, or we may be working in an office that operates a computerised reservation system.

Let's do a checklist of the sort of questions we may be asked by the customer, and the sort of information we should certainly supply to the customer.

Checklist

- Has the travel insurance and motor insurance been fully explained?
- Has the correct fare been charged for the length of the client's vehicle?
- Should the client take a warning triangle?
- What other items are compulsory?
- What are the speed limits for the countries to be visited?
- Is the motorist entitled to a reduced fare or excursion?
- Are motorway toll taxes payable? How much will they be?
- Have reporting times been entered on the ticket?
- Is the passenger's driving licence valid for all the countries to be visited?
- Has the passenger been correctly briefed regarding his passport, visa and health requirements?
- Does the car require rear seat belts?

Place the travel ticket and useful information – leaflets, maps, etc. – in a travel wallet to provide a good presentation.

That just leaves you to wish your clients 'bon voyage' – happy sailing!

Railways

Understanding rail travel, the calculation of fares and issuing of tickets, like air travel, is a specialised job and most travel agencies either obtain their tickets from a representative of the railways or, if they wish to develop direct links, they employ fully qualified staff. The majority of travel agents in the UK do not deal with independent rail travel at all but concentrate on package tours based on the railways. It is necessary, however, to be able to read timetables and understand the maps and services available in order to provide a complete service for the client.

At the turn of the nineteenth century, the railways were mainly used to transport goods, coal from mines, slate from quarries in the Welsh mountains, mail, and so on. By 1865 the railways in Britain carried 252 million passengers, not including commuters – travel was now within the reach of all but the very poorest.

Towns, hotels, seaside resorts all sprung up due to the advancement of the railway system, and by 1880 the British railway network was almost complete with 15 000 miles of mainly double-track route in operation. The period known as the Golden Age of Railways was between 1880 and 1919. Many factors have contributed to a demise in the railway system today – an increase in private car ownership, goods being transported by road, the growing popularity of air travel, and a lack of investment in the railway system, to mention just a few. For several passengers travelling together, train travel can be expensive compared with, say, four or five passengers in one car.

Why travel by train? People have always been fascinated with train travel, and still are today. They like to travel on steam trains; use trains for holidays; some package holidays are based on rail travel, and people enjoy independent travel by train (many specially reduced fares reflect the encouragement for travel during off-peak times for holidaymakers, senior citizens, students, etc.). There is an endless choice of routes, types of train and fares available.

Have you thought of travelling on the Orient Express with its 1920s theme and elegance? Or through the magnificent Canadian Rockies by train? Perhaps the Glacier Express would appeal – a train taking you over the roof of Switzerland: the 'slowest' express in the world will take you between Zermatt and St Moritz or Davos through the most spectacular scenery passing through Alpine meadows and dramatic mountain peaks.

Speed is often a reason for rail travel, especially on short journeys. The difficulty and frustration of congested roads and where to park the car on arrival at the destination can be very offputting for the motorist.

With the development of high-speed trains, rail travel across Europe will present strong competition to air travel. Although the rail travel from, say, Brussels to Paris is approximately $2\frac{1}{2}$ hours and the flight is approximately 50 minutes, the train service begins in the centre of Brussels and arrives in the centre of Paris. The time gained by air travel is soon lost in travelling to and from the airport in both countries, and the necessary pre-flight check-in times, and custom/baggage clearance.

Travellers can also find rail travel relaxing, with the facility of being able to move around the train, enjoy lunch with a view of picturesque scenery, and business travellers have the space to work.

The motor-rail service, also known as 'car sleepers', is excellent for travellers who wish to use both car and train. The car is boarded onto the train, and the driver and party have accommodation in the passenger part of the train. They collect their car on arrival at the destination. This takes away the long, often boring part of a journey, and leaves the driver with a shorter journey by car, and the freedom of independent transport during the remainder of the holiday. Unfortunately the motor-rail service is not widely available in every country, least of all in Britain, and it is expensive.

For example: French Motorail operates from Calais to Avignon/Nice, and to Brive/Toulouse/Narbonne. For a car plus four passengers in a couchette, peak return fare to Nice travelling Friday/Saturday in August costs up to £1148.0 and off-peak Monday to Wednesday in August up to £928.00.

In more recent years, there are the 186 mph *train à grand vitesse* (TGV) trains operating in Europe which are fast and efficient. Let's take a quick look at what different countries have to offer.

Germany's railway system – Deutsche Bahn AG – was privatised in 1994, and safety has become the biggest issue since the 1998 crash in Eschede in which 101 people died. DB spends over £100 million annually on maintenance and signalling upgrades. DB is a public limited company with the government as sole shareholder. If a train fails to arrive within five minutes of the scheduled time passengers get an instant 10 per cent refund.

France's state-owned railway system is fast, efficient and realistically priced. Trains are 98 per cent punctual. The 500-mile journey from Paris to Marseilles takes under 3 hours on a TGV train at speeds of 166 mph and costs around 8 pence per mile. By comparison, the 545-mile journey from London to Aberdeen takes 7 hours at an average speed of 78 mph, and using a saver return ticket costs 17 pence per mile. Where there is no TGV network, France uses the luxurious 120 mph Corail trains. Eighty per cent of these are less than 7 years old. There has been a high level of government funding which totals £2 billion a year.

Where speed is concerned, comparing France with Britain is not a like-for-like comparison. Britain is densely populated, especially in the south-east, and it is not acceptable to bulldoze countryside, towns and villages in order to make way for high-speed rail links, as was done in France. Problems with planning orders, protesters' objections and compulsory purchases are in place. Britain has inherited its railway system from the Victorian era and a large amount of the infrastructure has remained unchanged since then. Running an intensive service on an antiquated infrastructure creates many problems.

Let's take a quick look at Spain's state-run RENFE railway. It is one of Europe's best run systems. In 2000, 98.1 per cent of passenger trains were on time. On the high-speed AVE link between Madrid and Seville, passengers receive a full refund or a voucher for another trip if the train arrives more than 5 minutes late. The AVE does the journey in 2 hours 25 minutes and has three classes of travel – tourist, preferential and club. There are great fare deals for commuters, linking rail to tube and bus fares.

Japan's privatised railway system has the Shinkansen bullet train, running at speeds of 190 mph. It has a reliable safety record, and after thirty years of operating at the highest speeds in the world there have been no accidents or deaths to date. A train making the 300-mile journey from Osaka to Tokyo will take $2\frac{1}{2}$ hours, with 16 carriages holding 1300 passengers (double that of an Inter-City train).

The USA has never had an extensive passenger railway system. The popular forms of transport are coach or air and trains are used mainly for the transportation of goods. The railway companies offering transcontinental (Atlantic to Pacific coasts) passenger services are Amtrak in the USA and Via Rail Canada (VIA). At the time of writing, Amtrak is suffering financial difficulties and, like many railways around the world, is in a state of change.

Let's look at some great trains around the world.

The Blue Train

This is a luxury express train that operates in South Africa between Cape Town and Pretoria. It was introduced in 1903 in connection with sailings of Union Castle mail steamers from England. The Blue Train offers five-star luxury accommodation for a maximum of 84 guests in gleaming new carriages. All meals and beverages are included onboard, except certain imported beverages which can be purchased from a butler. Two types of accommodation are offered, both with the highest degree of comfort. There are 36 deluxe suites with twin or double bed, bath and shower, and six luxury suites with twin or double bed, bath, shower, CD and video machines. This five-star hotel on wheels travels 1000 miles in approximately 25 hours. This is a lovely way to see the landscape between Cape Town and Pretoria, and is usually combined with a sightseeing tour of the many other interesting and beautiful places to visit.

In Cape Town, a trip up Table Mountain is a must. It's flat on top, and when shrouded in cloud looks as if it's covered with a table cloth! The Cape Peninsular has the Cape of Good Hope Nature Reserve, Simonstown (a naval base with a penguin colony), and the Winelands (vineyards and beautiful valleys). The journey from Cape Town to Port Elizabeth is known as the Garden Route, travelling over the Outenoqua Pass. Clients travelling on the Blue Train because of an interest in trains may like to go to George, a beautiful place, and take a return trip on the Museum Line steam train to Knysna, and visit the Railway Museum there. This is a very scenic journey as it crosses the ocean via the Kaaiman's Bridge and the Knysna Lagoon by a long bridge.

Rovos Rail

Some clients may like to experience the classic atmosphere of a bygone age by travelling on the Rovos Rail. It carries a maximum of 72 passengers and is drawn by steam, electric or diesel locomotives. In July every year the restored Victorian coaches travel for thirteen days through South Africa, Zimbabwe, Zambia and Tanzania, making it the ultimate safari in complete luxury, comfort and security. At other times of the year, Rovos Rail does various trips to different parts of the country, often with a theme.

Assignment 7.4

Look up and write down some tourist attractions of South Africa.

The Canadian

Another famous train is The Canadian – a beautiful train originally built in 1954, and since refurbished in Art Deco style. The Canadian travels from coast to coast – Vancouver to Toronto – passing through some of the most beautiful scenery on earth – the Rockies, Jasper, Lake Louise and Banff. It has two classes of travel, Economy and Silver & Blue, both with observation dome windows.

Assignment 7.5

Look up and write down some tourist attractions of Canada.

The Orient Express

The Venice-Simplon Orient Express service was inaugurated in June 1883 to provide a connection between Paris and Istanbul, but used a package steamer for part of the journey from Varna on the Black Sea. It was not until 1889 that the whole journey was made by train. With the opening of the Simplon tunnel in 1906, The Orient Express changed its route to reduce the journey by approximately 14 hours.

With the demise of the railways, and two world wars, the carriages of the Orient Express were sold off and dispersed. The train made its last trip in May 1977 until on 25 May 1982 when James B. Sherwood reintroduced the glamorous, more modern version of the Orient Express which we know today, giving his inaugural speech standing on platform 8 of Victoria Station just before it set off for its first London to Venice journey. Mr Sherwood is an American-born businessman who was inspired to relaunch the Orient Express when five of the original 1920s sleeping cars (used in the film *Murder on the Orient Express*) were auctioned by Sotheby's in Monte Carlo in 1977. Sherwood was struck by the huge media interest – there were three buyers and 500 journalists! People's fascination for the Orient Express convinced him that there might be a market for a revival, and he managed to buy two carriages and spent five years scouring Europe for more. Since then, Sherwood's train interests have expanded to the Far East. He has acquired the Great North Eastern Railway (GNER) and has been responsible for running Peru's national railway.

If you are interested and would like to learn more about this fascinating train, I recommend you read *Venice-Simplon Orient-Express – the return of the world's most celebrated train*, written by Sherwood and published by Weidenfeld & Nicolson. It really is a lovely true story. Today the Orient Express has 1920s elegance, each carriage is different and has its own history. It is still possible to travel from Paris to Venice, and around the United Kingdom – often on celebration journeys. Passengers often dress in 1920s style, and the atmosphere is very jolly. It should be mentioned that nowadays it is not possible to travel from London to Venice on the same train. Leaving London, a Pullman takes passengers from Victoria Station to Folkestone, where they board coaches to travel on the Shuttle through the Channel Tunnel to Calais. Upon leaving the Shuttle terminal, passengers travel by coach to the station, where they finally board the wagons-lits coaches that take them to Venice on the Orient Express.

The Trans-Siberian Express

This is the longest through-journey on the railways in the world. The distance between Moscow and Vladivostok is 9297 km (5778 miles) and takes approximately 8 days. There are two classes – 'soft class' equivalent to first class, providing upholstered seats, and 'hard class' equivalent to second class with plastic or leather seats that convert to sleeping accommodation for night-time travel. This journey is, for many holidaymakers, an educational adventure. It is not to be recommended to tourists wishing to be pampered – no five-star hotel on wheels here, but nonetheless very exciting!

Assignment 7.6

Study the brochures giving details of holidays by rail. Look in your travel guides and *Travel Weekly* for operators. The following details may help:

Travelsphere Worldwide Escorted Holidays by Train	Tel: 0800 191418	www.travelsphere.co.uk
World of Rail, Leisurail	Tel: 0870 7500246	www.leisurail.co.uk
Bridge Rail Holidays	Tel: 0870 010 2456	www.bridge-travel.co.uk
Great Rail Journeys	Tel: 01904 521946	www.greatrail.com

Travel agent/client: providing information on various routes

Train travel in India is very popular. Travelling on the Palace on Wheels, passengers enjoy the splendour of the carriages used by the Maharajahs and princes of India, an excellent way to see the pink city of Jaipur and the Palace of the Winds. Some may prefer the hill stations of northern India, such as Shimla and Darjeeling, built by colonial rulers as a retreat from the summer heat. This spectacular journey is made travelling on a very narrow gauge railway line used by the Raj.

Another exotic rail journey is from Thailand to Singapore on the Eastern & Orient Express. From Chiang Mai in the north of Thailand, down through Malaysia to

Singapore, there are 1600 miles of fascinating scenery and cultures to enjoy. The journey includes Bangkok, the River Kwai (with its infamous 'death railway'), and Kuala Lumpur.

Discussion

After studying the various rail journeys throughout the world, brainstorm routes and interesting sightseeing places en route.

Private steam railways are a great tourist attraction in Britain, often run completely by enthusiasts and heritage groups. They are often included in package holidays, and are therefore worth adding to your product knowledge.

The three 'Great Little Trains of Wales' are Ffestiniog, Talyllyn and Snowdon Mountain rack railway (from the base of Mount Snowdon to the top). Some others are:

Sittingbourne to Kemsley	– Kent
Romney Hythe to Dymchurch	– Kent
Ravenglass to Eskdale	– Cumbria
Bure Valley Railways	– Norfolk
Severn Valley Railways	– 16 miles from Bewdley to Kidderminster and Bridgnorth
Dart Valley Railway	– Devon
Blue Bell Railway	– Sussex
Isle of Wight steam railway	– Hampshire

Eurotunnel

People wishing to take their car across the Channel by train use the Eurotunnel, which opened to the public in 1994 and runs through a tunnel 25 to 45 metres below the seabed between Folkestone in the United Kingdom and Calais/Coquelles in France. Passenger vehicles and their occupants are transported through the tunnel in enclosed wagons which are brightly lit and air conditioned. Crossing time is 30 minutes. There are up to four departures per hour 24 hours a day, 365 days a year.

Eurostar

Eurostar accepts foot passengers only and operates fast rail services which take only 6 hours from Waterloo Station, London, to Avignon, one of the most historic cities in Provence. Eurostar also travels to Paris (3 hours), Lille (2 hours) and Brussels (2 hours 40 minutes). A connection with Belgian railways and a one-hour onward journey takes you to the beautiful medieval town of Bruges.

The growth of the cross-Channel market has increased considerably over the years with the increase in car ownership and the single European Community. The Channel Tunnel offers speed and reliability as the service is not affected by weather conditions. Eurotunnel and Eurostar are used in great volume by tour operators organising holidays by rail, coach and self-drive transportation to include accommodation and sightseeing tours.

Most of the railway systems around the world offer rail passes providing good value travel. They usually have a variety of passes with flexible conditions that are relevant to the passenger's itinerary, age, and so on. Rail passes can also have links with other forms of transportation and accommodation, offering bargain tariffs.

Discussion

Are the ferry services threatened by the Eurotunnel route? What steps have been taken for the ferry services to remain in business?

Describe the benefits of travelling by ferry and the benefits of travelling by Eurotunnel.

Exercise 7.3

Research of brochures and travel destinations worldwide

1 Where would you expect to use the Austrail Pass, Austrail Flexipass and the GSR International Pass?
2 Name two tourist attractions at Oudtshoorn along the Garden Route in South Africa.
3 Norway has a breathtaking rail journey between Myrdal and Flam.
   (a) Name the railway.
   (b) How many tunnels does it pass through on a one-hour trip?
   (c) What facility has been provided in order to admire the breathtaking views?
4 Name the train, still operated by steam, which is used for celebration trips. (Its original steam run was from London to Edinburgh.)
5 Name Amtrak's premier train which runs along the Pacific Coast.
6 Where is the California State Railroad Museum located?
7 Describe three attractions at San Francisco.
8 Where are the Great Columbian Icefields located?
9 Before boarding the train at Chiang Mai, what tourist attractions would you recommend your client to see?
10 Describe the facilities onboard the Eurostar.

Where in the world?

1 This city is built on seven hills, has a history of more than 2700 years and is often known as the eternal city. It is one of the world's great cultural centres and has many ancient ruins. One ruin was an open-air arena where gladiators fought and Christians faced lions.

   Name the city and the open air arena.

2 This city is the only city in the world situated on two continents. It has over 500 domed mosques, and among the most famous is the Blue Mosque because of the interior decorations of blue tiles. Cruise ships claim safe anchorage in the four-mile inlet of the Golden Horn.

   Name the city.

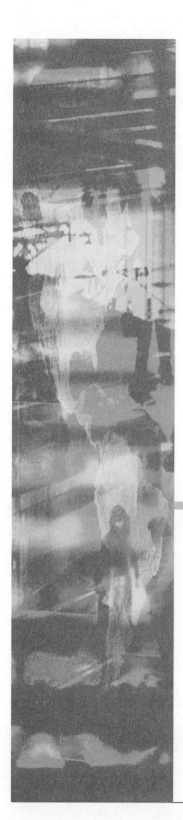

CHAPTER 8

Airlines

In this chapter we are going to discuss:

- IATA Worldwide Travel and Tourism Course
- IATA Traffic Conference Areas
- Most logical routings
- Aircraft types
- Fear of flying
- Deep vein thrombosis (DVT)
- Seat pitch
- Charter airlines
- Time differences and elapsed flying time
- Passport, visa and health regulations
- Special services for passengers
- Airport information
- Stopover holidays
- Route planning

Introduction

IATA Travel and tourism course

Many readers will be studying an IATA Travel and Tourism Course, either by distance learning or by attending one of the classroom courses held in more than 230 authorised training centres around the world. Computer-based training is also available in either CD-ROM or Internet format. More than 200 000 students have successfully completed the IATA/UFTAA International Travel and Tourism Training Programme, which has been established for 25 years and is a globally recognised and well-respected travel and tourism qualification. Details of the topics covered by IATA/UFTAA are given in Table 8.1.

Some useful addresses are as follows:

MONTREAL
IATA
Aviation Training and Development Institute
800 Place Victoria
PO Box 113
Montreal
Quebec
Canada
Tel: +1 (514) 390 6840

GENEVA
IATA
Aviation Training and Development Institute
Route de l'Aeroport 33
PO Box 416
CH – 1215 Geneva
15 Airport
Switzerland
Tel: + 41 (22) 799 2582

SINGAPORE
IATA
Aviation Training and Development Institute
77 Robinson Road
05–00 SIA Building
Singapore 068896
Tel: + 65 239 7251

BEIJING
IATA
Aviation Training and Development Institute
12a Floor, Building 12, Xibahe Beili
Chaoyang District
100028 Beijing
China
Tel: + 86 10 6423 8684

Table 8.1 IATA/OFTAA Four Level Career Path Programme

LEVEL 4   SENIOR MANAGEMENT DIPLOMA
Marketing 2
Law and regulations 2
Technology in the travel industry 3
Managerial skills 2
Finance and business planning

LEVEL 3   MANAGEMENT
Managerial skills 1
Negotiation skills
Tour packages 3 special interest tours
Meetings, incentives, conferences and exhibitions
Administration and accounting
Marketing 1
Technology in the travel industry 2

LEVEL 2   CONSULTANT DIPLOMA
Geography in travel planning 2
Land transport – rail 2
Land transport – bus and coach
Accommodation – other than hotels
Water transport – cruises and private charters
Tour packages 2
Law and regulations 1
Selling skills
Air fares and ticketing 2

LEVEL 1   FOUNDATION DIPLOMA
The business environment of the travel and tourism industry
Geography in travel planning 1
Travel formalities
Land transport – rail 1
Land transport – car, camper, hotels
Air fares and ticketing 1
Water transport – ferry
Tour packages 1
Air transport essentials
Customer service
Technology in the travel industry 1

IATA traffic and conference areas

So what is IATA? It is an association created in 1919 when six airlines agreed to set up the Air Traffic Association to foster collaboration between air transport operators. It has since grown to include about 188 airlines worldwide which are either active or associate members of what is now known as the International Air Transport Association.

One of the Association's rules is to impose standardisation in the air travel industry. Imagine the chaos if airline personnel from 188 different airlines used different languages, different safety regulations, different methods of documentation! The IATA's international language is English and all pilots and air traffic controllers give and receive instructions in English.

Travel personnel, whether based in Tokyo, Sydney or London, all work in accordance with standardised documentation, rules governing fare calculation and ticketing. Air space throughout the world is strictly controlled with regulations governing the right to fly over another country, land in another country and to collect and deliver passengers from/to another country. Noise pollution is controlled and monitored. The IATA has been instrumental in getting airlines to work together in many areas, for example:

Safety	Finding joint solutions to problems beyond the resources of any single company
Environment	Noise and smoke emissions
Security	Protection for passengers
Medical	Physiological and psychological factors affecting safety, comfort and efficiency of air crews and passengers
Legal	Concern for the liability of air carriers and their legal relationship with their customers
Finance and accounting	Simplifying accounting, including matters relating to currency and exchange, taxation and insurance
Standardisation	Of fares, documentation and code of ethics

IATA has come a long way since 1919, adapting to the vast changes in aviation and the travel industry over the past 50 years.

IATA has divided the world into three air traffic conference areas and has three main offices in Geneva, Montreal and Singapore.

Geneva office	Europe, Africa and the Middle East
Montreal office	The Americas
Singapore office	The Far East and Australasia

Exercise 8.1

Study a map of the world. Divide it into three areas to include the following countries:

Area 1   North, South and Central America
         Hawaiian Islands
         The Bahamas
         Bermuda
         Greenland
         All the Caribbean Islands

Area 2   Europe (including Iceland, Russia to the west of the Ural Mountains)
         Islands adjacent to Europe
         The Azores
         Canary Islands
         The Middle East (including Iran)
         Africa and adjacent islands

Area 3   Asia (including Russia to the east of the Ural Mountains)
         Islands of the Pacific Ocean west of the International Date Line
         Australasia

Area 1 is referred to as the Western Hemisphere, areas 2 and 3 are referred to as the Eastern Hemisphere. The International Date Line separates area 1 and area 3.

Exercise 8.2

Jot down the IATA area to which the following cities belong, also naming the country.

CITY	COUNTRY	IATA AREA
e.g. Bogota	Colombia	1
1 Athens		
2 Madrid		
3 Beijing		
4 New Delhi		
5 Pretoria		
6 Nairobi		
7 Budapest		
8 Jakarta		
9 Tehran		
10 Maseru		
11 Caracus		
12 Tokyo		
13 Lima		
14 Los Angeles		

A knowledge of geography is very important if you have chosen a career in travel and tourism. You can learn by studying maps, reading travel articles, watching travel programmes on television, and generally being up to date with what is going on in the world. Listen to clients – they often have up-to-the minute-information.

Exercise 8.3

To test your geography knowledge, try to write down in which countries the following cities are located:

CITY	COUNTRY
Madras	
Istanbul	
Beirut	
Damascus	
Kuala Lumpur	
Montevideo	
Manila	
Colombo	
Osaka	
Blantyre	
Chittagong	

Each city and airport has an internationally recognised three-letter code. When more than one airport serves a city, both codes are used: for example, London = LON. London has several airports: London City Airport = LCY, London Gatwick Airport = LGW, London Heathrow Airport = LHR, London Luton International Airport = LTN, London Stansted Airport = STN. The complete list is published in the *Airline Guide*.

The three-letter code is not always the first three letters of the city because many cities begin with the same spelling – for instance, Madras, Madrid, and so on. It is essential to learn the codes or look them up in the *Airline Guide*. Do not guess them! Several countries have cities with the same name, such as Hamilton, which can be found in Canada, New Zealand and Scotland.

Most logical routings

There are several factors to consider when putting an itinerary together, including the client's choice, the regulation surrounding the fare construction, the availability and accessibility of flights and acceptable departure and arrival times.

It is useful to develop a sense of direction. The client's route should be as direct and logical as possible, without back-tracking. For example, a passenger wishing to fly on a one-way journey from Athens to Brussels, Helsinki and Paris would be routed as follows: Athens, Paris, Brussels, Helsinki.

Exercise 8.4

Whether a one-way or return, it is important to know which city is the furthest from departure and make that the turn-around point. Look at your map and write down the most logical routing for the following:

1 A one-way journey from Japan to Baghdad, Taipei, Lisbon, Osaka, Madrid
2 A one-way journey from Australia to Durban, Manila, Cape Town, Bombay, Sydney
3 A return journey from England to Amsterdam, Karachi, Istanbul, London, Berlin
4 A return journey from Greece to Rome, Madrid, Athens, Oslo, Vienna
5 A return journey from America to Paris, Munich, New York, Madrid, Amsterdam, Brussels
6 A return journey from France to Nairobi, Perth, Mauritius, Athens, Bombay, Athens, Paris

Aircraft types

Consider an airline network. A large international airline will operate services to perhaps 150 destinations in about 80 countries. That could be about 2000 services a week. There could be 150 aircraft in the fleet. Just stand near a busy airport for half an hour and note the number of aircraft taking off and landing. This is happening all day every day throughout the world!

As an example, when terrorists attacked the World Trade Center in New York on 11 September 2001, it took 120 air traffic controllers three hours to clear the skies of the 6000 aircraft in the vicinity to make way for military aircraft.

Some 50 million passengers pass through London Heathrow Airport every year – about 100 000 people every day. On average, 1600 aircraft take off and land a day and 3 billion litres of fuel is supplied to the airport each year. Heathrow serves the public around 23 500 cups of tea and coffee, more than 6500 pints of beer and 11 500 sandwiches daily. These statistics may give you an insight into the scale of the operation.

Aircraft have long-, medium- and short-range flying abilities, and are not easily interchangeable between routes. The aircraft type and distance to be flown are major considerations when planning routes, as are the costs of running an airline and the fares charged.

The *Airline Guide* publishes details of aircraft types. Take time to read this section of the reference book. You will see each aircraft has a code denoting its type – jet (J); prop-jet (T); propeller (P); helicopter (H); amphibian/seaplane (A). (The amphibian plane has wheels and can touch down on land or sea.) Some descriptions give the number of passengers permitted onboard. Only codes are used in the timetable, but you will find the meanings of each code listed at the bottom of the page.

For various reasons, some clients like to know the type of aircraft they will be flying in, and it is good service to supply this information – there are many aircraft enthusiasts out there! For example, the aircraft coded 747 is a Boeing 747 jet (often referred to as a jumbo because of its size) which has a capacity for 400 passengers. The 747 cruises at 30 000 feet at 575 mph and has four engines, all mounted on the wings.

The aircraft coded SSC is a British Aerospace Concorde (BAC). This is a supersonic aircraft which flies at an altitude of 50 000 feet (avoiding any bad weather conditions) at twice the speed of sound. Carrying up to 100 passengers (the body of the aircraft is long and narrow), and cruising at speeds in excess of 1450 mph, flying times are halved in Concorde. This aircraft is used on long journeys and charter flights. Tour operators charter Concorde for special flights such as anniversaries, birthdays, fun days, etc. Concorde held an unblemished safety record until the fatal accident which befell an aircraft departing from Paris, and all Concorde aircraft were grounded. Modifications were subsequently made to the aircraft design, and Concorde was, for a while, back in the air (see Figure 8.1). Sadly, at the time of writing, plans to ground the aircraft and place it in a museum have been made. Richard Branson of Virgin Atlantic is currently negotiating to keep Concorde flying.

The age of 'hypersonic' is almost here. Hyper-X – the flying machine of the future – has been unveiled by the American space agency (ASA) and aircraft manufacturer Boeing. Hyper-X will run almost entirely on fresh air, scooping up oxygen from the atmosphere. It is expected to be about half the size of the current Boeing 747 and will carry 250 passengers. The aircraft will not have windows, but 'virtual windows' may be incorporated, showing images of sky and clouds, to prevent passenger claustrophobia. The flight time from London to New York is expected to be around 40 minutes, while London to Sydney will take 2 hours, and an around-the-world flight will take just 4 hours. The aircraft will be used initially for military and cargo purposes, but by 2016 should be carrying passengers – an interesting prospect for future air travel.

Fear of flying

Statistically, flying is still one of the safest forms of transport. Although they are ten times more likely to be killed in a car crash – and travel by car every day – many people have a real fear of flying. One in ten people avoid travelling by air, and around 20 passengers a day turn up at London Heathrow but are unable to board the plane. Help is provided by airlines in the form of one-day courses to help combat the fear of flying. Often by the end of the day participants can bring themselves to board an aircraft and take a short flight. They might not enjoy the flight but they have learned to control the fear. If you have clients who suffer from fear of flying it might be useful to find out about the courses, using the following contact information:

British Airways (through Avia Tours)   Tel: 01252 793250
Britannia Airways   Tel: 01582 424155
Virgin Atlantic   Tel: 0800 0835300

Deep vein thrombosis

Are you sitting comfortably? There has been a lot of publicity recently about deep vein thrombosis (DVT). The condition is a blockage of the main veins caused by blood clotting. Anyone can suffer from DVT but there are factors which make passengers more prone to the condition when flying, including immobilisation (due to restricted seating space), increasing age, pregnancy, use of contraceptive pills, varicose veins, and a previous heart attack.

To lessen the risk of developing DVT, passengers should exercise during the flight and drink plenty of liquid (not alcohol). Some passengers wear support socks which

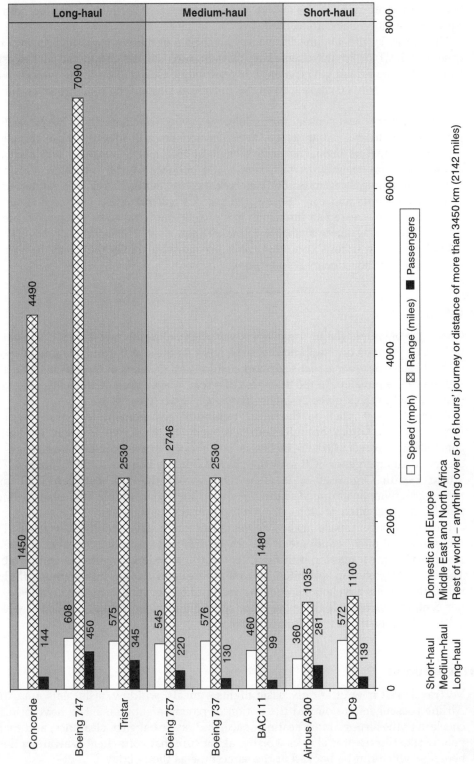

Figure 8.1 Aircraft speed, range and passenger capacity by aircraft type

because they are tight at the ankles and less restrictive further up the leg help to squeeze the blood back up to the heart.

The World Health Organisation has launched a definitive investigation into the causes of DVT in air travellers. Part of the study will be conducted at Leicester University. The British government has contributed £1.2 million to the project, with an additional £600 000 coming from the European Union. The final report is due in 2006.

Revolutionary seat-sensor technology is being developed to warn airline passengers who are in danger of DVT. The sensors will identify those travellers whose poor posture or inactivity puts them at risk, and a computer will alert the cabin crew. This technology has been made possible by the invention of 'smart fabrics' containing thousands of tiny electrical components. The cloth is connected to tiny circuit boards and can be powered using small batteries. The Civil Aviation Authority has expressed an interest in this project, but it has to be rigorously safety-tested before being made available to the airlines.

DVT is a very serious condition, and anyone who thinks they may be at risk should consult their doctor before flying.

Seat pitch

One of the big issues for air travellers is seat pitch on the aircraft. This is the distance between a point on one seat and the same point on the seat in front. Passenger space is the distance between a seat's support cushion and the back of the seat in front. The difference is equivalent to the thickness of a seat. A seat pitch of 28 inches when the seat is 2 inches thick gives 26 inches passenger space (see Figure 8.2).

A 26-inch seat pitch is the legal minimum requirement. A report by ICE Ergonomics in Loughborough, commissioned by the Civil Aviation Authority, concluded, however, that 26 inches is not enough space to allow passengers to escape in an emergency. ICE says the pitch should be increased to 29.4 inches. The World Health Organisation is also investigating the link between DVT and passengers flying in cramped seating. Some airlines, for example Ethiopian Airlines, publish the seat pitch of all its aircraft types in their timetable.

More passenger space means fewer seats on board, and higher fares. The minimum seat pitch requirement was set in 1989, and since then the 'average' body size has increased, making it difficult for people with long legs to get comfortable. There is a difference in seat pitch, as well as fares and class of travel among flights. Scheduled flights have an average load factor of 60 per cent, compared with 90–100 per cent for chartered flights which are normally used for package holidays where a 10- or 12-hour flight is no longer unusual.

Charter airlines

MyTravel/TUI now offer only basic flights – meals, window/aisle seats are extra. Airline passengers are offered the option of paying a supplement to have priority check-in at the airport, more seating space, and faster baggage clearance, and many people take this up. It is always worth making sure that your client is aware of these benefits, which can be booked at the same time as the holiday.

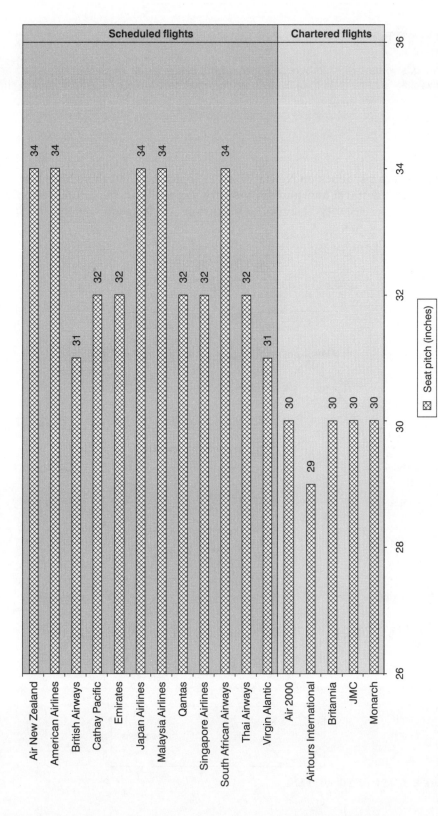

Figure 8.2 Seat pitch

Discussion 8.1

Discuss with other members of a group what steps the airlines, tour operators and travelling public could take in order to improve air transport comfort, and explain the outcome of each action.

Since the terrorist attack on New York on 11 September 2001 there have been many changes in the travel and tourism industry, especially in the airline sector. These include tighter security at airports, restrictions on baggage content and lengthy

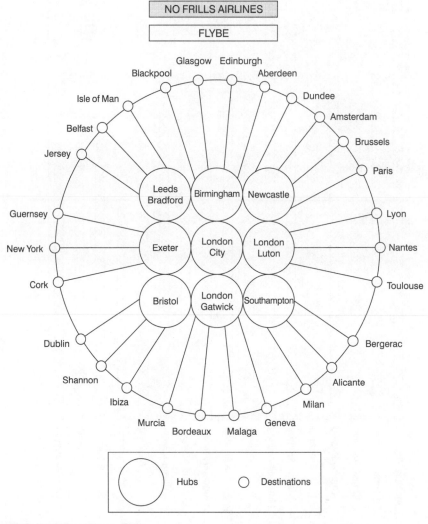

Figure 8.3 No frills airlines: Flybe

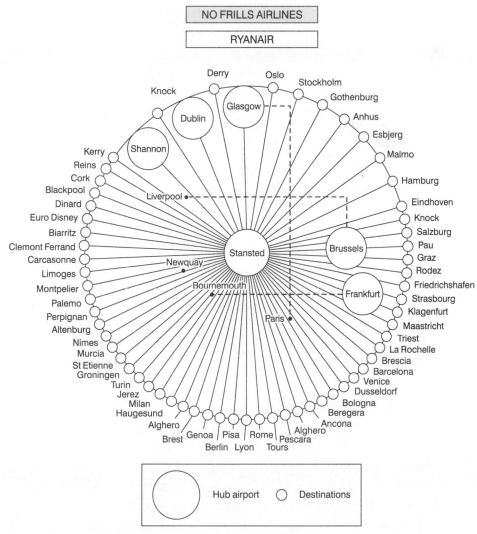

Figure 8.4 No frills airlines: Ryanair. Ryanair has now taken over Buzz

check-in procedures. The large scheduled long-haul airlines have faced heavy financial losses: conversely the 'no frills' short-haul budget airlines have gained strength (see Figures 8.3–8.7). The main complaint is that the budget fares clients see advertised are subject to availability, and often the low fares are not available on the dates and routes required. Fares are also subject to supplements and taxes, and do not include the cost of food and drink on board. The free baggage allowance may also be reduced.

When booking a flight, remember to check the budget airlines, charters (airlines used by tour operators) and scheduled airlines because they have slashed air fares to many destinations as a direct competitive response to the 'no frills' airlines.

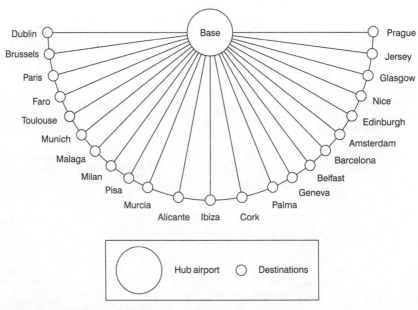

NO FRILLS AIRLINES

BMI BABY

Routes from its East Midlands

Figure 8.5 No frills airlines: BMI Baby

Some useful contacts include:

British Airways	Tel: 0845 773 3377	www.ba.com
BMI Baby	Tel: 0870 264 2229	www.bmibaby.com
EasyJet	Tel: 0870 6000 000	www.easyjet.com
Flybe	Tel: 0870 5676 676	www.flybe.com
Ryanair	Tel: 0870 569 569	www.ryanair.com
GB Airways	Tel: 0870 850 9850	www.gbairways.com

Assignment 8.1

Choose six destinations from the capital city of the country in which you live, and compare fares, routings, baggage allowance, flight times and flexibility between all the different airlines that service your chosen routes.

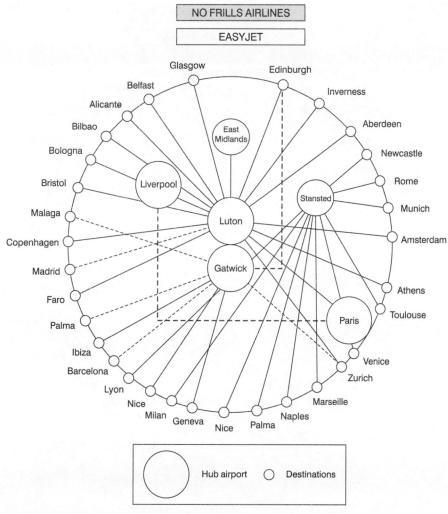

Figure 8.6 No frills airlines: easyJet. easyJet has now taken over Go. easyJet have 105 routes between 38 key European airports

Organising an itinerary

We will shortly be planning a stopover holiday, but first list all the topics you think should be considered before organising an itinerary that includes air travel and stopovers en route. The following headings may help:

Facilities at airports
Transport to/from airports
Flight details
Passport and visas
Minimum connecting times
Time differences
Hotel accommodation

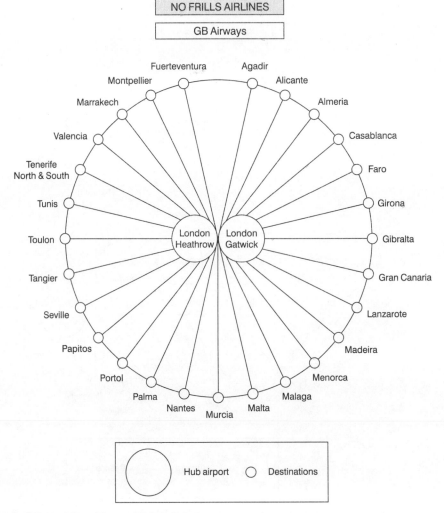

NO FRILLS AIRLINES

GB Airways

Hub airport   Destinations

Figure 8.7 No frills airlines: GB Airways

Class of travel
Attractions of each stopover
Security/air rage
Age and safety of domestic aircraft/airline (some are high risk)
Applicable surcharges and taxes
Special services for passengers

Add any more headings you can think of and build up on each category.

Let's first consider connecting flights. These are needed if there are no direct flights between each stopover. Minimum connecting times for every airport in the world can be found in the *Airline Guide*. There are numerous reasons why passengers might miss a flight. At some airports the passenger has to go through immigration, and baggage has to be cleared by Customs. Weather conditions can delay a flight, and the passenger may also have to change airport before arriving at the final destination. Useful terminology includes:

Domestic flights   = flights within the same country
International flights = flights from one country to another
Online   = a transfer from one flight to another without changing airline
Interline   = a transfer from one airline to a flight on another airline

Time differences and elapsed flying time

Next, let's look at time differences and elapsed flying times. First, it is essential to be familiar with the 24-hour clock.

0100 hours   1.00 am (early hours of the morning)
0200 hours   2.00 am
0300 hours   3.00 am

and so on

1200 hours   12.00 noon (mid-day)
1300 hours   1.00 pm
1400 hours   2.00 pm
1500 hours   3.00 pm

and so on

2400 hours   midnight
2359 hours   one minute to midnight
0001 hours   one minute past midnight

Using the 24-hour clock eliminates mistakes or uncertainty about whether the time is am or pm. For instance, by '8 o'clock' do we mean 8 o'clock in the morning or 8 o'clock in the evening? By using 0800 hours or 2000 hours the time is perfectly clear.

Time differences

The world is divided into 24 time zones, each of 15° longitude, with the Greenwich meridian being point zero (GMT). The time used in each country, whether it is the time of the corresponding time zone or modified, is an hour fixed by law. Time is known as legal time, standard time or local time. Certain countries modify their legal time for part of the year, especially in summer.

Study the international time calculator from your *Airline Guide*. Here you will see all countries listed, and whether their legal time is plus or minus GMT and whether the time is modified. If the time is modified, the dates are given under DST (daylight saving time). For example, look at Albania and note that the legal time is plus one hour, except during the summer months, when the time is plus two hours.

Imagine it is now 1500 hours (3.00 pm) in Tokyo on 22 December. What time is it in Copenhagen? Denmark's standard time is GMT + 1, and Japan's is GMT + 9. It is therefore 8 hours earlier in Denmark than in Japan. Subtract 8 hours from 1500 hours to arrive at 0700 hrs in Denmark on 22 December.

It sometimes helps to draw the face of a clock and move round the dial to assist with the calculation. Let's try another one.

It is 0800 hours in Athens on 12 October. What is the time in Barbados? Check the international time calculator: Greece + 2, Barbados – 4. Add 4 and 2 together to make it 6 hours earlier in Barbados than it is in Greece. Then deduct the 6 hours from 0800 hours to reach the answer – it is 0200 hours (2.00 am, early hours in the morning) in Barbados.

Some large countries, such as the USA, Brazil, Australia and the Russian Federation, do not have the same standard time throughout the country. Details are published in your *Airline Guide*.

How long does the journey actually take? In your *Airline Guide*, you will find a table giving average journey times between major cities. This allows you to see quickly the approximate flying times between two cities, but you might need to work them out for individual journeys.

Then find the actual flying time for a journey where the city of departure has a time different from that of the city of arrival. You will need to convert both times into GMT.

Step One: Establish the departure and arrival times in local time. These are published in the timetables. Example travel is in August:

Depart Rome   1415 hours
Arrive Port au Prince   1915 hours

Step Two: Look at the international time calculator to establish the time variance to GMT.

Rome – Italy   = GMT + 2 (DST March – September)
Port au Prince – Haiti   = GMT – 4

Step Three: Convert local times to GMT

Depart Rome   1415 hours + 2 hours   convert to GMT (–2 hours) = 1215 hours
Arrive Haiti   1915 hours – 4 hours   convert to GMT (+4 hours) = 2315 hours

Now that you have both departure and arrival times in GMT it is easy to work out the actual flying time:

From 1215 hours to 2315 hours = 11 hours

A word about the international date line

Look at the map for the Fiji Islands and Hawaii in the Pacific Ocean. They are not a great distance from each other and yet there is a 22-hour time difference. This is

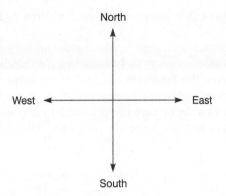

Figure 8.8

because Fiji is at the eastern extreme of the time zone (GMT +12) and Tahiti is at the western extreme (GMT – 10). When we travel across the International Date Line going from the eastern hemisphere to the western hemisphere we gain a day. Travelling from west to east, we lose a day (see Figure 8.8).

Passports, visas and health regulations

Passports

Passengers travelling overseas need to have valid travel documents. Everyone always needs a passport, often a visa, and less frequently a vaccination certificate to meet health regulations. Full details can be found in the *Guide to International Travel*. Care should be taken when checking a passenger's documents, making sure in particular, that they meet with:

(a) Validity requirements
(b) Exit requirements
(c) Transit requirements
(d) Destination requirements

It is important to understand the terminology used for different types of passport in order to give the correct information to the client.

- **Citizen** A citizen is a person who owes allegiance to that country's government. Citizenship can be decided by birth or awarded through naturalisation.
- **National** A national is a person who owes allegiance to a government, with his or her passport declaring him or her to be a national, not a citizen, of that country. People generally become nationals of a government by (a) treaty; (b) international mandate: (e.g. UN), (c) Right of Discovery, or (d) obtaining a country by conquest.
- **Alien** An alien is a person in a country of which he or she is not a citizen. He or she could be an immigrant, non-immigrant or resident.
- **Non-immigrant** A non-immigrant is an alien who enters a country temporarily as a tourist or for business.

123

- **Tourist** A tourist is a temporary visitor staying at least 24 hours in the country visited.
- **In transit** A person in transit is passing through a country – usually because their aircraft has a stop en route or because they must change flights. He or she is not allowed to leave the international area of the airport.
- **Stateless person** A stateless person is outside the country of his or her nationality and is either unable or unwilling to obtain a passport because the country no longer exists, or because he or she no longer owes allegiance to the government in power.

One final word on passport types – passports for pets! The Pet Travel scheme was introduced in 2000 and to date around 40 000 pets (cats and dogs only) have travelled under this scheme. The pets have to be vaccinated in the UK, a process that takes seven months. The official requirement for dogs and cats returning to the UK is that they should be treated against ticks 24 and 48 hours before their journey and this is strictly enforced. The Pet Travel scheme covers most of Europe and 28 rabies-free long-haul destinations, including Australia, Singapore and Japan.

Visas

A visa is an entry in a passport made by a consular official of a government to indicate that the bearer has been granted authority to enter or re-enter the country concerned. The granting of a visa, however, does not guarantee entry. The main types of visa are: tourist, transit, immigrant and diplomatic.

If you are applying on behalf of your client, allow plenty of time because at peak holiday times there is often a backlog. If your client is applying, advise them of the possible delay.

Not all visas have to be stamped in passports. In some instances the information is stored electronically. Biometric data can be used, including a fingerprint code or a scan of the iris of the eye. This is not as futuristic as it sounds. Hand biometrics is used at many US airports, and various other airports are conducting trials with iris and retina biometrics. Where relevant, make sure your client knows the cost of obtaining a passport and visa as this can considerably increase the cost of the holiday.

Health regulations

Some countries require travellers to present a certificate of vaccination for certain diseases. We need to check the validity of our client's certificate for:

Cholera   6 days to 6 months
Yellow Fever   10 days to 10 years

Study the map for infected areas of the world in your *Airline Guide*. With the upsurge of last-minute travel, often people do not have time to seek appropriate medical advice. The adverse side-affects of anti-malarial medication have been well publicised in recent years, and this has discouraged travellers from taking the necessary medication. There are now more than 2000 cases of malaria among British travellers every year, resulting in between 10 and 20 deaths.

The *Airline Guide* also provides information about Customs restrictions, airport tax, climate, public holidays and business etiquette and cultural customs. Take time to read the details of several countries.

Exercise 8.5

Choose a country, and provide information to answer the following questions:

1 What currency is used?
2 What are the banking hours?
3 What is the expected temperature for August?
4 What are the Customs restrictions?
5 Who needs a visa?
6 What language is spoken?
7 What are the health requirements?
8 What is the distance between the airport and the town centre?

Special services for passengers

Airlines are able to make special arrangements for certain passengers, such as:

- Young fliers (unaccompanied children)
- VIPs (very important persons) such as royalty, government officials, etc.
- People with mobility problems such as invalids, infirm passengers, expectant mothers
- People who require special meals and diets

Arrangements, however, must be made in advance. Each airline sets out its own regulations and conditions of booking for each circumstance, so it is important to check with the airline being used. Let's think about the kind information required for each case.

Young fliers

What is the permitted minimum age of a child travelling alone?
What is the maximum age?
At what age is the passenger considered an adult?
Do any forms need to be completed?
Who will be taking the child to the airport?
Who will be meeting the child on arrival at the destination?

VIPs

What security arrangements should be made?
How many people are there in the party?
What are their special requests?
What can the airline offer in special services?
What are the formalities?

Special meals

What type of food is required (e.g. medical, baby, vegetarian, Moslem, Hindu, Kosher)?
Does this need to be confirmed before departure?

Invalid and infirm passengers

Is the passenger able to ascend/descend the aircraft steps?
Is the passenger completely immobile?
Is a wheelchair required?
Is the passenger on a stretcher?
Will any medical apparatus be required?
Does the passenger have a medical certificate confirming fitness to travel?
What are the formalities?

Expectant mothers

Does the passenger need a medical certificate confirming fitness to travel?
What is the maximum number of weeks into a pregnancy allowed by the airlines for expectant mothers to fly?
What are the formalities?

Escort services

Who would need an escort? (children travelling without parents)
Medical escorts?
What would they do?
How much would they pay?
What are the formalities?

Most airlines produce excellent manuals and information brochures. Obtain all the material available from each airline and take time to read and understand it. If necessary, take the literature home to read, and query any point you do not fully understand.

Free baggage allowance

Clients will need to know how much baggage they are permitted to take onto the aircraft with them. This information can be found in the *Air Transport Manual*, and many airlines also provide a quick reference chart. Generally, the free baggage allowance depends on the class of travel and the route. For some journeys, the 'piece' system is used – e.g. two suitcases. For other routes, the 'weight' system is used, e.g. usually 15, 20 or 30 kg.

Restricted articles

You should also be able to advise your client on restricted articles – items not permitted onboard an aircraft. Since 11 September 2001 this has included sharp objects. Also, it is not permitted to use mobile phones or other electronic equipment during flight.

Airport information

Manuals and information booklets give accurate information on the facilities available at airports. There are many points you should advise your client about, including how to get from one airport terminal to another if needs be – for example, to change planes. You should also be able to advise on the following:

- Car parking facilities and cost
- Public transport – length and estimated time of journey
- Information desk and meeting point
- Check-in desk
- Banks
- Business centres
- Baggage security and left and lost baggage
- Post office
- Nursing mother's room
- Public telephones
- Restaurants, bars, lounges
- Traveller's welfare (staffed by social workers)
- Hotels
- Medical services
- Porters and trolleys
- Customs formalities
- Duty-free shops
- Chapel (open day and night)

An international airport is rather like a small town, and reflects all the activities that would go on there, plus the specialised work that air transport involves. An airport is split into 'landside' and 'airside'. The public is allowed to move about freely landside, but airside is strictly for passengers and employees only.

Before boarding their flight, travellers must first check in at the airline's check-in desk landside and show a valid passport and ticket to travel. In return, the passenger is issued with a boarding pass. Also at check-in, the traveller's luggage is weighed and taken away to be loaded onto the plane and a luggage receipt is issued to the passenger. After check-in, passengers go airside. For security, passengers are obliged to pass through a metal detector and have any hand luggage put through an X-ray machine. On occasion, a passenger may be 'frisked' or patted down by a security officer.

There is a wide variety of jobs to be done by the staff airside, including:

- Ground movement control services (movement of aircraft vehicles on taxi-ways)
- Catering staff to replenish aircraft
- Aircraft cleaners
- Refuellers
- Aircraft tug drivers
- Dispatchers

- Bird scarers (yes! It's true! If birds get into the engine the result can be catastrophic so people are employed to scare away the birds)
- Security: police, fire and emergency services
- Animal welfare staff (for animals in transit)
- Staff for passengers with special needs
- Drivers to transfer passengers between terminals by coach
- Drivers of buses for crew
- Runway cleaners and sweepers (although this is done mechanically, operators are required. Debris left on the runway can cause catastrophe as shown by the Concorde crash at Paris)
- Customs excise and immigration officials
- Cargo handling (with special security for high-value cargo)
- Passenger baggage handlers
- Meet and greet services for VIPs
- Aircraft are kept in large hangers for maintenance and repair by engineering staff

As this book is explaining 'life in a travel agency' and the many aspects of work to be processed, there is not sufficient space to give details of the complex subject of air fares. The best advice is to take a recognised airline course; details of some of the qualifications available are mentioned in Chapter 1.

Stopover holidays

A stopover holiday is the name given to packages that allow clients flying long-haul to break their journey and see another part of the world. It's a great way of making a long boring flight exciting with two or three days spent in interesting places along the way. Stopover holidays can be tailor-made by many airlines or long-haul operators, making them ideal for business travellers and holidaymakers. They are also excellent value for money.

The first step in selling a stopover holiday is to consider the client's journey. Perhaps there is a specific choice of airline? Suggest making stopovers along the way to make the maximum use of the airfare from commencement of the journey to the final destination.

Study the brochures provided by the airlines. Check the hotels used by reading the information and studying the city map in the *Hotel Guide*. Also, consider the client's interests. Is the stop over for business or for sightseeing? Does your client wish to stop over for shopping, or perhaps just to rest part-way through a long flight, or for all these reasons?

After you have investigated your client's needs, you are in a position to recommend an airline, suggest which stopovers to make and how long to spend at each place. The package will be limited by the flight schedule. Study the map of the world shown in Figure 8.9.

There are thousands of combinations, but let's just look at a very simple journey, starting in Sydney and finishing in San Francisco, with stopovers.

Sydney to Singapore – flying time about $8\frac{1}{2}$ hours
Shopping for Thai silk, jewellery and made-to-measure dresses perhaps

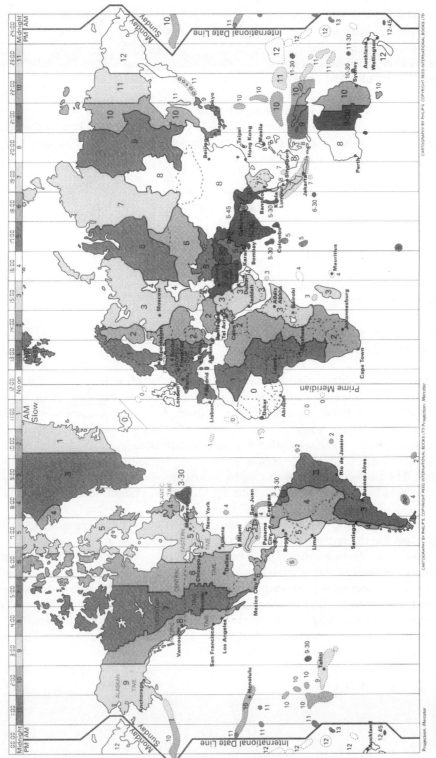

Figure 8.9

Visit the Tiger Balm Gardens
Singapore to Bangkok – flying time about $2\frac{1}{2}$ hours
Visit the floating market
Travel along the waterways
Visit the temples and shrines

Bangkok to Rome – flying time about 13 hours
Visit the Vatican, the independent state (0.17 mile) ruled by the Pope – the beautiful paintings by Michaelangelo, the Sistine Chapel and Vatican Palace guarded by Swiss Guards in sixteenth century uniform.

Rome to New York – flying time about 9 hours
Visit the Empire State building for the best view of New York
Enjoy a ferry trip
See the Statue of Liberty
Walk along Fifth Avenue

New York to San Francisco – flying time about 6 hours
Visit China Town
Wander around Fisherman's Wharf
Take a trip to Alcatraz Island
Drive over the Golden Gate bridge

Apart from building product knowledge about the attractions of possible stopover locations, it is important to study the conditions attached to any offers, bearing in mind the stopover package offers great reductions. In many cases, certain services are complimentary, such as car rental, extra night's accommodation or city sightseeing tour. So check with the airline in question.

Here are a few questions to ask yourself when selling a stopover holiday to a client. The answers can be found in the airline stopover holiday brochure, as well as the travel information manuals, your computerised system, and the Internet.

- **About the client:** Interest – reasons for travelling – time available – maximum budget for the trip – nationality (to obtain visas)
- **About the destinations:** Flying time – climate – location of accommodation – places of interest – best time of year to visit
- **About the stopover programme:** Booking conditions – which airline must be used and how many flights are allowed – what the cost includes – type of accommodation (single or double room, bed and breakfast or half-board) – cost for children – cost of an extra night's stay – cancellation charges – facilities of each chosen hotel – surcharges.

Exercise 8.6

1 Using the world map in Figure 8.9 place the following cities:
  (a) Bombay
  (b) Nairobi
  (c) Cairo
  (d) London
  (e) Rio de Janeiro

2 Advise the approximate flying time between:
  (a) Sydney and Bombay
  (b) Bombay and Nairobi
  (c) Nairobi and Cairo
  (d) Cairo and London
  (e) London and Rio de Janeiro

3 Use your international time calculator and advise the Standard Clock Time, plus or minus GMT for the following cities:
  (a) Sydney
  (b) Bombay
  (c) Nairobi
  (d) Cairo
  (e) London
  (f) Rio de Janeiro

4 Work out the time differences between the following:
  (a) It is 1700 hours in London. What time is it in Bombay?
  (b) It is 0800 hours in Nairobi. What time is it in Sydney?
  (c) It is 1400 hours in Cairo. What time is it in Rio de Janeiro?

5. Describe four tourist attractions for the following cities:
  (a) Sydney
  (b) Bombay
  (c) Nairobi
  (d) Cairo
  (e) London
  (f) Rio de Janeiro

Case study

Travelling by air

Mr and Mrs Cox are travelling to Perth, Australia, to visit family and will be away for six weeks, spending four weeks in Perth. They depart on 1 October from London Heathrow. This is a very big step to take for Mrs Cox because she has a fear of flying. She is also convinced that she will experience air rage (not hers, but another passenger's), and suffer DVT and be ill when she eventually arrives in Perth. It is the strong emotional pull to see her daughter and grandchildren that has allowed her to agree to travel.

Mr Cox has suggested two stopovers in each direction to help break the journey and to visit places she has read about. They have called into your travel agency to talk over the proposed trip in the hope that Mrs Cox will gain confidence about the forthcoming journey. It will not be an easy task because, apart from reading about DVT, she has also read about 'airports from hell', muggings in stopover cities and long delays at airports. Mr Cox has only one fear – the cost. He has read about the many supplements that are charged including a proposed 'green' tax.

Question

(a) What suggestion would you make to help Mrs Cox overcome her fear of flying?
(b) What information can you give her on DVT?
(c) Where would you suggest the four stopovers should be made? Give reasons for your choices.
(d) Explain the facilities at the airport en route, and the agreement most airlines have signed regarding care of passengers during delays.
(e) Which airline would you suggest for these clients? Take into account any special offers for sightseeing and hotel accommodation en route. Explain seat pitch and compare paying a higher fare for extra comfort and the use of the airline lounge at airports.
(f) Confirm the cost including the fare, supplements, possible visa charges, insurance and sightseeing tours you have suggested.

Discussion

Regulation and deregulation of the air industry

What are the benefits and disadvantages of regulation of the air industry? Some of the aspect you should consider are:

Passenger safety
Control of routes (overcapacity)
New routes (pioneer airlines)
Pooling airline services
Standardisation
Agreed fare structure
Routes and licences.

What are the benefits and disadvantages of deregulation of the air industry? Some of the aspects you should consider are:

Relaxing or lifting of the rules
Reduction in state control over airline operations
Withdrawing of fare fixing
Liberation for licenses
Employees' working conditions.

Discussion

Television programmes

Various television programmes have been made about life at an airport and the behind-the-scenes activities of some airlines. Discuss the programmes you have seen and answer the following questions:

(a) What did you learn from these programmes?
(b) Did they give you confidence in travelling by air?
(c) Did they inspire you to want to work for an airline or at an airport?
(d) Were questions left unanswered by these programmes?
(e) Discuss your views on training and security.

Assignment 8.2

The Civil Aviation Authority (CAA)

Research and report on the history and functions of the CAA. It has five regulatory functions. Describe the effect the CAA has on the air industry. A helpful address is:

Civil Aviation Authority
CAA House
45–59 Kingsway
LONDON
WC2B 6TE
Tel: 020 7379 7311

As a manager of a scheduled airline you have been requested by the director to prepare a talk on how to compete against the 'no frills' airlines. Your task is to explain your airline's costs under headings such as: fixed costs – variable costs – operational costs. You must then lead your audience into coming up with ideas on how savings might be made. You will need to do a considerable amount of research before preparing a 20-minute talk.

Dilemma

1 Use of private airport lounges

Miss Handley will arrive at Heathrow airport on a flight from Hong Kong and has a 4 hour wait before her onward flight. You have been asked by your colleagues at your company's Hong Kong office if Miss Handley may use an airport lounge. She is flying economy and is not a member of any kind of executive club.

Action

Research whether this passenger may use the facilities of a private airport lounge, and the services available.

2 Passport, visa

Mr Edmonds travelled to Northern Cyprus last year, and this year wishes to travel to Greece. He has heard that he will not be allowed to enter Greece with a Northern Cyprus stamp in his passport.

Action

Find out whether or not this is true.

3 How many airports in Britain and which is the busiest?

You have a client who takes a great interest in transport and, whilst making a booking to the USA, has asked you the above question.

Action

To offer an interested and personal service, and to increase your product knowledge, research the above question and record your findings.

Where in the world?

This city has a theatre where famous film stars have their hand- and footprints set in cement. It is known for film making and the homes of film stars. It is the stopover city for Disneyland.
Name the city, the theatre, and the area where famous film stars live.

CHAPTER 9

Technology

In this chapter we are going to discuss:

- The main functions of an agency system.
- The names of some of the main agency system suppliers.
- How technology can help suppliers to do their job better and more efficiently.
- The difference between viewdata and global distribution systems, and the different roles each performs in travel agencies.
- Hands-on experience working on a GDS.

Introduction

Technology is one of those subjects that you either love or hate. If you fit into the first category, you will enjoy working through this chapter; if not, don't despair. This part of the book is designed to familiarise students with the technology used in the travel industry, not to turn everyone into a computer expert.

The chapter will begin by looking at the history of travel technology and the way it has developed, before going on to focus on some of the various front and back office travel agency systems on the market. It will also focus on the role of viewdata and global distribution systems, or GDSs. By the end of the chapter, you should have an understanding about the role of technology in the travel industry and how it can help you to do your job better and more efficiently.

We will also touch on the Internet as it is such an important part of the way travel technology is developing, but specific information about booking on-line, how agents can harness the World Wide Web to their advantage and its future role in the travel industry will be covered in Chapter 10.

Understanding systems

One of the best ways of understanding the way a system works is to draw yourself a flowchart linking the database at the centre with the various operations it can perform, as in Figure 9.1. That way you are painting a picture in your head of the functions of the system, which it is important to understand. Remember that you will be using a particular system to make a booking; you will not be expected to fix it when things go wrong.

Several types of systems are used in the travel industry. Travel agencies use what are known as agency systems. These handle the office management, accountancy and reservations administration; many these days also link into the viewdata booking system. There are also tour operator systems. These handle all a tour operator's office management but also hold all the company's inventory – that is the term used to describe the actual holidays the operator has for sale.

If you go to work for a leisure travel agency, you will have to learn to use viewdata, a 20-year-old booking system that nevertheless remains a favourite with agents because they are familiar with it and it is simple to use. In a business travel agency, you will find yourself using a global distribution system, or GDS. These contain huge numbers of air fares, hotel and car rental rates and much more. There are four big GDSs used worldwide – Amadeus, Galileo, Sabre Travel Network and Worldspan.

Travel agency systems

Until the 1980s, many travel retailers relied on pen and paper to do their work. Something called the 'back office system' was available, but it was new and unproven. They were basic products anyway, mainly a computer-based accounting system, and few travel agents could see the point in spending money on a system to do a job they had been doing manually for years.

Attitudes started to change as technology started to improve. By the early 1990s back office systems transformed into complete management systems, combining

Vertical Group, the travel industry's first one-stop-shop for technology and telecommunication systems

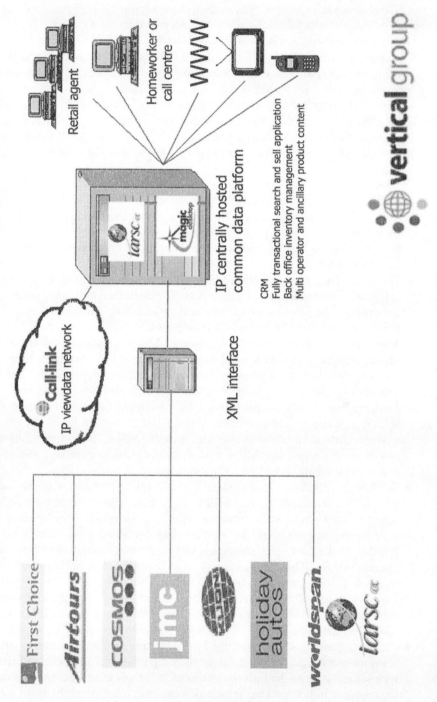

Figure 9.1 The only 'one stop' Multi channel ASP solution for the UK Leisure Travel Industry

front and back office functions. Staff in the back office could use the system to look after the accounts while sales staff working in the front office could store details of a client's booking electronically rather than relying on paper files. Once a booking was made, all the client's details were retyped into the system.

The next obvious development was a system that could connect to viewdata or a GDS and automatically 'grab' the client's details from the booking, saving time and eliminating the chance of error. Compiling daily management reports and the ability to monitor cash flow suddenly became a lot easier.

The final stage so far, for technology never stands still, was to add booking capability to the agency system. There are several integrated management and booking systems on the market, and each works in a slightly different way. The following list gives you some examples of the systems available and the way they operate:

- *TravelCat.* This uses a booking system called EasySell to search via the Internet for holidays on viewdata. Using EasySell, agents can search by date or operator, or they can find out if a specific holiday is available, and get the price, by entering the brochure code. The holiday information can be viewed in either viewdata or Windows format.
- *Traveleye.* This was developed by NTL Business (Travel Division). Traveleye integrates management and reservation functions, and also offers e-mail and Internet access, on-line brochures and links to the Holiday Autos, Gold Medal Farebank and Hotelbank and BCP websites.
- *Magic Desktop.* Developed by Call-Link, Magic Desktop is a travel portal that allows agents to search for holidays on viewdata via Internet, then transfer the booking details to the agency system without any rekeying. It also has a link to the Worldspan global distribution system for scheduled air fare bookings. Magic Desktop, which sits on the agent's PC desktop ('desktop' refers to the opening screen on a computer) also has a Magic Palette that can be used to customise the system with their shop name and brand. Magic Brochure Shelf taps into a selection of on-line brochures and there's a travel resource centre with foreign office, visa, weather and other information.
- *Dolphin for Windows.* This system from Dolphin Dynamics allows agents either to select a holiday by requesting a specific operator or use an availability search. The system links transparently into viewdata ('transparent' means the user is not aware that the system has switched into viewdata). Once the holiday is booked, the information is automatically handed to the Dolphin agency system. The company says agents can book a holiday in 5 minutes and make a costing in 30 seconds. Dolphin Dynamics also has a product called Dolphin Wave. This connects to the Galileo global distribution system via the Internet, and also provides access to viewdata and the Dolphin for Windows agency system.
- *Endeavour Search.* Developed by Telewest, this stores holidays in an extranet, a term used for a closed community of companies that are accessed using Internet technology. Agents go into the extranet, which is managed by Telewest, and can search for a holiday based on various criteria. Clients might want a hotel with a children's club, for instance, or a lively resort, or they might want only a short transfer from the airport. Compare this to viewdata, where you can find holidays

only by typing in a date and the name of the resort. If clients know exactly what they want, Endeavour Search allows you to skip the search, check availability and make the booking.

Viewdata

Viewdata was the first industry-wide booking system, introduced back in the 1980s. More than 20 years later it is very out of date but it is still the trade's favourite reservation system.

There are several reasons why it has stood the test of time – much to the amazement of most technology experts. Top of the list is the fact that it was a made-to-measure system that does exactly what it was built to do, namely to access tour operators' booking systems and take reservations.

The other reason why it is still going is that there has not been anything to replace it, despite the great advances that have been made in on-line booking on the Internet. That is because industry-wide, computer systems are not yet able to talk to each other.

To understand that better, imagine a group of people in one room. One speaks French, the other speaks German, the third speaks English and the fourth speaks Italian. Because they all speak different languages, they cannot communicate. Technology systems are the same. A tour operator's reservation system has to be able to 'talk' to the system that agents are using to make their bookings. But agents cannot fill their offices with a large number of systems, each able to talk to a specific operator. They need one system that operates using what we can call a universal language, which is what viewdata does.

As this book went to print, the Travel Technology Initiative, made up of many of the leading travel companies and associations, announced the development of a common XML (eXtensible Markup Language) that allows tour operators to distribute holidays over the Internet, using one language and bypassing viewdata and the global distribution systems. There is a lot of work to be done before it can replace viewdata, but it is believed to signal the true beginning of the end for viewdata.

There are other developments, TUI UK, which as Thomson pioneered the use of viewdata, has developed a system called Genie. Launched in all Lunn Poly shops at the end of August 2002, this enables sales consultants to book direct in the TUI UK Tracs system without using viewdata. Genie is web based and guides agents through the sales process, so little training is needed. Unlike viewdata, the system looks good, so agents can turn the computer screen round to allow clients to follow the booking process and choose elements of their holiday. It remains to be seen whether this can be developed for use by other agencies.

How does viewdata work?

Before looking at why viewdata needs to be replaced, let's pause and consider the system itself and how it works.

Viewdata is what is known in the industry as an order-entry tool. It works from a dumb terminal, which means the hardware has just one function – to provide access to viewdata. Compare that to the different functions available on a personal computer – accounting, word processing, e-mail and Internet access and so much more.

You access viewdata through a hard wire, like a telephone line, that dials straight to one of the databases hosted by the travel network specialists. Which database depends on which network your agency is signed – the biggest are NTL Business or Telewest (usually known under the former names of Istel and Fastrak).

To find and book a holiday, you key in a code that identifies a specific tour operator or travel supplier and dials into their reservation system. Most companies on viewdata have two codes, so they can be accessed over both travel networks for maximum distribution, although Thomson uses T# for both. Unijet uses UNI# for Istel and UNI for Fastrak, while car rental broker Holiday Autos uses 'cars'# for Istel and 'car'# for Fastrak.

Once into the operator's pages, you type in the holiday code listed in the brochure to check availability. If the client is happy with the holiday, you can go ahead and make the booking.

Remember, because viewdata is going into the operator's own reservation system via NTL or Telewest, it is searching in what is known as real time. That is important because it means you can sell a holiday from the system without phoning to check with the operator that the holiday is available, which is time-consuming.

Also, once a reservation is made, that holiday is removed from the operator's inventory straight away, so there can be no danger of it being booked a second time by another agent at the other end of the office, or indeed the other end of the country.

One of the early problems for operators trying to sell on the Internet was that the holidays shown on their web pages were 'posted' manually every day so anyone wanting to make a booking had to e-mail the company first to check there was still availability because those holidays were also being booked by the trade via viewdata.

Exercise 9.1

Know your viewdata codes

Find and write down the viewdata codes for the following tour operators and travel suppliers

Irish Ferries
Bridge Travel Service
Kuoni
Suncars
Cosmos
Airtours Holidays
Stena Line Holidays
Superbreak
Thomas Cook/JMC
Brittany Ferries

Why does viewdata need to be changed?

Imagine the following scenario. Mr Jones comes into your travel agency to book a holiday he has found in operator A's brochure. You go into viewdata to check availability and price. The good news is that there is room at the chosen hotel; the bad news is that the price of the holiday has gone up since the brochure was printed.

A quick flick through a rival brochure shows operator B has the same hotel, so Mr Jones asks you to check availability. You come out of the viewdata pages of operator A and dial into operator B. Sure enough, operator B has availability and the holiday is a bit cheaper but the flight times are not so good. So Mr Jones asks for a third quote. Each time, you have to come out of one operator's pages and start the search again. And in the end, Mr Jones decides the first quote was the best, so you have to start from the beginning because there viewdata has no mechanism for saving holidays. You have made a sale, but it has taken nearly an hour.

In addition, during the sales process, you have had access only to the information in the brochure and shown on viewdata, and both are limited. Unlike the Internet, viewdata has no colour pictures of the destination, resort or hotel, and no room plans to help clients decide what standard of accommodation they want.

From your dumb terminal, you cannot dial into massive databanks of destination information, weather forecasts or travel advice to pass on to clients. As was said before, viewdata is purely an order-entry tool. It was not designed to help with the sales process.

The cost of viewdata is also a disadvantage. Agencies pay a one-off connection fee to viewdata network suppliers of about £5000, but otherwise operators have to shoulder the cost of the system, paying per hour that agents are connected to their pages rather than per booking. Compare that to bookings via the Internet, where you pay only for the cost of a local phone call.

A future for viewdata?

This chapter has already looked at the new generation of agency systems that integrate the booking and management functions. These systems have to rely on going into viewdata because the majority of operators' systems are still plugged into it, but they speed up access by moving it from a dial-up hardwire to an Internet Protocol application.

The best way to understand that is to look at a couple of systems in detail.

- *Magic Desktop*. We have already mentioned this system. It sits on an agent's PC desktop and gives agents access to the Internet, where they can show their clients resort and brochure information, but it finds and books holidays in viewdata. Operators pay Call-link per passenger booked rather than for the time spent searching for a holiday, so you can see there are financial incentives for encouraging agents off viewdata proper.
- *Viewdata Express*. Developed by TARSC, this allows multiple operator searches. In other words, you can type in the required resort or hotel and the system will search through viewdata for all the holidays that match the client's requirements. You can display as many pages as is practical, but realistically eight at once is more than enough to cope with.

Global distribution systems

When they were first introduced in the UK in the late 1980s, global distribution systems, or GDSs, were known as computer reservation systems. Some still refer to them as CRSs, although more usually that term is used to mean the operator reservation systems. The GDSs Amadeus, Galileo, Sabre Travel Network and Worldspan were set up by competing airlines as a means to distribute their fares electronically to business travel agents. All are still used by business travel agents who will select one of the GDSs rather than use all four.

To get an air fare, you go into the system, tap in a code to denote the required date and time of travel, and the departure and arrival airport, and the system comes back with availability. You then select flights and the system comes back with a list of flights and fares.

It sounds simple enough, but consider this. Codes vary between GDS systems. Not only that, airlines use a host of different codes for the same thing, so Q, Y, M, B, S, L, V, W can all mean economy, C and J are among those used to denote business class and F and P are used for first class. L stands for lunch, D is for dinner, X can sometimes mean Air Miles, and so on. And then you have to remember the airline and airport codes. BA and AA for British Airways and American Airways are easy enough, but what about CY, AZ and VS? They are actually Cyprus Airways, Alitalia and Virgin Atlantic.

Exercise 9.2

Know your GDS codes

1 How many letters can be used to denote service classes?
2 How many different codes can represent business class?
3 What is the difference between a non-stop and direct flight? What numbers are used to denote non-stop and direct?

Over the years, hotel and car rental rates, ferry fares and rail travel were added, enabling business travel agents to book each component of their corporate clients' trip individually. Note how this differs from viewdata, which is aimed at the leisure travel market and therefore is used to book package holidays as well as some seat-only charter flights and car rental companies.

Exercise 9.3

More GDS codes

Write down the GDS codes for the following companies:

Hilton International	Avis
Inter-Continental	Stena Line
Hertz	Elgar (rail booking system)

Thankfully, the look and feel of the GDSs has changed over the years. The first major development was to introduce a Windows-based point-and-click system of moving around the screen. Rather than have to spend weeks learning the dreaded GDS codes, agents familiar with using computers could get a fare and make a booking with the click of a mouse and very little training.

There are now also systems that combine the best of both worlds, for instance Vista, Amadeus' browser-based front office booking system. This allows you to switch from command mode – where you need to use codes – to the graphical mode, where you point and click with a mouse. That is useful for anyone familiar with flight codes but less sure about hotel and car rental entries. Amadeus believes the system can be used by anyone after just 30 minutes' training.

The next important enhancement enabled agents to access the GDS databases via the Internet rather than through a hardwire link – like the hardwire link between an agency and viewdata.

A hardwire link is still the most common way for agencies to access their GDS, but it is also the most expensive because agents have to pay not only for the line to be installed but also a monthly rental charge, much like a telephone line rental. At the same time, travel suppliers – the airlines, hotels, ferry companies and others hosted on the systems – pay the GDS for every booking made.

By using the Internet, agencies can connect to their GDS for the price of a local telephone call. The drawback is that connections via the Internet are still not 100 per cent sound, with the risk that the system could crash during a booking.

This would be a good time to look at the Worldspan's Internet site, *www.worldspan.com*. Click on 'training' twice and then enter the global learning centre. Click on e-learning and from here you can register for on-line GDS courses. See how many you can work through.

GDSs and e-commerce

GDSs still carry out their original database functions, but they have also moved into the world of e-commerce, providing the content, search and booking engines for high street and on-line travel agents and other travel companies that want to offer their own web pages.

The GDSs have also developed self-booking systems for corporate clients. That might sound as if they are trying to bypass the agent, but in fact the GDSs make these available for business travel agents to pass on to their corporate customers. Clients can then make their own flight, hotel and car hire reservations, entering the GDS via the Internet.

The benefit is that business travellers can make simple bookings quickly – maybe a flight from London to Paris or New York, or two days' car hire in Berlin – leaving agents more time to use their skills to put together complicated itineraries and handle ticket fulfilment.

If you are going to work in a business travel agency, you should also be aware of GDS web products such as Worldspan's My Trip and More and Galileo's ViewTrip. These automatically create itineraries on the web when a GDS booking is made, so both agents and clients can log on to check details. Any changes to the flight schedules are immediately shown, which is useful for clients who are travelling as they don't need to keep checking details with their agent.

Exercise 9.4

Round-up – Viewdata versus GDS

Write down as many differences between viewdata and GDSs as you can think of. Then note as many benefits as you can think of for using the Internet.

Useful contacts

Free advice on technology-related issues is available by calling the ABTA technology helpline on 020 8349 0099.

Travel Technology Initiative – tel: 0870 904 1521; e-mail: *admin@tti.org*; www.tti.org

Genesys – The Travel Technology Consultancy – tel: 0870 704 0870; e-mail: *enquiries@genesys.net*; www.genesys.net

Amadeus – tel: 0870 990 9199; www.amadeus.com

Galileo – tel: 01628 822111; www.galileo.com

Sabre Travel Network – tel: 020 8577 4615; www.sabretravelnetwork.com

Worldspan – tel: 020 8745 1900; www.worldspan.com

Dolphin Dynamics – tel: 020 7381 7261; www.dolphind.com

TARSC – tel: 0161 929 1200; www.technologyreview.co.uk

Call-link – tel: 0800 983 0100; www.call-link.net

Farebase – tel: 01322 280011; www.farebase.co.uk

Comtec (for Travelcat and Easysell) – tel: 01633 627500; *www.comtec-europe.co.uk*

Where in the world?

There is a village in Europe that has performed an all-day biblical play every ten years since 1634 after the plague ended in the village. From the 5000 inhabitants, often 900 actors can be on stage at one time. Thousands of people book often two or three years in advance to experience this theatrical, emotional and religious scene.

Name the village and the country.

The Internet

In this chapter we are going to discuss:

- Frequently used Internet terminology.
- How to get on-line and find our way around a web site.
- How to search for information on the Internet.
- The benefits of the Internet – how to see it as a friend, not an enemy.

Introduction

Most young people these days are familiar with using the Internet – how to get on-line and search for information on the World Wide Web, and how to send e-mails to friends and colleagues. But how many know how the Internet works? That is one of the issues that will be covered in this chapter, along with the role of the Internet in the travel industry.

We also look at some of the major issues facing the retail sector since the advent of the Internet, specifically the fact that clients now have the option to book on-line, by-passing the traditional high street distribution channel. We will examine how agents can combat this and make the Internet work for them.

One of the ways to do this is to become familiar with the web sites set up by tour operators and travel suppliers for agents to use. This chapter looks at some of these dedicated sites, including the information available and, where relevant, how to make a booking.

A brief history

A history of the Internet is short in terms of years because the technology hasn't been around that long. But during its short life it has had a roller-coaster of a ride where travel is concerned.

It was in the late 1990s that dot.com mania reached its height as investors poured millions of pounds into one on-line travel agency after another. Companies called Dreamticket, Destinex, u-travel and many more appeared, only to disappear, along with the investors' millions, in the dot.bomb at the turn of the century.

But they didn't all collapse. There is a core of so-called 'clicks and mortar' agencies – as opposed to 'bricks and mortar' agencies on the high street – which have built strong brands and whose names you should be familiar with. They include Expedia, Travelocity, e-bookers, Lastminute.com, Web Weekends and Online Travel Corporation. The public can log on to these sites and find and book flights, hotels, car rental, travel insurance and other travel components.

Online Travel Corporation offers something it calls BYO, or Book Your Own, which allows customers to book flights and hotels at the same time. But generally, components on these sites have to be booked separately, which can be a drawback. Imagine spending half an hour finding a suitable flight, then going into other pages to find a hotel, only to go back and find the flight is now booked up.

Spend some time looking at these sites, to see how they work and what they offer. Think how you, as a travel agent, can provide a better service by selling a package. But don't, whatever you do, dismiss the Internet. Research companies reckon travellers in Europe will book £10 billion of travel on-line in 2002 – a huge leap up from the £4 billion spent on-line on travel in 2001 – and 30 percent of that will come from the UK.

How the Internet works

The Internet, or 'net' for short, can be divided into two. On the one hand, it provides the technology that allows you to send e-mails around the world at the touch of a button; on the other, it is the technology that allows you to search the massive database of information known as the World Wide Web.

The best way to try to picture the web is to imagine a huge warehouse full of information filed in different sections. When you go on-line, and we shall see what that term means in a minute, you are going into that warehouse through a telephone line. That is why you can go on-line anywhere in the world and get the same information.

If you know the location you want in that warehouse, you can type in an address – these are the long lines of text that begin with www., meaning World Wide Web. If you don't know the address or you want to browse for information, you can ask one of the Internet search engines, rather like 'keepers', to offer some suggestions.

You can use the warehouse analogy in respect of e-mails. When someone sends you an e-mail, it doesn't go to your computer but is stored in that warehouse under your address until you go to fetch it. That is why you can pick up your e-mails from any computer across the UK. To access your e-mail outside the UK, you need to use an Internet Service Provider that can be accessed over the web, like AOL and Hotmail. There is more on ISPs in just a moment.

Getting on-line

So what does getting on-line mean? It is the term used when you are reading information at the moment that it is piped down the phone line from the 'warehouse' to your computer. Note the difference between that and downloaded information. That is where you go on-line and save information into a folder in your computer's hard drive. It can then be read off-line.

Before going on-line for the first time you must set up an account with an Internet Service Provider, or ISP. These are the companies that provide the access into that warehouse. ISPs in the UK include Demon and Freeserve. Hotmail and AOL, as we have seen, are global ISPs. All ISPs provide a local or freephone number for you to dial into the Net. They also charge a monthly fee. This might allow you to go on-line for a limited number of hours a month, but most also have unlimited-access tariffs. This is the most-sensible option given the growing role of the Internet in the agent's life.

Whether you are going to work for a leisure or business travel agency you should find the Internet set up and ready to use. What you need to know is where to find the most useful information to help you in your job and how to send and receive e-mails. Your office manager will explain how your precise system works.

It is important to remember that both the web and e-mail are excellent work tools if used correctly. Unfortunately, too often they are not, leading to issues of time-wasting during working hours and questions over the suitability of e-mails that are being sent. Many big companies now monitor every e-mail leaving their system to make sure they do not contain unsuitable material or confidential information.

Tour operators and the Internet

Like travel agents, tour operators have been looking at how the Internet will affect their businesses. But while agents have viewed the net as a threat to their livelihoods, tour operators see in it an opportunity to expand their distribution outlets – in other words, to get their products, namely their holidays, in front of more potential customers – while also cutting costs.

After all, if more bookings are made via the Internet, operators can reduce the number of staff taking phone reservations, and as more people use the web as an information resource, they can print fewer paper brochures. That is the theory, at least; it has yet to become a reality.

Most travel suppliers have a presence on the Internet and although still small, the number of on-line bookings they are taking is increasing. However, evidence so far suggests that consumers like to go on-line to research their holidays, and even to make simple bookings, maybe a flight from London to Paris or New York. They are less happy to book and pay for the family's two weeks in Spain or Greece over the net. Long-haul specialist Kuoni's web site leads customers by the hand through every stage of choosing and booking their holiday, but so far it has limited success in getting people to book on-line.

But most believe booking habits will change and as a result a growing number of operators are making their sites interactive – in other words you can make a booking on-line, taking holidays directly from their reservation system.

While keen to develop their on-line presence, operators realise they must not alienate agents, who remain their most important distribution channel. The solution has been to develop so-called dedicated travel agent web sites. They are packed with product information and many have training sections and sales tips. Most also allow agents who have registered to book on-line. By issuing passwords, tour operators can recognise the agency that is making the booking while agents can be sure of earning their commission.

This is a good moment to look at some of these dedicated web sites and how to use them.

www.disneytravelagents.co.uk

You have to register the first time you use this site, using your ABTA or IATA number. This gives you a login name and password. Once logged on, you go into the home page, and from here you can check out details about Walt Disney World in Florida, Disneyland in California, Disneyland Resort Paris and Disney Cruise Line.

Clicking on one of the buttons opens a box from where you can find out about that particular park's rides, its hotels and shopping and dining options, including a price guide for the restaurants, and the range of entrance tickets available.

Itinerary planner produces a day-by-day schedule for your clients, even including the likely weather for the time of year they are travelling. You can make changes to the itinerary; when you and your clients are happy, print it out.

Resort selector helps you choose the right hotel for your client based on various criterion, and you can see a 360° view of the hotel room before making a final decision.

The cruise line button on the home page contains details about onboard activities, shore excursions, itineraries and selling tips. You can also open stateroom and deck plans.

From the home page you can get selling tips, details about agent training, plus much more.

www.funwayholidays.co.uk

Once registered, click through to the reservations menu. To book a flight, enter travel dates and departure and arrival airport, if known. Otherwise enter departure airport and the system will suggest all possible arrival airports. This feature also works the other way around. Tell the system whether you are booking an inbound or outbound flight.

Click Continue to enter the hotel screen. Enter dates, number of nights and the system lists all Funway hotels in the destination and cost for duration of the trip. Add the hotel to the itinerary or click on the name for more details.

Click Continue to move to other options, including car rental, theme park passes and travel insurance. Click button to choose.

Click Continue for total price. Confirm the booking or there is an option to go back and change any or all of the itinerary.

www.stenalineagent.com

Once registered you arrive at the home page. From here you can navigate to the booking section, timetable details, special offers, news and frequently asked questions.

The booking section opens with a route map. Just click on the route you want, insert the dates and times of travel and the number of passengers, and whether the clients want seats in the Stena Plus lounge. The system then provides a quote. This far takes just four screens. You input the client's details on a fifth screen.

The news section has details of on-line booking incentives and how to obtain Stena's new self-study training pack.

You can find details of the Stena fleet and onboard facilities, and a clever availability check allows you to make sure there is space in the chosen crossing before getting a quote. Ferrycheck in the news section shows up-to-the-minute weather conditions on each route, any delays and whether roadworks are causing problems around the ports.

www.superbreak.com

The home page is full of search options and looks a bit bewildering when you first go in, but the site is just giving you lots of different ways to search for a hotel. Whichever you choose, you will get the same information. So you can look for London hotels only, by star rating or get the full list, or you can look through the international hotels section.

If you know the code of the hotel your client wants to book, enter that in the relevant box. Or open a map of the UK and select an area. A list of hotels in that area will then come up on-screen.

Once you have the hotel name on screen, click to check availability, select a room type and get a quote. Then fill in the client's details and book. For details about the hotel, click on its name.

From the home page you can click into sections on theatre breaks, airport hotels (for clients who want to book a hotel near the airport the night before their flight) and special offers. A useful agent support section allows you to order brochures, meet the sales team and find out about training and concessions.

www.holidayautos.co.uk

This site proves the point that the simplest is often the best. The pages are uncluttered so you can see immediately what you are doing.

To make a booking, just click on make a new booking, select the country, pick-up location, dates of travel and the system will come back with a quote for various size cars. Click on i next to the car to see a picture and capacity details. Then just choose the required vehicle, fill in the driver's details and book.

A huge section on small print is full of useful information such as what's included in the price, age limits and out-of-hours collections. A news section has details about agents training and incentives – always worth checking out – and you can click through to Travel Information to get weather reports, a route planner and other useful facts.

Exercise 10.1

Disney

Mr and Mrs Jones are taking their three children (aged 7, 9, and 12) to Walt Disney World in Florida. It will be their first visit and they want to organise the holiday to have 10 days in the park. They want to stay on-site, want to know if there is a good time to go and which hotel to choose. They are prepared to spend what it takes for this holiday of a lifetime, but want a hotel the children will enjoy and two of them love tennis. Mum would also like a heated swimming pool for times when they are not in the park and Dad is into fitness. They would also like to know about the restaurants in their hotel – they particularly want a character breakfast one morning – and the cost of dining.

1 Use the Disney web site to find out which hotels to recommend, and details about the restaurants.
2 Produce an itinerary, making sure it includes all the Jones' requirements. Are there any things you would change?
3 What is the likely weather in April, July and December? Which month would you recommend?

Note: Disney's travel agent website is a password protected site dedicated to travel agents. If you are employed as a full-time travel agent, you can register by using your agency ABTA or IATA number. If you are a student and are not affiliated to a travel agency, please use the following Disney web site ID number: GB99999. On the log-in page, you will need to enter this ID number under the 'Identification Number' field in the 'First Time Visitors' box. Remember to select 'Disney Website ID' in the scroll down bar below too, before you hit 'Submit'.

The Internet as a marketing tool

So with the advent of the Internet and the growing number of opportunities for customers to book on-line, is there any future in becoming a travel agent? Three years ago, most agents would probably have answered 'No'. Now, having lived with the Internet for some time and had a chance to see its strengths and weaknesses, most would answer 'Yes'.

But retailers can't afford to put their heads in the sand and carry on with business as usual. The Internet is a very real competitor, just like the travel agency on the other side of the high street. In the case of the rival agency, you have to monitor their discounts and provide an added-value service; in the case of the Internet, you need to use the power of the web to your advantage.

All travel agencies these days must have their own presence on the web – not a few pages on the Internet to tell the world that Joe Bloggs Travel exists and its opening hours, but a fully interactive site that potential clients can visit any time of the day or night to research holidays and, if they want, to book a holiday.

That booking will be directed to the travel agent for fulfilment, so you don't lose the business. More to the point, customers are only likely to make simple bookings on-line – a flight or hotel maybe. If you give them the option to make that booking at your site, there is a good chance they will come to your agency when they want to book a more complicated holiday package.

Figures from Sabre Travel Network, the global distribution system, show that in the UK, agents with web sites have seen a 30 per cent increase in the number of calls to their call centres, indicating that a sizeable proportion of people are going on-line to book.

The site should have a prominent position on one of the leading search engines. That costs money but there is no point having a web site if no one can find you. Remember that warehouse? The dusty piece of information in the corner is the one that no one can find. ABTA agents' web sites can also be listed on the Association's public site using their choice of key words – it might be a destination or subject they specialise in like the USA or cruising. .

Your site should feature a lot of different holidays and also have hyperlinks to other travel suppliers' web pages – companies that specialise in car hire, airport parking, airport hotels or travel insurance, for instance. That way, you are providing clients with a complete service so they don't have to go anywhere else to make a booking.

Agencies should also aim to make the most of any e-marketing tools developed for agents. Here are two examples:

- Traveleye, the integrated management and reservation tool from NTL Business (Travel Division), allows agents to request specific information on behalf of a client. The request is entered into Traveleye with the client's name and e-mail address and relevant information is sent out on a regular basis.
- TARSC has created a brochure database from which call centre or homeworking agents can e-mail brochure pages to clients while they are on the phone. It gets over the problem of customers not being able to see a photograph and details of the hotel or location in a brochure before they make a booking.

Travel portals

Travel portals are best described as gateways, accessed over the Internet, that provide access to other companies' databases. It means the user gets a wide choice of products and prices at one address rather than having to go into three or four different airline or hotel sites for a range of prices and to check availability. There are travel portals for both the trade and consumers, as the following examples show. Familiarise yourself with these sites and how they work.

For the trade:

- *www.cyberes.co.uk*
  This site hosts both negotiated and published air fares – the latter from the Sabre global distribution system. Both types of fares – and there could be up to 200 for any one flight sector – are shown on one screen, so agents can scroll through and find the best deal for their customer in a couple of minutes.
- *www.farebase.co.uk*
  This gives agents access to an on-line search and reservations section with published air fares from the Galileo global distribution system and consolidated air fares provided by Unijet, Travel-Centre, Lupus Travel, JTA and Stratford Air Fares. Fares, shown in price order, can be accessed for free by any agent who registers at the site. Agents who subscribe to the original off-line Farebase can now also search for fares on-line from more than 120 consolidators but you have to phone to make a booking.
  For consumers/business travellers:
- *www.orbitz.com*
  This was set up by five US airlines and promises the lowest-cost air fares and flight options anywhere on the web. It also offers hotel, car rental, cruise and package holiday bookings.
- *www.opodo.com*
  This is a European version of Orbitz, set up by nine European airlines to provide a low-cost distribution vehicle to fill their airline seats. It has some very low prices, but there are also gaps in the routes it offers.
- *www.andbook.com*
  This is a joint venture Internet company set up by the Accor, Le Meridien and Hilton International hotel groups and targeted at business travellers. There are also 14 partner hotel groups featured, between them providing more than 7700 hotels, and all get equal priority when clients are searching for a property. Consumers can widen the search to non-partner hotels, which gives them access to more than 55000 properties worldwide.

Exercise 10.2

Brittany Ferries

Mr and Mrs Berline want to visit Normandy, travelling with their car. They want to take a night crossing to France, but return in the day. They want to tour Normandy, staying in small hotels. A restaurant is not necessary as they like to go out in the evenings, but they do want parking and a bar. They want to visit interesting sights including anything connected to the D-Day landings in the Second World War. Use the Brittany Ferries' agents web site (*www.brittany-ferries.co.uk/agents*) to answer the following questions:

1 Which route and crossings would you recommend. How long does each crossing take?
2 What facilities can they expect to find onboard their ferry?
3 Which hotels would you recommend and why?

Exercise 10.3

Superbreak

1 Your client wants to book a short break in Cambridgeshire through Superbreak, staying in a four-star city-centre hotel. Which would you recommend?

2 You need to book a hotel in the West Country, not far from the North Devon coast. Which area would be suitable? What hotels would you recommend?

3 (i) How many countries outside the UK are featured on the web site, and where are they?

 (ii) How many hotels in Switzerland can you book and where are they?

 (iii) How many hotels are featured in France, and in how many regions?

Where in the world?

There are three islands in this state, all close together in the Mediterranean Sea. During the Second World War this island was subjected to fierce bombardment and the people of the island were awarded the George Cross by King George VI for their bravery. It has a beautiful harbour and a 'silent city'.

Name the island.

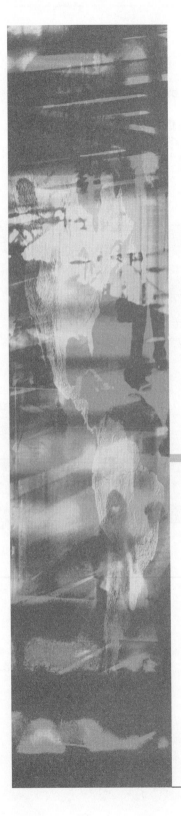

Insurance

In this chapter we are going to discuss:

- Holiday insurance
- Comparisons between different independent insurance policies
- Comparisons between different package tour insurance policies
- What is included in a travel insurance policy
- Exclusions
- The need for travel insurance
- Specialist insurance – pre-existing illness, dangerous activities
- E111 coverage
- Association of British Travel Agents (ABTA) code of conduct
- Terminology
- Making a claim
- Information required before issuing a policy
- Insurance tips for travel agents

There are many different types of insurance available. We can insure our homes against fire or theft, we can insure a car against damage, we can have life insurance making a provision for our dependants in the event of our death. If we are organising an event to take place outdoors, we can insure against loss of earnings in case of rain. Pianists insure their hands, models insure their legs – the opportunities for insurance are endless.

Holiday insurance

We are going to discuss holiday insurance, and the need for this insurance within our travel and tourism industry. Insurance exists to compensate people who suffer a loss or accident. Let's think about the type of misfortunes likely to happen whilst on a holiday or business trip, and the insurance cover required.

Assignment 11.1

(a) Collect travel insurance details from three different insurance companies
(b) Visit the post office and collect:
1 Travel Insurance booklet
2 Health Advice for Travellers (T6)
3 E111 form at the back of the Health Advice for Travellers (T6)
Or visit www.postoffice.co.uk and www.doh.gove.uk/traveladvice
(c) Compare premiums – what is covered and what is excluded with each policy

As you can see, cover and exclusions together with premiums will vary between insurance companies. We are going to look generally at the events that could happen and are included in a travel insurance policy.

What is included in a travel insurance policy

- **Medical expenses** In the event of sickness, medical expenses can be very high in most countries. The medical condition may mean spending months in an overseas hospital or being sent home by air ambulance.
- **Cancellation charges** As the date of departure draws closer, so cancellation charges become greater. In the event of your client cancelling the travel arrangements for 'reasons beyond their control' the insurance company will pay those charges.
- **Curtailment** Curtailment is when the client has travelled to the destination but has had to return home early.
- **Personal baggage and personal money** Considering the volume of traffic in the tourism industry, very little baggage is actually lost, stolen or damaged. Comedians like to joke 'I went to Florence but my baggage went to Sydney!' and if this really does happen to your client they will tell you it isn't very funny. Even small items can be expensive to replace and a change of clothing is definitely necessary.

- **Personal accident** The risk of personal accident is greater when on holiday than when following one's usual routine. Young people skiing or mountain climbing, elderly people dancing the night away – we often tend to put a lot of energy into enjoying ourselves on holiday!
- **Personal liability** This covers your client's liability in respect of accidental injury to third parties or accidental damage to their own property during the trip or holiday.
- **Medical emergency, repatriation and associated expenses**.
- **Missed departure** Due to public transport not running to timetable or vehicle policy holder being involved in an accident or breaking down.
- **Departure delay** Compensation if flight, international train or sea vessel is delayed at its departure point. Small payment is usually made for several hours' delay. £20 for every 12 hours' delay is a typical amount of compensation.
- **Hijack or mugging** This is one section everyone hopes never to claim against.
- **Catastrophe cover** Catastrophe cover is for occurrences such as fire, flood, earthquake, avalanche or storm during the journey. If accommodation is not inhabitable as a result, extra accommodation and any transport costs involved will be provided for under catastrophe cover. In Chapter 2 Exercise 1, you were asked to list deterrents (such as these events) that have taken place around the world during the last three years. You may have been surprised by the frequency of these events.
- **Avalanche closure** At the ski resort.
- **Homecare** This will cover emergency repairs necessary to secure the home following a burglary, or damage caused by serious fire, storm, flood, explosion, subsidence, vandalism, fallen trees, impact by aircraft or vehicle at the policy holder's home when on their journey.
- **Legal advice and expenses cover**.
- **Scheduled airline failure**.
- **Weddings** There has been an increase in marriages taking place abroad and this section will cover gifts, fragile items and so on.

We can say that insurance offers peace of mind to the traveller . . . if the traveller is fully covered.

The traveller may wish to have increased coverage – and therefore pay a higher premium – to include all hazardous sports which may be enjoyed during the holiday. All pre-existing medical conditions must be disclosed on taking out the policy.

Exclusions

Due to the spiralling costs of medical claims, many insurance companies have introduced medical screening. Insurance companies will not meet any claims arising from a pre-existing condition that was not originally declared. According to a report by Direct Line Travel Insurance, many holidaymakers are not being asked the relevant questions when taking out travel insurance. Many are buying the wrong policies and are under-insured. Direct Line Travel Insurance estimate that 8.5 million travellers would be out of pocket if they needed to make a claim as 75 per cent of those people who bought travel insurance with a holiday spent little or no time discussing the policy. Insurance is a serious business and needs to be fully understood. This takes time. The person selling the insurance policy, i.e. the travel consultant, has a responsibility to give and receive all the required information to ensure the customer understands and has adequate insurance for their needs.

All policies have an exclusion clause which states that not only must the policy holder notify the insurer of any health problems of their own but also those of 'any person upon whose health the trip may depend'. Medical treatment, a lengthy hospital stay, repatriation, legal fees and so on could all amount to thousands of pounds, and if the insurance policy were invalid most people would suffer trying to pay those costs.

Specialist insurance – pre-existing illness, dangerous activities

Should your client have a pre-existing medical condition, does that mean that they will be unable to obtain travel insurance? No. Most insurance companies provide insurance at a higher premium, bearing in mind that the risk of a claim is greater. If the condition is serious there are fewer insurance options, but companies specialising in this field include:

Medicover   Tel: 0870 735 3600
Folgate Insurance   Tel: 01202 668 066
Free Spirit   Tel: 08452 305000

The Multiple Sclerosis Society (tel: 0808 800 8000) have launched a travel insurance that includes cover for loss or damage to wheelchairs or walking equipment and payments to replace a carer if they fall ill or are injured.

People are living longer, and with improved health, more disposable income and free time, so there is a greater need for specialised travel insurance. Insurance premiums are often doubled for those aged 65 years and over. Bearing in mind that retired travellers will often take long-stay holidays to sunny climes during the cold dark winter months, selling insurance can be very profitable for the travel agent. Some useful contacts include:

Age Concern   Tel: 0845 601 2234
Club Direct   Tel: 0800 074 4558
Flexicover Direct   Tel: 0870 990 9292
Perry, Gamble & Co   Tel: 01404 830100
Free Spirit   Tel: 08452 305000
Leisurecare   Tel: 01793 750150

The cost of insurance for frequent travellers can be reduced by having an annual insurance that allows multiple trips. Contacting clients when the premium is due each year will ensure renewal is not overlooked.

Credit car companies also offer travel insurance but care needs to be taken that full cover is offered, especially if specialist cover is required.

E111 coverage

The European Economic Area (EEA) consists of 15 member states of the European Community plus Iceland, Liechtenstein and Norway. If a citizen or a dependant of a citizen of the United Kingdom is suddenly taken ill or has an accident during a visit to any of these countries, free or reduced-cost emergency treatment is available, in most cases on production of a valid Form E111.

The emergency treatment offered under Form E111 is state-provided and on the same terms as that offered to nationals of the country being visited. Private treatment is generally not covered, and state-provided treatment in other EEA countries may not cover all services received free of charge under the UK National Health Service. The E111 therefore is not a replacement for private travel insurance, but a back-up. The Form E111 needs to be completed and stamped by a Post Office to be valid. Fewer than 60 countries worldwide have any sort of health care agreements with the United Kingdom, so the need for a fully comprehensive, appropriate insurance policy cannot be emphasised enough.

Association of British Travel Agents (ABTA) code of conduct

The Association of British Travel Agents (ABTA) have a code of conduct between members and between members and clients.

Assignment 11.2

(a) Obtain from ABTA (tel: 020 7637 2444 email: abta@abta.co.uk) the Code of Conduct. It contains:
Aims of the Code of Conduct
Principles of the Code of Conduct
Definitions
1 CONDUCT BETWEEN MEMBERS AND BETWEEN MEMBERS AND CLIENTS
  Standard of service
  Minimum standards of brochures
  Advertising and promotion
  Booking procedure
  Booking conditions
  Insurance facilities
  Confirmation of bookings, tickets and other documentation
  Travel documents
  Alterations to travel arrangements and emergency contact
  Privacy and data protection
2 CONDUCT OF PRINCIPALS IN RESPECT OF CONFIRMED TRAVEL ARRANGEMENTS
  Cancellation by principal
  Significant alterations to travel arrangements by principals
  Cancellation of travel arrangement by client
  Overbooking
  Building works
  Principals' liability

3 CONDUCT BETWEEN MEMBERS AND CLIENTS AND MEMBERS AND THE
ASSOCIATION
Transactions and correspondence
Correspondence from the Association
Disputes
Arbitration
4 GENERAL CONDUCT
Misleading use of the ABTA symbol etc
Trading and website names
Notice to customers – financial protection
Payment of debts
Refunds
Vouchers
ABTA gold training award
Single payment scheme
Surcharges
Incentives
On-line transactions
5 INFRINGEMENT AND ENFORCEMENT CLAUSES
(b) Study 1.7 – Insurance Facilities
(c) Outline in your own words each point made in sections:
(i) a, b, c, d
(ii) a, b
(iii) a, b, c

Terminology explained

Let's just make sure we are clear on some insurance terminology, by studying Table 11.1.

Which insurance policy should you choose? There are many insurance policies on the market, and it will take time to compare best value for money. You are looking for a policy that meets your client's needs, and a company that will settle claims quickly and accurately and will not have to be constantly 'chased' to bring the claim to a successful and speedy close. Some operators require proof of insurance before they sell a holiday, and some tour operators provide their own insurance cover for their clients. The percentage revenue earned by travel agents from insurance companies is high. It is a worthwhile service to promote.

Let's also be clear on the terms 'broker', 'underwriter' and 'loss adjuster' (Table 11.2).

Table 11.1 Insurance terminology: 1

Premium	The amount of money a person pays to be insured.
Insurer/Underwriter	The company which receives the premium. This money goes into a common fund and is paid to the clients who have suffered a misfortune and make a claim. There is no refund for clients who have not needed to make a claim.
Intermediary	The company which travel agents deal with, rather than dealing direct with the underwriter or broker.
Policy holder	The person who pays the premium for the insurance.
Policy	The legal document providing written evidence of the contract between the insurer and the policy holder.
Claim	The request made by the policy holder for payment under the terms of the policy.
Exclusion	An event that is specifically not covered by the terms of the policy. Although exclusions are often found in small print in the insurance company's brochure, it is essential that they are fully understood. It is too late after the event has happened to tell your client that their circumstances are excluded from the policy.
Consumer	A person, company or firm acting in a personal or business capacity.
Force majeure	Circumstances where performance, or prompt performance, of the contract is prevented by reasons of war or threat of war, riot, civil strife, industrial dispute, terrorist activity, natural or nuclear disaster, fire or adverse weather conditions.
Principals	A member or other person, company or firm who enters into a contract with, or who holds himself out as being able to enter into a contract with, the client under which he agrees to supply services, or a member or other person, company or firm who supplies services, or who holds himself out as being to supply services, under the terms of an Air Tour Operators Licence (ATOL).
Excess	The initial amount required to be paid by a policy holder when making a claim. The excess applies per benefit not per policy.

Table 11.2 Insurance terminology: 2

Broker/intermediary	Insurance agent, holding a qualification licence, that arranges matters for a client. Looks for the best value, represents many different insurance companies.
Underwriter	The term originates from marine insurance. When a merchant was prepared to accept part of the risk he would write his name under the details of the risk with the proportion of the sum insured which he accepted.
Loss adjuster	Deals with all claims from clients made with the insurance company when there is a dispute. Otherwise claims are handled by a claims handler.

Exercise 11.1

Study any one of the insurance policies you have collected in Assignment 1 and find answers to the following questions.

1 Geographical areas – which countries are covered in 'Europe'?
2 Cancellation and curtailment – does the policy cover cancellation or curtailment due to:
   (a) not having the correct passport or visa?
   (b) the death of any pet or animal?
   (c) not enjoying the holiday?
3 Name at least four factors that can affect the cost of travel insurance.

Making a claim

To make a claim, a completed form will be required plus written evidence of the incident or reservation confirmation details. There will also be a written procedure on the policy for the policy holder to follow should the case be an emergency. Many insurance companies have a payout guarantee, perhaps within five days, of the claim being settled. Some useful contacts where information can be obtained are:

General Insurance Standards Council
110 Cannon Street
London EC4N 6EU
Tel: 020 7648 7800

Financial Ombudsman Service
South Quay Plaza
183 Marsh Wall
London E14 9SR
Tel: 020 7964 1000

Facts and figures supplied by the Financial Ombudsman Service regarding complaints

The Financial Ombudsman Service deals with complaints regarding personal pension plans, mortgage loans, motor insurance, buildings insurance, credit cards, permanent health insurance, and endowment policies linked to mortgages – to mention just a few. In the year ended 31 March 2002 the customer contact division referred 43 330 new cases to their case handling teams for detailed dispute-resolution work – a 38 per cent increase on the previous year.

Table 11.3 shows the number of enquiries received from clients for year ended 31 March 2002, 2001 and 2000 respectively.

Table 11.4 shows the volume of complaints for year ended 31 March 2002 for endowment policies linked to mortgages, motor insurance, building insurance, travel insurance and credit cards.

Table 11.5 shows the outcomes of those complaints for the years ended 31 March 2002 and 2001 respectively.

Table 11.3 Enquiries received from clients

Initial enquiries	Year ended 31 March 2003	Year ended 31 March 2002	Year ended 31 March 2001
Telephone enquiries	265 554	242 168	259 848
Written enquiries	196 786	146 071	154 874
Total	462 340	388 239	414 722
Complaints referred on to their case-handling teams	62 170	43 330	31 347

Table 11.4 Volume of complaints

	Year ended 31 March 2003	Year ended 31 March 2002
Endowment policies linked to mortgages	13 570	14 595
Motor insurance	2372	1609
Buildings insurance	1285	985
Travel insurance	1088	884
Credit cards	864	372

A few selected referred complaints from the 43 330 cases in year ended 31 March 2002.
There is a 38% increase on previous year.

Table 11.5 Outcomes of complaints

Outcome of cases	Year ended 31 March 2003	Year ended 31 March 2002
Resolved by mediation or conciliation	40% of which 13% mixed outcome (part win/lose for both sides) 18% in favour of consumer 69% in favour of the firm	45%
Resolved after investigation by a case-handler		40% of which 10% mixed outcome (partial win/lose for both sides) 23% in favour of the consumer 67% in favour of the firm
Resolved by the final decision of an ombudsman	11% of which 15% mixed outcome (part win/lose for both sides) 39% in favour of the consumer 50% in favour of the firm	15% of which 15% mixed outcome (partial win/lose for both sides) 29% in favour of the consumer 56% in favour of the firm

Exercise 11.2

Check some general information from the insurance details you obtained in Assignment 11.1.

1 (a) Can the insurance policy be extended if the original policy has not expired?
  (b) If the answer is yes, what procedure would you need to take?
2 Can this particular insurance be issued to a customer travelling from abroad to the UK?
3 Can this insurance be sold to non-UK residents?
4 If a tour operator alters a holiday and offers cancellation with full refund, will there be a refund of the premium?
5 Change of departure date – if a tour operator alters a holiday, are you allowed to change the date of the policy?
6 Can the policy holder increase the cover of the policy?
7 If the coverage for jewellery, cameras, video equipment was not sufficient what would you advise the policy holder to do?
8 Dangerous activities – are sports (such as hang-gliding, mountaineering, etc.) covered by the policy?
9 Can the policy holder pay more to be covered for hazardous activities?
10 What is the excess amount for personal accident in the event of a claim?

Build up your product knowledge by checking the following. Discuss the information given by each insurance company, and where they vary from the coverage below.

- **Luggage** It is appreciated that any settlement is only based on indemnity, which takes into account prior wear and tear, and not replacement value. The insurance company does not pay for any journey or expenses made with the replacement of the items. Check the policy to see the single item limit. Although the payment for personal possessions and personal money may be, say, £1500, it may pay no more than £300 per single item. As previously mentioned, policies vary with regard to conditions, excess and exclusions.
- **Goods lost or stolen** Should the incident happen whilst the goods are entrusted with the carriers (air, land or sea operators) then this must be reported to them, and a Property Irregularity Report obtained, or the carrier's confirmation. In other instances, the matter should be reported to the police, and a written report obtained to forward with any claim. Without this the claim could be prejudiced.
- **Money** It should be appreciated that the loss adjuster requires some quantification in support of the amount lost or stolen. The length of holiday and the day on which the money was lost or stolen must be taken into account as the insurers are always subject to audit and have to satisfy not only themselves but other bodies also that the claim has been correctly determined.
- **Hospital benefit** This only relates to the person confined to the hospital, and is applicable only during the holiday period, and not after the original return date.

- **Cancellation** When you have a party booking and one member drops out by way of an insured contingency it is not necessarily accepted that the whole party can then cancel. Cover relates to necessary cancellation and often when there are two or more couples involved and one person cancels there is normally no reason why the remaining couples cannot travel. Cancellation due to redundancy is covered only if the customer is being made redundant under the terms of the Employment Protection Act. Their employer should be able to advise on this.
- **Death benefit** Death benefit is normally reduced for children under the age of 16 years.
- **Illness** Pre-existing illness is not always excluded from the policy as long as the customer is not travelling against doctor's orders. People who have a terminal prognosis are not necessarily excluded from coverage. As previously advised, there are specialist type insurance companies who will insure people with terminal illnesses.
- **Medication** If medication is in use before commencement of the holiday it is only covered if it is lost or stolen. If the traveller does not take enough medication for the duration of the holiday then the cost of replenishing the supply is not covered.
- **Pregnancy** This may not be covered under the Medical Section if the customer is within two months of her expected due date.
- **Policy excess** This usually applies per person per benefit (where applicable) and not per policy.
- **Limits** In respect of valuable items, the limit usually applies to the whole of such property. For example, if a customer lost a camera, gold watch and diamond ring valued at £500 in all, the maximum amount the customer would receive would be the amount stated for the whole.
- **Bicycles/wheelchairs** Some policies may only cover bicycles and wheelchairs whilst they are being transported as luggage and only up to the limits within the policy. Once they are in use, bicycles/wheelchairs may not be covered if lost, stolen or damaged.
- **Skis, boots and poles etc.** These are covered under a winter sports policy. There are dedicated winter sports policies where other intermediaries have a winter sports section that can be added for an extra premium.

Information required before issuing a policy

The information required before issuing a policy is as follows:

(a) Name of insured person
(b) Age
(c) Area required
(d) Total premium
(e) Your agency validation (to obtain commission for the booking)
(f) Your initials
(g) Date of issue
(h) Client's address
(i) Trip duration
(j) Date of travel of the client

With this information you can quote for the insurance.

Insurance tips for travel agents

1 Ensure that the cover is what the client needs.
2 Ensure that the policy you are using is valid for issue, valid for travel dates and that the client is eligible to take out the insurance sold to them. Ask the client if they have any medical conditions that need to be reported.
3 Make sure that you give the client a copy of the policy document.
4 Remind the client to take the insurance policy with them when they travel.
5 Advise client that if they have an accident or are hospitalised they should contact the 24-hour medical emergency service detailed on the policy immediately. Tell client not to delay or look for alternative solutions.
6 If the client needs to make a claim please bear in mind the following:
    (a) The client should have acted in a reasonable way to protect their property – i.e. not left valuables or other items lying around.
    (b) Insurance policies demand a police report in respect of stolen property. This helps to substantiate ownership of the item.
    (c) Claims, along with supporting documentation, should be made as soon as possible after returning to the UK.

Insurance is a specialised field, and you cannot expect to be an expert in it. Do not hesitate to contact the insurance company if in doubt. Do not guess. You owe it to your clients to see that the correct information is given to them.

Assignment 11.3

You have a client who is travelling independently from London to Morocco and will be on holiday for 21 days. Your client is hesitating over taking out insurance and does not understand the benefits. Write an explanation for your client.

Assignment 11.4

Collect three tour operators' brochures that offer fly–drive holidays.

(a) Read carefully the information given on financial risks in the countries to be visited. For example, some US drivers carry little or no insurance.
(b) Explain fully the benefits of additional supplements and the tariff.
(c) Describe Supplementary Liability Insurance (SLI).
(d) Describe Loss Damage Waiver (LDW).
(e) Describe Uninsured Motorist Protection (UMP).
(f) Explain why it is a good idea to pre-book all-inclusive rental.

Assignment 11.5

Collect four package tour operators' brochures and study the details given on the insurance they offer. Make comparisons.

(a) Compare cost between domestic, European and long-haul holidays.
(b) Compare tariffs for children's reductions and qualifying ages.
(c) Compare tariffs for clients under 69 years of age and 70 and over.
(d) Is Annual Multi-Trip insurance available?
(e) Can the client pay a supplement to avoid paying any excess in the event of a claim?
(f) Can the insurance policy be extended for stays over 30 days?
(g) Compare each item. Do some offer more items and higher coverage than others?
(h) Does each policy cover repatriation?

Dilemma

Insurance USA

Your client is going on holiday to Las Vegas. There have been changes in treatment of serious incidents as a result of car crashes or muggings. You are checking the travel insurance policy to confirm the client has adequate cover.

Action

Name the section you are checking in particular and explain why.

Where in the world?

1 This city has a prison as a tourist attraction. The area is prone to earthquakes as it lies on the San Andreas fault line. Fisherman's Wharf is world famous for sea food of the highest quality.
   Name the city and the prison.

2 This city has hosted many successful musical and theatrical productions. It is a waterfront city built on three major islands. In 1884 the French presented this city with a now-famous statue. It has a famous park and shopping area.
   Name the theatreland area, the famous statue, the park and the shopping area.

CHAPTER 12

Finance

In this chapter we are going to discuss:

- How travel agencies earn their income
- Franchising
- Operational costs of a travel agency
- Security
- Legal and regulatory requirements
- Handling cash, cheques, credit cards and traveller's cheques
- EFTPOS (electronic funds transfer at point of sale)
- Foreign currency
- The Euro countries
- Disposable income

Introduction

There are many different types of travel agency. An agency may be one of a large chain of travel agencies owned by one company, often known as a 'multiple', such as Lunn Poly, Going Places, Thomas Cook, etc. There are also independent travel agencies that form a consortium; truly independent agencies; hypermarkets (usually owned by a multiple); agencies working on a franchise basis, and so on. A travel agency may offer every service, or specialise in a certain type of business.

The correct location is vital. If the travel agency business relies on clients calling into the shop, a high street location is important. If business is mainly conducted by telephone or Internet, however, an off-the-street location, perhaps above a shop, would be suitable. If the agency is concerned chiefly with making travel arrangements for one particular company only, an 'implant' travel office may be based at the client company's office or factory site.

When working on a franchise basis, the franchisee owns the office property and equipment and is responsible for debits and credits from the business. The franchisor offers back-up by providing a well-established and trusted name, and a successful blueprint for the franchisee to follow, plus help with training schemes, marketing, advertising, technology and so on. In return, the franchisee makes one initial payment to the franchisor and pays monthly royalties from the business profits. A contract signed by both parties binds this arrangement for an agreed number of years.

How travel agencies earn their income

Most travel agencies work on a commission basis receiving a percentage of the cost of the product ranging from 7 per cent to 40 per cent plus. It is possible for travel agencies to earn incentive commission. This is a higher rate for being loyal to one or several selected tour operators. After the agency reaches an agreed sales figure, a higher rate will be paid.

British Airways have introduced a fresh approach to agency remuneration by offering a fee-based payment system which is linked to the ticket. It is recognised that the work involved in selling an airline ticket is not always reflected in the total cost of the journey. The Booking Payment is a 'per sector' payment and the sector is based on class of travel and length of journey. For more details, log onto www.britishairways.com

Some airlines have an agreement to pay the credit card transaction charges for the travel agency.

Travel agencies can also be tour operators. In packaging their own tours they ensure that they receive the full mark-up. This will be a higher rate than the commission earned from a tour operator.

Charges can be made for services such as obtaining passports and visas. This saves the client a lot of time and trouble and to be relieved of this chore for a small fee can be worthwhile from the customer's point of view. Some agencies charge for supplying information, as compensation for agency time spent on something specific when no booking is the outcome.

Income is also gained from investment of customer's money between the time it is paid to the travel agency and the time it is paid by the travel agency to the principal. The money is deposited at higher interest bank rates. The fluctuation of exchange rates for travel agents dealing in foreign currency can also be advantageous.

Some travel agencies sell travel-related goods (hair dryers, travel irons, suitcases, etc.), tourist gifts and books in order to boost sales.

Discussion 12.1

Franchising

Research and think this situation through and discuss the advantages and disadvantages of having a travel agency on a franchise basis. Your discussion should include topics such as:

(a) What happens to the franchisee if the franchisor goes into liquidation?
(b) Is this a good system for first-time company ownership?
(c) If the business is a great success will the franchisee resent paying a royalty to the franchisor each month?

Useful address: BFA website www.british-franchise.org.uk or call the National Franchise Helpline on 0870 161 4000.

Operational costs of an independent travel agency

Salaries
National Insurance
Pensions
Staff travel
Staff training
Petty cash (tea, coffee, etc.)
Rent
Council Tax
Water, light, heating
Insurance
Cleaning
Computers, telephone
Postage
Hire of equipment
Advertising and publicity
Publications
Timetables
Credit cards
Bank charges
Auditing and accounting
Legal fees
Bad debt
Depreciation of building and equipment

Assignment 12.1

Fixed costs and variable costs

From the list of travel agency expenses decide which are fixed costs – that is, costs that have to be paid regardless of income earned, and which are variable costs – those that will vary in relation to the volume of sales.

At the end of the day it may seem that a travel agency does not have a large profit margin. However, it must be taken into consideration that the products of the travel agency do not have a high risk value because those risks belong to the principals. There is nothing to become outdated as there is with, for example, the clothing industry. There are no goods to deteriorate as with, say, the butcher, the greengrocer or the baker.

The travel agency manager's job is to forecast future trends. This can be done by comparing travel transactions over the past couple of years with the present sales figures. Analysing changes in products, the marketplace and consumer demand can help to decide where to build on strengths and correct weaknesses.

A computer print-out will show sales figures and expenditures, giving the state of the business in detail. It is important to keep a close eye on total sales made per day, the totals of receipts issued, details of products sold, bank statements, receipts and bills for every expenditure concerning the agency. Figures are reported on a daily basis to the management in order to keep them up to date with the information required to make constructive decisions.

Security

Because a travel agency sells valuable services great care must be given to the handling of cash, cheques and other accountable documents. Probably the most valuable accountable documents held in a travel agency are the IATA airline tickets. These blank tickets are entrusted to the travel agency. All accountable documents must be kept in strict numerical order and locked away in a fire-proof safe. Strict control must be exercised and a record kept of who has removed a ticket and which tickets have been sold.

Legal and regulatory requirements

Apart from 'direct sell' tour operators and travel companies that rely exclusively on their own retail outlets, most principals appoint travel agents to promote their product and administer bookings. The majority of travel agents are members of the Association of British Travel Agents (ABTA) and must abide by its code of conduct. All ABTA members are required to provide a bond to ensure protection for customers in the event of their financial collapse. A bonding arrangement requires three parties: the operator, the bank or insurance company that provides the bond, and an approved body responsible for calling in the bond and distributing the funds to consumers in the event of insolvency.

The travel agency represents the client and the principal and provides a convenient location for the public to make travel arrangements. When the client books a package tour, for example with a travel agency, the client is required to sign a contract. The contract is between the tour operator and the client. A contract is a legally binding agreement between two or more parties. A guide to the European Union regulations for travel agents can be obtained from ABTA and the Department of Travel and Industry at 1 Victoria Street, London SW1H 0ET.

European Union laws are in place regarding, among other matters:

- Descriptions in brochures must not be misleading
- Requirements as to the brochure
- Information to be provided before contract is signed (by travel agent and principal)
- Circumstances in which particulars in brochures are binding
- Transfer of bookings
- Price revision
- Insurance for client
- Responsibilities of travel agent, tour operator and service providers

Assignment 12.2

Research, read, think, write the answers to the following questions. The following organisations should be contacted for information packs:

Civil Aviation Authority
ATOL Section
CAA House
45–59 Kingsway
London WC2B 6TE

The Association of Independent Tour Operators (AITO)
Tel: 020 8744 9280
www.aito.co.uk

The Passenger Shipping Association (PSA)
Tel: 020 7436 2447

The Travel Trust Association (TTA)
Tel: 020 8876 4458
www.traveltrust.co.uk

(a) Are scheduled fares covered by ATOL?
(b) Is it enough protection if the tour operator is a member of ABTA?
(c) When is an ATOL needed?
(d) Are all bookings with AITO members protected?
(e) Will the PSA protect a fly/cruise package holiday?
(f) What is the limit of protection given by TTA (per passenger)?
  (i) £20 000   (ii) £11 000   (iii) £6 000

What thoughts have you on the following topics?

(a) Define a Retail Travel Agency
(b) Explain the difference between Business and Leisure Travel
(c) Describe three possible codes of conduct for a travel agent

Handling cheques and credit cards

Payment for travel services are usually made by cash, cheque, credit card or EFTPOS (electronic funds transfer at point of sale). Payment for each item must be recorded. Usually only smaller purchases are paid by cash. This must be counted in front of the client and large amounts checked by a colleague. Never leave cash unattended.

Dilemma

Balance of payment shortage

You work at a small branch of a multiple travel agency. The manager of a branch thirty miles away telephoned to say a valued client would be calling at your office to pay £3200 cash as balance on a cruise. You count the money out in front of the client and give a receipt for £3200. With just two members of staff on duty during the busy lunchtime your colleague is not free to check the money. Later on when preparing to make all payments to the bank you discover there is £20 missing. What action could you, and the manager from the other branch, take?

Cheques

You have to keep to very strict rules when accepting a cheque for travel arrangements. If you accept a cheque and hand over the travel documents before the cheque has been cleared (i.e. before the bank has paid your travel agency) you could have a situation where your client does not have sufficient funds in the bank account and the cheque is returned to you unpaid. Meanwhile your client is enjoying the thrilling experience of climbing the Great Wall of China at the expense of the travel agency.

Usually a travel company will rule that it requires 8 days to clear a cheque, and travel documents should not be handed over before that time has elapsed. Another point to bear in mind is that weekend and public holidays will bring delays. Your client can pay for a special clearance to speed up the process of cheque clearance. Some points to keep in mind when accepting a cheque are outlined in Table 12.1.

What happens if a booking has been made at the last minute and the client must have their travel documents today? They do not have a credit card, and you cannot accept a personal cheque because it is not possible to allow clearance period. The value of the travel arrangements is well above the limited amount guaranteed by the cheque card.

The client can pay by cash or, providing your client has sufficient funds in a building society account, they can call at the building society and have a cheque

Table 12.1 Accepting a cheque

Correct date	The date must be that on which you accept the cheque. Do not accept a postdated cheque as this is an indication that there may be insufficient funds available. The validity of a cheque is six months from the date of issue. However, it is important to bank cash and cheques every day.
Amount in figures and words	Look carefully at both – they must agree.
Travel agency name	Occasionally a client will be unsure as to whom the cheque should be written – the tour operator or the travel agency. If the travel agency is accepting payment the agency name must appear on the cheque.
Signature	Cheques should always be signed in your presence. See that the signature agrees with the name on the cheque. On joint accounts, usually either signature is acceptable so it is not necessary for both signatures to be obtained. Single accounts however, can only be signed by the person named on the cheque: Mr D. Gunning may not sign for Mrs D. Gunning.
Mistakes and illegible signatures	Any alterations must be initialled by the person writing the cheque, otherwise the cheque will become void and the bank will return the cheque to you unpaid. A large error would be best corrected by cancelling the cheque and writing a fresh one.
Cheque card	Banks issue a cheque card to accompany a cheque book. A cheque card is a guarantee by the issuing bank branch that it will pay cheques up to a limited amount. Once again there are certain points to check when accepting payment. The cheque card, account number and sort code must match those on the cheque. The name of the bank appears on both cheque and card. Check the signature on the cheque card with the signature on the cheque, and check the expiry date on the card. You (not the client) must write the cheque card number on the back of the cheque. A cheque card normally guarantees payment up to £50 or £100.

made payable to your travel agency immediately. The cheque will be signed by the building society representative. There will be no need for a supporting cheque card, and there is no need to wait for clearance.

When the cheque is presented at the travel agency, however, a quick telephone call to the building society should be made in order to confirm that the cheque has been issued for this client. This is because building societies do not guarantee payment on any cheques stolen and subsequently represented.

It is also possible to e-mail cash, a scheme where an on-line bank lets customers transfer sums ranging from £1 to £200 to any UK bank account. The use of cheques has declined by 34 per cent since 1990 and, with the growth of technology, is set to decrease even further.

Stopping payment on a cheque

The occasion may arise when it is necessary to stop payment on a cheque. Perhaps the cheque has been lost or stolen. Speed is required here to supply the bank with the following information:

- The cheque number
- The date it was written
- The payee's name
- The amount

Providing the cheque card number has been entered on the cheque, this information will be entered into the computerised system and the computer will automatically reflect that entry or issue a warning to the customer's own bank.

Credit cards

Credit cards offer credit to a preset limit depending on the card holder's income. There may or may not be an annual fee. The card holder can settle each monthly statement in full, or take credit to a preset limit at a monthly interest rate, subject to specified minimum monthly repayment. The two main credit cards are Access and Visa. Various banks and other organisations act as issuing principals and agents.

Charge cards

These cards offer credit for the period between making the purchase and receiving the statement. The card holder is then expected to settle the statement in full. An annual fee is generally charged. Although they are interest free, charge cards offer no credit and a high penalty is imposed on overdue accounts.

Debit cards

A safe way to accept payment for goods purchased. The funds are taken directly from the client's bank account.

All credit companies issue leaflets explaining their own conditions of use and can be collected from banks, post offices, stores, etc.

Assignment 12.3

Credit and charge cards – advantages for the card holder

Think through and write down at least six advantages for the customer using a credit/charge card for the payment of goods and services.

What are the advantages to the retailer, or travel agency?

1 The agent can offer a complete range of travel services such as car rental, insurance, all travel tickets, holiday and business travel – to be paid immediately by the plastic card.
2 There is no clearing delay as with cheques. Payment is guaranteed providing the usual points are checked.
3 Clients with cards have a great deal of spending power, and this can be to the travel agency's advantage. Payments made to the travel agent by credit card are safer than other forms of payment.
4 Clients do not have to make a journey to the agency but can pay balances, for example by telephone, giving credit card details.
5 Added security and convenience for client and retailer.
6 Cards are swiped through an automatic machine which then gives approval of the client's credit rating.

The disadvantages of credit card use include keeping an eye open for stolen cards. Also, credit card companies charge the retailer a percentage of the turnover of the business for the privilege of the payment being made by credit card. Many travel agencies pass this cost on to the client.

Many clients will choose to shop where the credit card is acceptable rather than pay cash or cheque. Therefore, as a retailer, if you do not accept credit card payments there is a strong possibility of not getting the business.

Checks to be made are:

- Check the agency accepts this type of card
- The card has not expired
- The card is not listed as lost or stolen
- The card has the client's name on it
- The client's signature and the sales voucher match
- Obtain an approval code if not using an automatic card swipe machine, or if going above the agency's merchant limit
- For all transactions a sales voucher must be completed and signed by the client

EFTPOS (electronic funds transfer at point of sale)

Basically, EFTPOS machines are card swipe terminals connected to a bank computer. Approval can be sought immediately, therefore guaranteeing the funds to the travel agency. The benefits of Switch and Barclay Connect for the client are:

- No cheque to write
- No cheque guarantee limit
- No need for cash or cheque books
- Printed details appear on the client's bank statement in due course

The benefits for the retailer are:

- No 8-day bank clearance required
- Quick and easy to process
- Payment guaranteed

Foreign currency

Many travel agencies have their own foreign exchange department. It makes a lucrative contribution to the revenue of an agency, and is very convenient for the client.

Buying and selling rates

When dealing with foreign currency it is important to know the difference between the buying and the selling rate of exchange. Think of it this way. Any retailer will buy something at a certain price and sell it at a higher price in order to make a profit. It is exactly the same for buying and selling foreign currency. The rates of exchange in Table 12.2 are fictitious and should be used as an example only.

Table 12.2 Rates of exchange

Country	Currency	We sell	We buy
Australia	Dollars	2.77	3.10
Canada	Dollars	2.50	3.40
South Africa	Rand	15.36	16.80
Thailand	Bahts	60.50	64.20
USA	Dollar	1.38	1.94

Equals one pound sterling (£1.00)

A client enters your travel agency and requests £120.00 worth of Thailand Baht. Because you are selling the foreign currency to your client, the rate of exchange would be 60.50: £120.00 × 60.50: = Baht 7260. Perhaps something has happened and the client can no longer travel and has decided to return the Baht to your office. You are now buying the currency: Baht 7260 divided by 64.20 = £113.08. Your client has lost £6.90 on the whole transaction. That profit, like any other profit on goods, will go towards the cost of transacting that piece of business.

Let's try another example. Your client wishes to purchase £200 worth of South African Rand. Multiply £200 by 15.36 = South African Rand 3072. The trip has been cancelled and the currency returned. Divide South African Rand 3072 by the buying rate of 16.80 = £182.85. The client has lost £17.15.

It is important to keep in mind when dealing with foreign currency that many countries impose export and import restrictions. Also, exchange rates fluctuate, so be sure that the correct rate is being used for the business transaction.

Exercise 12.1

Foreign currency

Using the previous fictitious rates, calculate the amount of (a) foreign currency you would give the client before departure and (b) the total in pounds sterling you would give them on their return.

1 Client requires £90 worth of Canadian dollars and returns with Canadian dollars 35.
2 Client requires £400 of Australian dollars and returns with Australian dollars 45.
3 Client requires £290 worth of US dollars and returns with US dollars 120.

Travellers' cheques

What are the benefits of taking travellers' cheques? They are the safest method of carrying money whilst travelling at home or overseas. In countries throughout the world, notably the USA, travellers' cheques can be exchanged for purchases made at shops, restaurants, hotels and airlines – just like bank notes. Each cheque has a number of special security features. The cheques are numbered and, providing they have been signed, are self-insured in the event of being lost or stolen.

Travellers' cheques are issued in many currencies: for example, Hong Kong dollars, United States dollars, Canadian dollars, Japanese yen, euro cheques and British pounds sterling.

When cashing travellers' cheques the client should show their passport as identification. Most bureaux charge a handling fee the amount of which can vary considerably. There have been many complaints about the high charges when changing euro cheques. If cashing travellers' cheques into another currency it is advisable to compare rates of exchange and handling fees.

The euro

In January and February 2002, twelve European countries replaced their national currency with the euro. They are Austria, Belgium, Finland, France, Germany, Greece, Italy, Luxembourg, the Netherlands, Portugal, the Republic of Ireland and Spain.

One euro is made up of 100 cents. There are seven different euro notes in different colours and sizes and denominations are 500, 200, 100, 50, 20, 10 and 5 euros. The design on both sides of the notes is common to all member states. There are 96 different euro coins in total; that's twelve European Economic and Monetary (EMU) countries with eight different coins per country. The coins carry a common European face but the reverse of the coins differs from country to country.

The exchange rates against the euro for the participating countries are listed in Table 12.3. Many of the European currencies were re-established due to (a) high inflation and (b) the end of Second World War.

When travelling on holiday, should card, cash or travellers' cheques be taken? A combination of all three is the best option. This combination is recommended but some countries are less likely to take credit cards. Agents should check the situation and advise clients.

Plastic cards are popular because they are widely accepted in many countries, offer a competitive exchange rate and, by keeping a note of the emergency contact number and reporting any lost or stolen cards immediately, the money is relatively safe. Lost cards can normally be reissued within a day or two. There is a charge for cash withdrawals from an overseas cashpoint, but the exchange rate is usually good. The downside is fraud.

Fraudsters net more than £100 million a year from cards belonging to British holidaymakers. Most losses occur in the USA, Spain and France. Shop assistants or restaurant staff may be dishonest, bribed, or threatened to note card numbers and details on payment slips. The information can be used for telephone or Internet purchases. Swiping the card twice also happens – once for the purchase and the second swipe to use the information on the magnetic strip to make a fake card with a false signature.

In countries where exchange rates to the pound are in the hundreds and thousands, watch out for an added zero. It is easy to overlook this error and be charged ten times more for the item.

Table 12.3 European currency replaced by the euro (rates for 1 euro)

Austrian schilling
Introduced in 1924, disappeared when Austria became part of the Third Reich,   13.7603
reinstated 1945.

Belgian franc
Introduced in 1830 when Belgium gained independence.   40.3399

Finnish markka
Introduced in 1862 when Finland became autonomous grand duchy under the tsars.   5.94573
(The only part of the Russian empire to have its own currency.)

French franc
Introduced in 1360 during France's Hundred Year War with England.   6.55957

German mark
Victim of hyper-inflation in the 1920s, rescued by currency aid after the Second   1.95583
World War from foreign nations.

Greek drachma
Europe's oldest currency dating from the middle of the sixth Century BC,   340.750
reintroduced in 1944.

Italian lira
Introduced in 1860. Also suffered from high inflation.   1936.27

Luxembourg franc
Introduced in 1848 but tied to Belgian franc since 1921.   40.3399

Netherlands (Dutch) guilder
Introduced in 1816 with fall of the Napoleonic empire.   2.20371

Portuguese escudo
Introduced in 1910 with the overthrow of the Portuguese monarchy.   200.482

Republic of Ireland punt
Introduced in 1928 as a symbol of independence from Britain, renamed the Irish   0.787564
punt in 1979 (previously the Irish pound).

Spanish peseta
Introduced in 1868 to replace the peso.   166.386

Discussion 12.3

Discuss ways of protecting against fraud when using plastic cards as money.

Travellers' cheques are safe and secure and are easily replaced if lost or stolen. The disadvantages are that they are cumbersome to carry around, and a commission is paid when obtaining them, and again when cashing them. A place to cash them has to be found, and the rate of exchange may not be good.

It is not a good idea to take all the holiday money in cash. If lost or mugged most insurers will only cover up to about £200 in cash – and then only if you can prove you had that much on you. It is necessary and convenient to have a small amount of local currency available at the start of the holiday. It may be required for porterage, snacks, taxis and so on. It is not good to be looking for a cashpoint on arrival at a destination.

As suggested earlier, a combination of all three methods – travellers' cheques, credit card and cash – may well be the best approach to taking money on holiday.

A very powerful motivator for travel and tourism is cost. The exchange rates between the tourism generating country's currency and that of the host country, and the rates of inflation in these countries, play an important role in being able to offer value for money. For example, if a country that is heavily dependent on tourism suffers inflation at a higher level than that of the countries it is normally competing against, tourists will often change their holiday destination to a cheaper country. The high-inflation country may be forced to devalue its currency in order to attract its tourists back.

There are occasions when the inflation rate may be so low in a destination country compared with that of the generating country that even unfavourable exchange rates will not discourage travel.

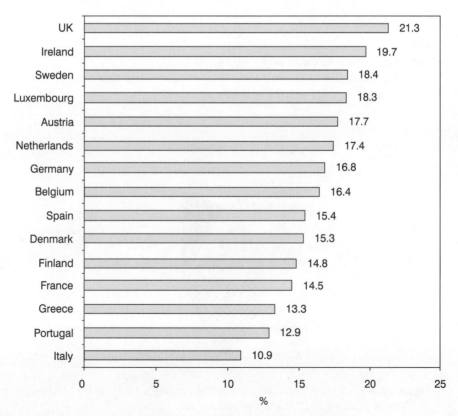

Figure 12.1 Europe – percentage of household spending on recreation

Discussion 12.4

In the 1970s the South African rand was 2 = £1. Today it is about 16 rand to £1. In the 1990s France became very expensive with 7 French francs to £1, instead of 10 or more to £1. Research and discuss other countries in a similar position. Discuss reasons for these changes coming about.

Disposable income

The British population spends more on leisure activities than their European partners and gross domestic product per head is 16 per cent above the average of the twelve euro countries. Figure 12.1 explains the percentage of household spending on recreation in Europe and Figure 12.2 gives the breakdown of UK leisure spending. Going out and taking holidays are the main recreations.

Dilemma

Stranded abroad with no cash

A client has presented you with the worst scenario. 'What happens if my car is broken into and I am stranded without a passport and holiday money?'

Action

(a) Advise the procedure for reducing risks
(b) Advise what to do if left with no money at all
(c) What is the procedure to replace travellers' cheques and credit cards?
(d) Advise the procedure for obtaining a new passport.

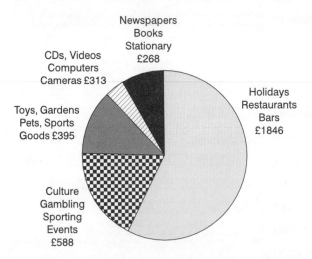

Figure 12.2 Breakdown of UK leisure spending (going out and taking holidays are the main recreation). Total = £3410 per household per year.
(Figures compiled by Oxford Economic Forecasting)

Where in the world?

This is the smallest European country. It lies on the River Tiber. It is only 0.17 square miles in area and has its own flag, seal, postage stamps, daily newspaper, television studio, radio station, army, police force and diplomatic service. It is dominated by the dome of the largest Christian church in the world.

Name this country.

Skills

In this chapter we are going to discuss:

- Skills required to work in a travel agency
- Converting enquiries into sales
- Product benefits for the client
- Sales techniques in the office
- Controlling the conversation
- Identifying the client's needs
- Closing the sale
- After-sales service
- Preparing to use the telephone
- Time management

Skills required to work in a travel agency

We are going to discuss the skills required to work in a travel agency, and generally when dealing with the public. In this situation life can be fun, stimulating, varied and even exciting – or it can be frustrating, tedious, emotional and a disaster! Which is it to be? Life being what it is, it will probably be a bit of both. With training and the right outlook on life, however, we should enjoy more of the former than the latter!

We all develop many skills just by getting up in the morning and tackling each day. Working in a travel agency can add to those skills. Issuing a ticket, collecting money, giving a receipt, using a computer, using the telephone, finding out information, reading instructions from a manual and understanding them, talking to clients, organising the day to the best advantage (managing our time), calculating the cost of a journey, advising clients on health and visa requirements, getting on well with our colleagues (not invading their space) – we take all these skills for granted.

Converting enquiries into sales

How can we convert enquiries into sales?

Product benefits for the client

We are trying to sell as many travel products as possible in order to have a profitable travel agency. It is difficult to do that unless we realise the benefits for the customer of the products or services we sell. We cannot use the 'hard sell' approach in the travel agency. We cannot make someone buy a holiday if they really do not wish to.

However, if a client is unsure of where to travel, or needs many items in addition to, let's say, an air ticket – for example, insurance, airport parking, hotel accommodation, etc. – this is where skills are used to do a professional job. A true benefit is a product or service that applies specifically to clients, meeting their individual requirements, as opposed to just selling the principal's package.

Assignment 13.1

Selling skills

(a) Explain the benefits for the client of the following products sold at a travel agency:
Car rental
Travel insurance
Flights
Escorted tours
Ferries
Cruises

Rail
Package holidays
Hotel reservations
Theatre bookings
Special interest holidays
Stopover holidays
Weekend breaks
Trade fairs and conferences

(b) Decide when you may have the opportunity to sell the following additional services:
Upgrading class of travel
Upgrading car group
Airport transfers
Airport parking
Priority check-in
Additional insurance cover (describe in detail)
Excess payment for claims waived
Excursions
Entrance fee to theme parks
Upgrading cabin
Upgrading hotel accommodation
Choice/change of airline
Pre-bookable seating arrangements and meals
Domestic connections
Obtaining passport and visa
Expert information
Traveller's cheques and currency
Extended holidays
Overnight accommodation
Advance registration service
Last-minute payment
Tickets on departure
Ticket delivery
Additional baggage allowance
Pre-departure pack (vouchers, guide books, etc.)
Upgrade to half or full board
Choice of meals on the aircraft
Order duty free in advance
Order champagne and chocolates for the flight
Airport lounge
Priority baggage collection at destination
Stay and park facility (stay the night before the flight and park the car for the holiday)
Order gifts (flowers, etc.) for special occasions
Single-room supplement
Chauffeur-driven car
National Express coach travel
Convenient outward and return travelling times
Travel guide books and videos

So! When using our selling skills at a travel agency, we need to think of all the products and services we sell. Consider the many benefits they provide, offer them to the client when appropriate, explaining the benefits, and making sure that we have up-to-date product knowledge in order to enhance those benefits.

Using the telephone

Using the telephone to conduct our business can be an asset – bearing in mind that if we are making the call we can prepare what we intend to say. This saves a lot of time and money on the cost of making the call. So we need to be organised, have all relevant papers to hand, and our conversation 'rehearsed' if necessary. We certainly need to list the points we wish to cover, otherwise they can be easily forgotten.

If the client is not available, keep trying. It is easy to give up when you have many other jobs on the list to do, but keep trying!

Incoming calls can take you by surprise. You could be asked anything, so you need to be organised. You need to be able to reach the client's booking details, or information on the products you sell or the services you offer. You need to have a pen and paper at hand to write down essential details.

Often your voice on the other end of the line is the client's first contact with the travel agency and within a few seconds an impression will have been formed. If you answer a direct line to the public you should introduce the travel agency's company name. Usually, 'Good morning/afternoon/evening, XYZ Travel, may I help you?' is successful for the following reasons. If you commence with the name of your company the caller may not hear it – either because it is 'clipped' or because the caller is not tuned in to listen to the first word. The salutation takes care of that problem. The name of the company, and the consultant's own name, followed by the question 'May I help you?' give the caller the opportunity to ask for a particular department or travel consultant, or perhaps briefly describe their purpose for calling. If the greeting is too long the caller is wasting money waiting for you to finish before getting on with the reason for the call. The caller may well be feeling relieved to hear a real live voice at the other end of the telephone having listened to repetitive music for ten minutes! Travel agencies need to action calls quickly in order to keep abreast of telephone bookings.

We need to identify the client's needs and project the right impression of our company in those first few seconds. Your voice is the key factor here. It must sound warm and friendly but not emotional. Try to keep a steady pitch, not singing the words. Practise using words that the client will understand – do not use travel jargon or slang words. The aim is to communicate as easily and as simply as possible.

The tone in which we speak words can alter the meaning of the sentence. You can sound aggressive, sympathetic, sarcastic, disinterested, helpful, hopeful, and so on. Volume also plays an important part in the call – if you speak too loudly you may sound aggressive, too softly and the caller will have to ask you to repeat everything because they cannot hear you properly. The pace of the conversation must also be considered. Allow yourself time to think, and give the caller time to write down the information you are giving. Don't forget, the caller may have hearing difficulties.

A call may take only a few seconds or few minutes, and may seem an easy transaction and natural process. By now, however, you will agree that it has to be well planned, organised and practised to be successful.

Let's run through making that telephone call again. It's all about preparation.

1 Decide what you are going to say
2 Make a list of points to be raised
3 Be ready with relevant papers
4 Be prepared with alternatives
5 Have a pen and paper at hand
6 Be organised with all relevant files, etc.

If for some reason you are nervous about making that call, go into the back office and have a rehearsal!

Exercise 13.1

Describe eight points to keep in mind when receiving a call.

It is not always easy to keep your tone of voice fresh, especially if you have said 'Good morning, XZY Travel, may I help you?' at least a hundred times already that day!

If you are in a position where you cannot help but have to pass the message on, double check that the message has been actioned. Many travel companies have lost business because of lax telephone procedures. Clients will not wait – they will book elsewhere.

Sales techniques in the office

Face-to-face selling, when the client is sitting or standing opposite you and looking into your eyes, requires a certain technique. Using the rules of investigating the client's needs, and listening to the client, begin by asking open questions. An open question seeks an answer that gives some information. You will then have the beginnings of a conversation on which to build the travel arrangements you hope to make. A closed question will receive the responses 'yes' or 'no', making the next step in the conversation harder to take. For example:

| Closed question: | Are you travelling alone? | Answer: | 'No.' |
| Open question: | Who will be travelling with you? | Answer: | 'My parents and young brothers.' |

This can lead onto the question of the ages of the brothers – they may qualify for children's reductions.

Exercise 13.2

Write down three open questions for each word beginning with the following:

(a) Where?
(b) When?
(c) How?
(d) Why?
(e) Who?
(f) What?

Exercise 13.3

Closed questions:

(a) Are you travelling to Japan?
(b) Have you been to Madeira before?
(c) Are you travelling with a friend?
(d) Are you travelling by train?

Change the above closed questions into open questions.

Our product knowledge should include the season of every country and destination, bearing in mind that many countries are so large the climate varies drastically at the same time of year from one part of the country to the other. When is high season and low season? This will affect availability and cost. This information can be quickly found by use of the computer or manuals.

Identifying the client's needs

It is important to know why people are travelling – and we are not just being nosy! People travel for different reasons, and if we know why we are able to offer alternatives should the first choice not be available.

Perhaps they are travelling for educational reasons. Consider colleges throughout the world, together with the subject covered and term dates as this will affect any alternative travel arrangements for the student.

Perhaps our client is travelling for business reasons, and has an important meeting to attend, therefore if the flight requested is fully booked a later one would not suffice. If you know why the business traveller needs a flight you are in the position to offer an earlier one that is available.

Is your client seeking the sun? Again, if this is the prime reason for travel the choice is enormous, and a suitable holiday should be possible.

Is the client travelling for health reasons? You should have details of the many health resorts, spas and medical schemes available around the world, and make useful and constructive suggestions. Your client may need medical assistance whilst travelling.

Perhaps your client is going to visit friends and relatives. Dates may be important here – perhaps to attend a wedding. Alternative routings may be necessary in order to get your client to the destination on time.

Body language plays an important part in looking interested in your client's needs. Inwardly, you may feel tired at the end of the day, or frustrated by a particular situation, but your body language should not reflect this.

Keep smiling! Throughout face-to-face selling it is important to demonstrate client care by using eye-to-eye contact. Use the client's name and be genuinely interested. Making travel arrangements should be an enjoyable thing for the client to do. Avoid giving the client the impression that you are 'too busy'.

Closing the sale

So far we have discussed selling skills by investigating the client's needs and listening to what the client has to say. Reservations have been made, and alternatives offered if the original request is not available. Other available services have also been suggested.

The next step is to overcome sales resistance! You cannot force your clients to accept the travel arrangements! They have, however, either telephoned the travel agency or made the effort to call in, and it is reasonable to suppose that the intention to travel is in their minds. So why is the client hesitating? Perhaps you didn't really listen, and have not offered what the client is really looking for. Perhaps you have not given enough information about the trip. Could that show a lack of product knowledge? Did you take enough interest in the client? Perhaps your attention was diverted by what was going on around you in the shop. Were you too pushy or perhaps not confident enough?

Having avoided these negative actions, you have won the client's confidence, and sold the holiday. This will include asking whether you may go ahead and book the holiday for the client. You need to collect payment, complete the booking form, and attend to all the other formalities such as passport, health and visa requirements, insurance and so on. This is known as 'closing the sale'. But does it end there? No!

After-sales service

Having attracted clients to the agency, demonstrated your product knowledge, gained their confidence and made many sales, you need to keep your clients. You would like them to book all their travel arrangements through you every time they wish to travel. And you would like them to recommend your travel agency to their friends and relations because they are satisfied with the service you have given them. There is little point in fighting for business, spending large amounts of money on costly advertising and market research, or racking your brains for new ideas when you do not look after the business you have already won.

That existing business offers us potential future business. The traveller is looking for a reliable, pleasant, efficient travel agency. Once they have found you, they will want to stay – so look after them! Keep them up to date by e-mail or by post,

whichever the client prefers, on all the latest information that is relevant – special reductions, country information, special interests for groups or individuals. Keep in close contact before, during and after their booking. Remember important occasions such as birthdays, weddings, etc. as a comfortable relationship is built over the years. A wedding card, champagne or flowers to the bride and groom when you have booked their honeymoon arrangements will mean a lot to them. You need to show that you care – by really caring!

Let's go through those steps again.

Step 1 Obtain information from the client – how? why? when? where?

Step 2 Make recommendations – suggest arrangements that may be suitable, check availability, offer alternatives if fully booked.

Step 3 Remember the benefits of the products and services you sell by offering additional services.

Step 4 Overcome sales resistance (without becoming aggressive). If the client is 'not sure' try to dispel their fears.

Step 5 Close the sale by confirming the reservation and collecting a deposit to secure it, and completing the booking form.

Step 6 After-sales service – keep in touch with the client. Do not make the booking then promptly forget about the client until six months' time when the balance is due – keep in close contact.

Client relations

It is all very well trying to follow these guidelines in theory but you don't know my clients! It is true, some clients are time wasters. It is all part of the day's work, I'm afraid. One may just be browsing through brochures, dreaming of sunnier climes on a wet and windy day. Another may be killing time before keeping an appointment. There are many reasons why someone walks into a travel agency but does not buy.

Mostly, clients really are very pleasant. If they are booking a holiday, it is a happy occasion for them. They need our help and the whole transaction can be enjoyable for both customer and travel consultant. But sometimes we need to be aware that stronger controls are required, and we must learn how to put them into practice. Don't wait for the client at the agency – practise on your friends and relations!

You may have a talkative client (or friend). Once they begin talking they are very hard to stop. Remember that the person asking the questions is the one in control. Be patient – they must surely take a deep breath some time. Be ready with a question to steer the conversation in the right direction. Be prepared to control the conversation and get on with the job as soon as possible. Out of the corner of your eye you may see several other clients waiting for attention.

Sometimes a client will be very irritable, or suspicious. Try to realise this. Is the service not really what was expected? Are you rushing them? Try to explain everything with confidence, and be patient. Have as much information as possible to hand to show the client in order to gain their confidence. They may have had a bad experience the last time they made a travel arrangement and are now very wary.

Perhaps the client is rude, or angry. Unfortunately there are some people who always expect to get everything they want and become very threatening when they realise it is not possible. Keep calm. Try not to take it personally. It is upsetting that you have come up against their problem, but try hard not to let it show. Be professional. Keep detached and try to meet the client's demands. Offer as many alternatives as possible. If the client is angry because something has gone wrong, again, keep calm. We will be handling complaints in Chapter 14.

Assignment 13.2

Comparing travel agencies

Visit three travel agencies and make a travel enquiry. It has to be the same question to be able to compare the response from each agency. Write a report on your impressions to include the following:

Appearance of the agency

- Was it easily recognisable as a travel agency?
- Did it make you want to go inside?
- Was it in a good convenient location?

Interior of the agency

- How many staff were there to help?
- Were the brochures well placed?
- What computerisation was available?
- Did the staff wear a uniform?
- How was the office furniture arranged?

Efficiency of service

- Were the travel consultants helpful?
- Were they accurate?
- Were they knowledgeable?
- Were you made to feel welcome?

Finally, the report should include:

- What client type were you?

Assignment 13.3

Controlling the conversation

Whenever the opportunity arises during the course of one week, practise controlling the conversation. Ask open questions, steer the conversation back to the point. When making telephone calls, either private or business, use control. Follow the points discussed in this chapter and record any changes in your style. Assess your success and failure rate and analyse why, when and how improvements could be made.

I wonder whether your friends will notice any changes? To seek an answer, ask an open question!

Time management

Not all the skills we acquire can be covered here, but managing time is an important one. Records need to be kept with the use of a diary and computer so that important jobs are not missed – jobs such as collecting a visa, reminding a customer the balance of payment is due, issuing tickets on a particular day, making telephone calls, and so on. The skills may follow the cycle shown in Figure 13.1.

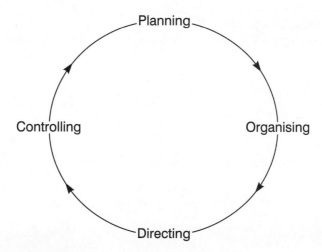

Figure 13.1 The skills cycle

- Planning what needs to be done, prioritising tasks, estimating how long each job will take. Allow for unexpected events.
- Organising by actioning the tasks. Keep an eye on the deadline.
- Directing if receiving help with a particular task. Make sure your helper understands exactly what is to be done.
- Controlling the day's work by adjusting when required.

It is rare that a planned programme can be strictly followed. In addition to the work planned, there will be telephone calls, queries to answer, talking to clients, plus many more unexpected situations to deal with. Monitor the success or failure of the planned day. Try to make adjustments. Remain focused on the priorities, and don't let those not so interesting jobs build up.

Easy to write about, not so easy to do! Acquiring the quality of being motivated and competent is a skill.

Where in the world?

1 This city has tree-lined streets and is one of the most beautiful cities in Europe. Not to be missed is the Alfama, an area of narrow winding streets dominated by the Castle of St George, once the home of kings. It also has a famous coach museum called Museu Do Coches. The most popular area in the country for tourists is the long sandy coastline.

   Name the city.

2 This country is in South-east Asia. The Kingdom has a population of about 50 million. In the mountainous north, elephants still work teak forests. It has a lively floating market where people trade their wares on small boats. The capital city has a breathtaking complex of temples and shrines. It also has a night market called Patpong. A village in the north is famous for hand-painted umbrellas, and a bridge and river have also been famous since the Second World War.

   Name the country.

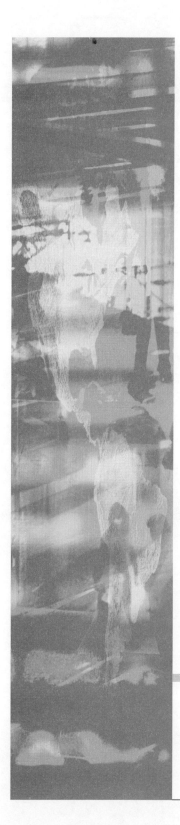

Handling complaints

In this chapter we are going to discuss:

- Guidelines to follow when faced with a complaint
- Some do's and don'ts
- Trade associations involved with codes of conduct
- Real-life problems to solve

Introduction

Unfortunately there will be times when we receive complaints. On some of these occasions these complaints could have been avoided if we had finalised our work accurately and thoughtfully. Some of the reasons for complaint will be out of our control, but we will be on the receiving end of the outburst!

There are a million different situations that can initiate a complaint: change of holiday dates; delays at airport; missed flight; inferior standards at hotel; increase in cost of holiday; travel documents incorrectly issued; lack of interest in reservations by travel consultant and many, many more.

It isn't easy to be face to face with a client who is absolutely furious, and is raising his voice and shaking his fist! What can you do? Put yourself in the client's shoes. He wants the matter put right. Your objective is to keep the business, to defuse the situation and to try to action the problem.

The Tourist Board of Wales conducted a survey on how custom is lost and the result was as shown in Figure 14.1.

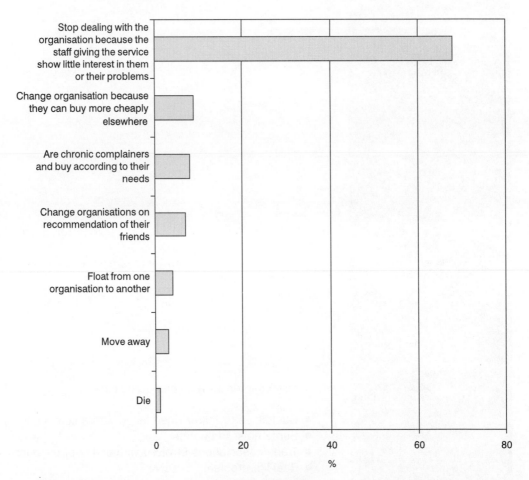

Figure 14.1 Reasons why customers leave companies

Were you surprised at the percentage that were dissatisfied with the service?

Should you be faced with someone with a complaint, you will need an area away from the main office. A scene becomes disruptive for the other clients and staff members. Be prepared to listen without interrupting. Ask the occasional question to establish the facts. Make short notes – this makes you look interested and shows you are listening.

Do not give the impression that you are rushed. Take as much time as you need. If there is any point you can explain to the client that will help, do so. However, do not argue with your client. You are there to establish the facts and to try to correct the situation. Can you offer an immediate alternative? You will not be in the position to make rash promises of compensation. Each complaint will have to be investigated and the offer of compensation may have to come from the tour operator, or airline carrier, or shipping company etc.

Let's think about some DON'Ts:

1 Don't lose your temper – it will not help!
2 Don't pass the blame onto someone else or the computer. The client is not interested in who is to blame. He or she is more interested in knowing what you propose to do about it.
3 Don't suggest it is the client's fault. It may be partly the client's fault, but this is not the time to say so.
4 Don't tell lies. It would be nice to smooth over the truth when we realise we have made a terrible error, but our clients are not silly and eventually they will realise what actually did happen. It is better to tell them now.
5 Don't take things personally. The client may be very angry, very rude or perhaps very frightened about an incident, and you are the first person to listen. Keep in mind that it is the situation that has become so upsetting – not you personally. You are their first point of contact.

Let's think about some DO's:

1 Do be as sympathetic as possible. Look and sound sorry for what has happened.
2 Do put yourself in your client's shoes. What would you like to be done about the problem?
3 Do ask questions and establish the facts.
4 Do promise to do something.
5 Do let clients talk the problem through.
6 Do keep a cool head!
7 Do thank the client for bringing the problem to your attention.
8 Do try to anticipate complaints before they happen in future.

Handling problems and complaints to everyone's satisfaction is not easy. Although we all know that practice makes perfect this is one side of the travel and tourism industry where we hope not to get too much practice! Handling problems and complaints can be a lot easier in theory: we know what we should do but in practice it is not always easy to follow the rules and situations can be difficult to control.

ABTA and arbitration

What happens if a client is not satisfied with the outcome of a complaint that has initially been made at source, then to the supplier via you, the travel agent? The first stage is for the travel agent to take up the matter with the tour operator or supplier involved. No one likes bad publicity and the complaint will be investigated by the tour operator or principal, and if found to be justified, an offer of compensation will be made to the client. Should the client feel the offer is unfair or insufficient compared with the distress suffered during the holiday, he or she may explain their case to the Association of British Travel Agents (ABTA) providing the travel agent or tour operator is a member.

Some background information on ABTA. The Association was founded in 1950 and formed into a company in June 1955. ABTA is a highly respected, independent, self-regulatory body that covers many different aspects connected with the travel and tourism industry. Its members are responsible for the sale of over 90 per cent of UK package holidays.

ABTA covers aspects concerning:

- Financial and Holiday Protection
- Quality Service and Code of Conduct
- Comprehensive Travel Assistance and Services
- Customer Information Line
- ABTA Phonecard
- Healthline and Health and Safety
- Internet
- Complaints Resolved

We discussed the role of ABTA in further detail in Chapter 2. Here we need to look at ABTA and the arbitration facility.

ABTA provides a low-cost, independent service to ABTA members' clients, administered by the Chartered Institute of Arbitrators. It is a simple, inexpensive way to reach a legally binding decision and does not require attendance at court as the process is entirely based on written paperwork.

All complaints from the client need to be received in writing. On occasions, video or photographic evidence is useful. The travel agent or principal must send an acknowledgement not later than 14 days from the date of receipt of the correspondence (not later than 5 days in the case of an e-mail). A detailed reply must be sent not later than 28 days from the date of receipt of correspondence.

Where a client wishes to refer an unresolved dispute to arbitration, the Chartered Institute of Arbitrators will forward the client's application form and Statement of Claim to the member. Within 21 days of receipt the member must ensure that the application form is signed and returned to the Chartered Institute of Arbitrators, together with a Defence to Claim and the appropriate arbitration fee.

The arbitration fee is based on the expectations of the client's compensation claim. A guide is as follows:

Up to £3000   = £72.85
Between £3000 and £5000   = £98.70

Between £5000 and £10 000   = £129.25
Between £10 000 and £15 000 = £164.50

The client must make the application for arbitration and Statement of Claim either within nine months of completion of the return journey or the events giving rise to the dispute, whichever is the later.

In the year 2000, ABTA received 15 503 complaints. In 2001, ABTA received 17 462 complaints. Of those complaints, only 10 per cent were not resolved and went to arbitration. Of those 10 per cent, 80 per cent were found in favour of the client.

Of course many complaints fizzle out before reaching this stage because the client declines to pursue the matter any further. With the single European market, there are many changes in the laws referring to travel and tourism. There are greater responsibilities placed on the tour operators and travel agents, and tighter control over standards.

Another route for a client to take is to pursue their grievances at the 'small claims court' if it is felt that any of the other organisations are unable to meet their needs.

Assignment 14.1

Handling complaints

Study the *Travel Trade Directory* for a full list of societies, associations and trade organisations. Familiarise yourself with the relevant organisation for your work, making a note of the areas for which each association is responsible. Each organisation will have its code of conduct or ethics (rules to follow which should minimise complaints). They will cover topics such as reservation procedures, training, issuing of documents, advertising, surcharges, mandatory information and safety. Use the following guidelines when handling complaints and answering questions. Then try solving the following problems (see Figure 14.2).

Discussion 14.1

Question A

You have to tell your client that arrangements have changed. Describe how you would do this.

Question B

You have received a complaint from your client: a mistake has been made and your client is furious. Describe how you will defuse the situation.

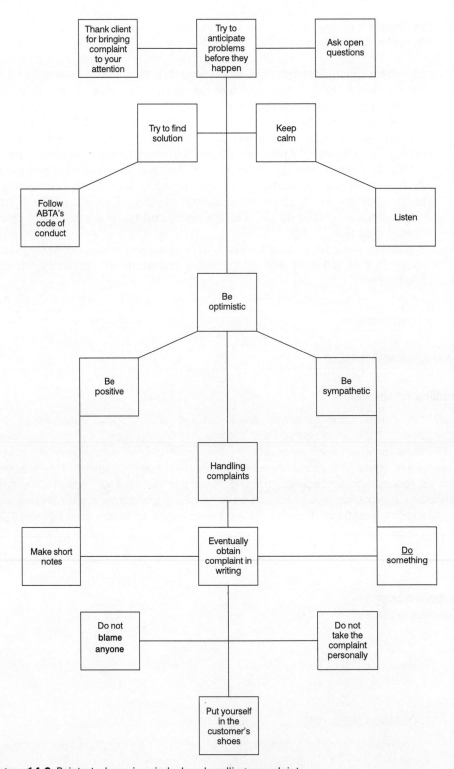

Figure 14.2 Points to keep in mind when handling complaints

Discussion 14.2

Complaints by travelling members of the public are on the increase. Discuss reasons for this with other members of a group.

Case study 14.1

Mr Benson – change of airport

You have booked an itinerary for Mr Benson, and part of the journey includes Paris with a change of airport. He arrived at Charles de Gaulle Airport, and departed from Orly Airport. At least four hours should have been allowed to travel between the two airports, but unfortunately you did not allow enough connecting time and Mr Benson missed his flight. He had to organise hotel accommodation at Orly Airport, stay overnight and continue his journey the following morning. This meant that he missed part of a very important meeting. On his return, he contacted you at your travel agency: he was still furious. He has threatened to remove his company business account from your travel agency.

What action will you take with this situation?

Case study 14.2

Mr Hart – no rail reservation

Mr Hart travelled from his home in Essex to King's Cross station in London to board the overnight train to Edinburgh, departing at 10.40 pm and arriving in Edinburgh at 6.20 the next morning. The journey from his home to King's Cross station takes about two hours.

Mr Hart has a conference to attend at 10.00 am on the morning of his arrival in Edinburgh. When Mr Hart arrived at King's Cross station he discovered that no reservation had been made for him, and the train was fully booked. He immediately telephoned his secretary at her home, who assured him that the reservation details were given to you. Mr Hart decided to return to his home in Essex. The time is now 08.30 hours and he should be in Edinburgh, but he is standing on the travel agency doorstep waiting for you to arrive! After the initial salutations, you look at the file and discover that the reservations have been made for the following night.

What action will you take in this situation?

Case study 14.3

Miss Jones and the cheque

You have made a last-minute booking for an employee of one of your biggest business accounts. You accepted a cheque for payment one day before Miss Jones departed on her holiday. This is not normal procedure but Miss Jones is known to you through business. The cheque has just been returned from the bank unpaid, and Miss Jones is at this moment sitting on a beach on the island of Mauritius having a lovely time!
What action will you take in this situation?

Skills for problem solving start at a stage before the problem. Careful planning is essential. However, once a problem develops, a plan of action must take place.

1 Identify the problem, the source, the areas it extends to
2 Collect all information on the matter
3 Decide on a possible plan of action
4 Consider alternatives and their implications

Some clients have problems before going on holiday and so it is not a complaint you are asked to sort out but research to find a solution to the problem. Here are two examples.
Find a solution to:

1 **Unaccompanied 16-year-olds** Several friends aged 16 years would like to go on holiday in England to celebrate the end of their GCSE exams. They have been told most holiday parks will not accept unaccompanied under 18-year-olds, partly due to licensing regulations. Research the facts and make some holiday suggestions suitable for these teenagers.
2 **Parents needing a holiday nanny** Exhausted parents are ready to book a holiday but want to know if they can hire a nanny just for the holiday. Research the options available to them.

It can be easier to handle a complaint made by letter. It gives us time to think, investigate and prepare. Try the following assignment.

Assignment 14.2

You have received the following letter from a Mr R. Arnez. You are employed by a travel agency called Mayflower Travel and you booked Mr and Mrs Arnez on their holiday to Majorca.

1 Reply to this letter
2 Explain the various actions that can be taken to solve this complaint

7 Avon Drive
London NW4
17 April 200x

Mayflower Travel
PO Box 33
London NW4

Dear Sir

Mr and Mrs Arnez – Holiday Number YSO/44/92
06 April – 16 April at Hotel Luna at Magaluf

We have just returned from the worst holiday ever experienced. Our departure date was changed three times before eventually leaving on 6 April. On arrival at Gatwick Airport we were advised of an 8-hour delay with the flight. No alternative arrangements were made for us and we had to wait at the airport for an additional 8 hours.

On arrival at the Hotel Luna, our rooms were not ready and we had to wait 3 hours before we could occupy our room.

The tour operator representative was nowhere to be seen. The Hotel Luna is listed as a three-star hotel, and yet we had hot water on only 5 of the 10 days we were there. The food was very monotonous with very little choice. We were not advised that extensive building work is going on at a site immediately next to Hotel Luna and we could hear all the noise of the building machinery all day every day of the holiday. We could not make use of the hotel pool because of the dust from the building site.

On arrival at Gatwick at the end of the holiday, my suitcase did not arrive. I completed a loss of baggage claim form at the airport, but to date have received no news at all of its whereabouts.

I look forward to receiving your reply and to learn what you intend to do about this disastrous holiday.

Yours faithfully

R Arnez

Where in the world?

1 This is a vibrant fascinating island, steeped in history. During the sixteenth and seventeenth centuries it was the richest island in the Caribbean. The strong Spanish influence can be seen through its architecture. The island produces cigars. Ernest Hemingway lived here during the 1940s and 1950s and set two of his novels on the island: *Islands in the Stream* and *The Old Man and the Sea*.

Name the country and the capital city.

2 This country consists of four main islands. Its culture includes flower arrangement (Ikebana), miniature potted trees (Bonsai), tea ceremony (Chano yo) and the traditional costume is Kimono.

The legend of the three monkeys – see, hear, speak no evil – originated at the Toshugo Shrine in Nikko.

Every February, a Snow Festival is held where hundreds of snow statues are sculptured.

Name the country. Where is the Snow Festival held? This country has a famous very fast train service – what is it called?

Solutions

Chapter 2

Solution to Dilemma

Aurora Borealis

The Northern Lights can be seen between November and March. One very good place is just outside Reykjavik, Iceland. Icelandair Holidays www.icelandair.co.uk
Tromso, Norway is also a good place to experience the Northern Lights. Tromso is a lively place, has many good restaurants and tours including ice fishing, husky safaris, cross-country ski-ing and polar walks. Scantours' Northern Experience www.scantours.co.uk

Solutions to Where in the world?

1 Mallorca/Majorca
2 Royal Observatory, Greenwich

Chapter 3

Solutions to Exercise 3.3

1 6 hours
2 A13
3 Disneyland Resort Paris and Parc Asterix
4 The Louvre
5 Walt Disney Studios Park
6 Bognor Regis, Minehead, Skegness
7 See brochure – approximately twelve activities

8 Famous comedians, country and western, sounds of the 1950s, 1960s, 1970s, etc., dance-sequence holidays and so on

9 90 per cent

Solution to Dilemma

Walking holiday in France

Belle France (www.bellefrance.co.uk) has a good range of independent walks for all levels. The company supplies route details and maps, and transports luggage between hotels, which tend to be small family-run properties.

Solutions to Where in the world?

1 The Rijksmuseum, Amsterdam, The Netherlands
2 South Africa

Chapter 4

Solution to Exercise 4.3

1 Greyhound
2 Convenience, low cost, worries gone, fixed outlay
3 See pages 47 and 48
4 A coach that transfers passengers onto the main coach going to the ultimate destination
5 Euro
6 Cairns
7 Alice Springs
8 Adelaide
9 Swan River
10 See pages 51 and 52

Solution to Dilemma

Clean beach

The European Union's 'Blue Flag' scheme is a reliable guide to the true state of a beach. Blue flags are awarded when the beach is clean, safe and well maintained and the water is clean and safe for swimming. Britain currently has 83 Blue Flag beaches – look up their details on www.blueflag.org

Solution to Where in the world?

Jaipur, India

Chapter 5

Solutions to Exercises

Exercise 5.1

1 31.59 area space; 3.08 passengers to one crew member
2 23.88 area space; 3.36 passengers to one crew member
3 41.69 area space; 1.67 passengers to one crew member

Exercise 5.2

1 Monorail, motorcoaches and boats are available
2 Yes. They can be rented at each park entrance
3 Language assistance is available. Personal translator units are available in selected attractions at the Theme Parks in Spanish, French, German and Japanese
4 All Walt Disney World Theme Parks have a First Aid Centre staffed by a registered nurse
5 47 square miles
6 There are designated areas in these Parks and Water Parks. It is prohibited in all dining areas
7 There are many different types of entry tariffs suitable for individual requirements
8 KinderCare Services are available for guests staying at the Walt Disney World Resort hotels

Solutions to Dilemmas

1: America by sea

There are weekly cargo ship voyages from Liverpool to Philadelphia, and from Thamesport in Kent to Montreal. Both trips take about ten days. Also the QE2 makes regular crossings during the summer. Fares range from £800 each way.

2: Upper deck refund

This seems a straightforward case. In sections 13 and 14 of the European Union's Package Travel Regulations it says 'the organiser shall compensate the consumer for the difference between the services to be supplied under the contract and those supplied'. The company has 56 days to deal with a letter of complaint. Remind the company of this legislation in writing.

3: Around the world without a plane

It is possible to travel from Tilbury in Essex to Auckland, New Zealand on a cargo ship. It takes approximately 40 days and costs approximately £2500 per person. Two ships depart monthly and call at New York, Jamaica, Mexico and Tahiti. For more information call The Cruise People (www.cruisepeople.co.uk or telephone 020 7723 2450).

Alternatively it is possible to travel from London to Beijing by rail, then to Auckland by cargo ship.

Solutions to Where in the world?

1 Italy
2 Alaska, 49th state of the USA

Chapter 6

Solutions to Exercise

6.1: Car rental abroad

1 According to Alamo, there is no problem taking a car hired in Canada into the USA as long as the client returns the car to Canada. The insurance is equally valid in the USA and there are no extras to pay.
2 Stop along the way on Route 2 at Head-Smashed-in-Buffalo-Jump near Fort Macleod, a World Heritage Site. It is an easy 200-mile drive with little traffic.
3 There is a cash US$6 fee per person to pay at the border collected by immigration officials. Advise your clients to carry their return air tickets as well as their passports to prove that they are returning to the UK after the holiday.
4 West Yellowstone is a good place to stay and an ideal entry point to the Park. If Mr and Mrs Ebanks have time, a visit to Cody and the Little Bighorn battlefield can be recommended.

Solution to Dilemmas

1: Car rental

The charity Tripscope Tel: 0845 758 5641 or www.tripscope.org.uk has an excellent information service for the elderly and disabled. Its database has details of rental companies in a number of countries where cars with hand controls can be hired. These include Australia, France, New Zealand, Portugal, Sweden and the USA.

2: Swiss motorway pass

It is best to buy the motorway sticker, called a 'vignette', in advance. It is obtainable from the Switzerland Travel Centre, 10 Wardour Street (10th Floor), Soho, London (tel: 0800 100 200 300 or www.myswitzerland.com). A vignette costs £17 and there is a £5 handling fee. Credit cards are accepted and it is posted out first class the same day.

In Switzerland, vignettes can be bought at border crossings but there can be long queues and payment must be in Swiss francs. On non-motorway routes, petrol stations sell vignettes and accept credit cards. If towing a caravan or trailer, two vignettes must be purchased.

3: Car rental upper age limit

Some car rental companies do have an upper age limit for drivers. This varies between locations because car rental is operated on a franchise basis so different outlets may have different contracts with insurance companies.

Hertz (tel: 0870 8484848; www.hertz.co.uk) confirms that none of its rental stations in the UK has an upper age limit. The driver must have a clean valid licence and it is advisable to inform the rental company of the age in case there is a change in policy.

The car rental broker Holiday Autos (tel: 0870 400 0010; www.holidayautos.co.uk) also confirms that they can arrange car rental with no upper age limit.

4: Taking a car abroad

In theory Mr and Mrs Bedford are supposed to be exempt but in practice difficulties have been experienced. To avoid delays it is better to use a conventional GB sticker as well.

Solutions to Where in the world?

1 Hawaii, Oahu, Maui, Kauai, Molokai, Lanai
2 Canada, Toronto

Chapter 7

Solutions to Exercises

7.1: Brochure work

1 (a) Portsmouth
  (b) Plymouth
  (c) Plymouth
2 (a) One sailing per day
  (b) 9 hours
3 (a) 130 mins (2 hours 10 mins)
  (b) Vitesse
  (c) 4 hours 15 mins
4 London/Plymouth   228
  Santander/Marbella   627
  Total   855
5 (a) 14 per day   1 hour
  (b) 3 per day   2 hours
6 (a) High-speed sea service
  (b) See brochure
  (c) Wales, Ireland
7 (a) See brochure
  (b) Log onto www.poportsmouth.com/entertainment
  (c) Yes, to France only
  (d) (i) 3; (ii) 2 hrs 45 mins
8 (a) Rodin
  (b) 15 (see brochure)
9 See map

7.2: Tourist destinations in The Netherlands, France and Germany

1 Luxembourg and Belgium
2 Kinderdijk
3 Miniature town where everything is built on a small scale and most models are actually working
4 Flowers – 66 acres of parkland and bulb fields
5 Cheese market
6 Versailles and Fontainebleau
7 Montmartre
8 Artists
9 Giverny
10 Elbe
11 The River Rhine
12 (a) Cuxhaven
   (b) Harwich to Cuxhaven. Dep. Wed., Fri., Sun. Dep. 16.00. Arr. 09.45 next day
       Cuxhaven to Harwich. Dep. Tues., Thurs., Sat. Dep. 18.00. Arr. 09.45 next day

7.3: Research of brochures and travel destinations worldwide

1 Australia
2 Cango Caves and Ostrich Farm
3 (a) Flam
   (b) 20
   (c) Some of the tunnels have open windows
4 The Flying Scotsman (the locomotive is called the Flying Scotsman and the carriages are called the Northern Belle – Orient Express of the North)
5 Coast Starlight
6 Sacramento
7 Could be: Golden Gate Bridge, Fisherman's Wharf, China Town, Alcatraz Island
8 Between Jasper and Banff
9 Elephant camp, temples and cottage industry village – well worth a visit
10 All coaches are non-smoking and air conditioned and every seat has a foot rest, reading lamp and magazine rack. There are a number of compartments designed for families with four seats facing each other, foldaway tables and space for a pushchair, as well as special disabled facilities. Two buffet coaches provide hot and cold snacks and a trolley service offers additional refreshments.

Solutions to Where in the world?

1 Rome and Colosseum
2 Istanbul

Chapter 8

Solutions to Exercises

Exercise 8.2

	City	Country	IATA area
1	Athens	Greece	2
2	Madrid	Spain	2
3	Beijing	China	3
4	New Delhi	India	3
5	Pretoria	South Africa	2
6	Nairobi	Kenya	2
7	Budapest	Hungary	2
8	Jakarta	Indonesia	3
9	Tehran	Iran	2
10	Maseru	Lesotho	2
11	Caracus	Venezuela	1
12	Tokyo	Japan	3
13	Lima	Peru	1
14	Los Angeles	USA	1

Exercise 8.3

City	Country
Madras	India
Istanbul	Turkey
Beirut	Lebanon
Damascus	Syria
Kuala Lumpur	Malaysia
Montevideo	Uruguay
Manila	Philippines
Colombo	Sri Lanka
Osaka	Japan
Blantyre	Malawi
Chittagong	Bangladesh

Exercise 8.4

1 Osaka, Taipei, Baghdad, Madrid, Lisbon
2 Sydney, Manila, Bombay, Durban, Cape Town
3 London, Amsterdam, Berlin, Istanbul, Karachi, London
4 Athens, Rome, Madrid, Paris, Oslo, Vienna, Athens
5 New York, London, Paris, Amsterdam, Brussels, Munich, Madrid, New York
6 Paris, Nairobi, Mauritius, Perth, Bombay, Athens, Paris

Exercise 8.6

2 (a) 15 hrs 20 mins
  (b) 6 hrs 20 mins
  (c) 4 hrs 35 mins
  (d) 5 hrs 20 mins
  (e) 12 hrs 25 mins
3 (a) +10
  (b) +5.30
  (c) +3
  (d) +2
  (e) GMT
  (f) −3
4 (a) London GMT, Bombay +5.30 mins, 1700 hrs in London = 2230 hrs in Bombay
  (b) Nairobi +3, Sydney +10, 0800 hrs in Nairobi = 1500 hrs in Sydney
  (c) Cairo +2, Rio de Janeiro −3, 1400 hrs in Cairo = 0900 hrs in Rio de Janeiro
5 Tourist attractions could include:
  (a) Sydney Opera House, Sydney Harbour Bridge, Manly Beach, Centrepoint Tower, Kings Cross, Bondi Beach, Blue Mountains
  (b) Ornate Archway called 'Gateway to India', Elephanta Island, Jehu, Versova, Mardu and Manori beaches, Malabar Hill with hanging gardens, Aurangabad for rock temples
  (c) Karen Blixen Museum, Railway Museum, African Heritage Gallery, the historic Norfolk Hotel, then head off to one of the many game reserves within a day's drive from Nairobi
  (d) The Goldfen Mask of Tutankhamun, the Cairo Museum, the Egyptian Museum, the Pyramids, and the Sphinx
  (e) Tower of London, Westminster Abbey, Theatres, Museums, Hyde Park, Green Park, London Organised Walks, the London Eye
  (f) Copacabana, Ipanema and Leblon beaches, Sugar Loaf Mountain, Corcovado Peak with its huge statue of Christ the Redeemer.

Solution to Dilemmas

1: Use of private airport lounges

Yes. ABC Holiday Extras (tel: 0870 844 4000, www.holidayextras.co.uk) can arrange access to 22 lounges in 13 UK airports including Holideck lounge at Heathrow. Entry to these lounges costs approximately £18 per person and this allows access for up to three hours before the departure of the scheduled flight. It includes free drinks and shower facilities and some lounges have Internet access and other business services.

2: Passport, visa

The Greek Consulate in London is adamant that there is no problem at immigration desks anywhere in Greece. A Turkish stamp in the passport has not been an issue since Greece and Turkey patched up their differences in the 1990s.

3: How many airports in Britain and which is the busiest?

There are 142 licensed civil aerodromes in the UK. The busiest is Heathrow carrying 63.0 million passengers in 2002.
In the year 2002:
Gatwick: 29.5 million
Manchester: 18.6 million
Stansted: 16 million
Source: Civil Aviation Authority

Solutions to Where in the world?

Los Angeles, Manns Chinese Theatre, Beverly Hills

Chapter 9

Solutions to Exercises

9.1 Know your viewdata codes

The viewdata codes are (Istel; Fastrak):

> Irish Ferries – IRF#; IFR
> Bridge Travel Service – BTG#, BOB#, BBI#; BTG, BOB
> Kuoni – KUO#; KUO
> Suncars – SUN# (both)
> Cosmos – COS#, 7#; COS
> Airtours Holidays – AIR#, 81#; AIR
> Stena Line Holidays – SEA#; SEA
> Superbreak Holidays – UKB#; UKB
> Thomas Cook/JMC – LTS#; LTS
> Brittany Ferries – FERRY#; not registered with Telewest

9.2 Know your GDS codes

1 There can be up to 26 classes shown (letters A–Z).
2 Depends on the route. For Europe the letters C or D are used for restricted business class (which means a portion of the ticket may not be refundable) but there is no difference in the onboard service. For the rest of the world the classes are J or D for restricted business class.
3 This might sound a silly question, but although a non-stop flight is literally non-stop, a direct flight maintains the same flight number from A to B but can stop for refuelling or pick up/drop off passengers. Generally 0 denotes non-stop, 1 means one-stop, 2 means two stops, and so on.

9.3 More GDS codes

Hilton International – HL
Inter-Continental – IC
Sheraton – SI
Hertz – ZE
Avis – ZI
Elgar – 9F

9.4 Viewdata versus GDS

Your answers should include:

- Viewdata is designed for leisure package holiday bookings.
- Viewdata is not interactive, which means you can't interrogate the system.
- Native (i.e. original) viewdata is slow to use.
- You need training to use viewdata.
- Viewdata has limited information and no graphics.
- GDSs are designed to book individual travel components such as flights, hotels and car hire, rather than a package.
- GDSs can be interrogated using Windows-style point and click technology.
- Agents can get a fare from GDS with hardly any training.
- GDSs provide minimal information.

Benefits of the Internet:

- Fast, easy access.
- Direct access to computer reservation systems for up-to-the-minute rates.
- Lots of information.
- Pictures to show resorts/hotels/bedrooms to clients.
- Very little training needed to make a booking.

Solutions to Where in the world?

Oberammergau, Bavaria, Germany

Chapter 10

Solutions to Exercises

10.1 Disney on-line

1 Contemporary should be your first choice, followed by Grand Floridian Resort and Spa. These have heated pools, tennis and fitness facilities. Contemporary restaurants are the Concourse Steakhouse, California Grill, Chef Mickey's and the Food and Fun Center. Grand Floridian restaurants are Victoria and Albert's, Citricos, Narcoossee's, 1900 Park Fare, Grand Floridian Café, Garden View Lounge, Wonderland Tea Party.

2 Check that your itinerary includes a character breakfast and gives your clients free time to take part in their favourite activities.

3 You can either draw up an itinerary for each month to get the weather, or advise clients that this is a year-round destination.

10.2 Brittany Ferries

1 You should recommend the Portsmouth–Caen route as this takes them straight to Normandy. The night crossing takes 8 hours; a day sailing takes 6 hours.

2 Facilities vary between ships, but there will be a restaurant, a self-service café and Salon de Thé. There will also be a bar, live entertainment, cinemas, shops and a children's playroom.

3 There are lots to choose from. The Hotel de Brunville in Bayeux is a good choice as the Bayeux Tapestry and the Second World War museums are here. Le Moulin de Ducey near Mont St Michel is a good base to visit the mount and Hotel I'lle de Sées is a quiet country hotel 5 km from Sées, noted for its Gothic cathedral.

10.3 Superbreak

1 Cambridge has two four-star hotels. The Crowne Plaza is nearest the city centre. The alternative is the De Vere University Arms.
2 Barnstable is the best choice. There are three hotels – the four-star Imperial Hotel and three star Park Hotel and Barnstable Hotel. All promote themselves as being close to the north coast.
3 (i) There are 20 countries – Austria, Belgium, Czech Republic, Denmark, Finland, France, Germany, Holland, Hungary, Italy, Latvia, Lithuania, Luxembourg, Norway, Portugal, Russia, Sweden, Spain, Switzerland and the USA.
   (ii) There are 12 Swiss hotels – in Geneva or Zurich.
   (iii) There are 85 hotels in France, in 14 regions.

Solution to Where in the world?

Malta

Chapter 11

Solution to Assignment 11.2(c)

(i) (a) Members (travel consultant) must draw their client's attention to the availability of insurance cover to suit their client's requirements.
     (b) The insurance policy must be appropriate for the client's requirements including any hazardous activities during the travel.
     (c) Members shall ensure that clients are aware of the need to comply with the insurance company's requirements and their duty to disclose to the insurance company all relevant information, e.g. pre-existing illness.
     (d) Members shall comply strictly with the terms of business with insurance companies, as required under the agreements.
(ii) (a) Retailers providing insurance which is not arranged through the principal concerned, shall ensure that within 48 hours of booking being made, clients are given an insurance document giving all details of the reservation.
     (b) In respect of packages, retailers must ensure that should the client not take the principals or their own insurance, details of the client's insurance must be passed onto the principal.
(iii)(a) Principals, when providing the insurance, shall ensure the clients receive all details of the insurance. In the event of a late booking when issue of this confirmation is not possible, the principal shall ensure full written details of cover are provided to the client at point of departure.
     (b) Where a client is insured under a master policy held by the principal under which cover is provided as soon as a confirmation invoice is issued then, for the purposes of this clause, such confirmation invoice will provide cover.

Where the effective start date of cover is other than the date of issue of the confirmation invoice, this shall be clearly indicated in writing to the client.

(c) Principals shall ensure that insurance policies detailed in their brochure are appropriate to any packages or other travel arrangements detailed within that brochure.

Solutions to Exercise 11.1(3)

The area, the duration of the holiday, the age of the policy holder, whether any dangerous sports are anticipated, any pre-existing illness

Solution to Dilemma

Insurance USA

Holidaymakers with serious injuries face being airlifted to hospitals in California, Arizona or Utah. The city's only Level One trauma centre closed after doctors resigned due to fears of excessive malpractice lawsuits. Patients may be accepted by other local hospitals, but the most serious cases may be airlifted. Visitors should ensure their travel insurance covers air evacuation.

Solutions to Where in the world?

1 San Francisco, Alcatraz
2 Broadway, Statue of Liberty, Central Park, Fifth Avenue

Chapter 12

Solutions to Assignments

Assignment 12.1: Fixed costs and variable costs

Fixed costs	Variable costs
Rent	Salaries
Council tax	National Insurance
Water, light, heating	Pensions
Insurance	Staff travel
Cleaning	Staff training
Equipment hire	Petty cash (tea, coffee etc.)
Publications	Computers, telephone
Timetables	Postage
Auditing and accounting	Advertising and publicity
Depreciation of buildings and equipment	Credit cards
	Bank charges
	Legal fees
	Bad debt

Assignment 12.2

(a) Scheduled seats bought direct from an airline or travel agent are not covered by the ATOL system, even if they are bought as part of a package. If a schedule airline ticket is bought through a travel agency or tour operator, that company acts only as an agent of the airline and the contract will be with the airline.

(b) For charter-based air travel, no. An ATOL is a legal requirement and membership of the Association of British Travel Agents is not, in itself, a substitute for the operator having an ATOL. There is of course still full protection against the tour operator failure if a booking is made with an ATOL holder by using a travel agent.

(c) An ATOL is needed by anyone who sells charter air seats, or package holidays which include charter air seats, to the public as a principal. 'Charter air seats' in this context mean not only seats on charter flights but also when scheduled airlines release seats to tour operators etc. on a charter basis.

(d) Yes, all bookings with AITO members are protected. AITO will underwrite any shortfalls in funds to ensure all consumers are fully reimbursed.

(e) No. The PSA bond protects cruise passengers and ferry passengers if part of a package. Fly/cruise passengers are protected through ATOL and CAA.

(f) Up to £11 000.

Assignment 12.3: Credit and charge cards

1 The convenience of purchasing without either a cheque book and cheque guarantee card.
2 The ability to make purchases by telephone or internet, by giving the credit card number.
3 The ability to draw cash on the card at home and abroad.
4 The facility to use a credit card for purchases or services throughout the world.
5 The flexibility to spread the bills.
6 The ability to make unexpected purchases, perhaps at a sale, making a large saving on the usual price, without using cash.

Solutions to Dilemmas

1: Balance of payment shortage

This was a real life dilemma and the outcome was dreadful!

The client was notified of the shortage, was offended and never booked with the travel company again. The client refused to pay the additional amount on the grounds that it had been checked by a member of staff. A loyal customer who had spent thousands of pounds over the years was lost. Flowers were sent to the ship to wish the client 'Bon Voyage' but the sparkle had gone.

With hindsight:

1 The manager should have met the valued client at the office and counted the money.

2 When the error was discovered the company could have written off the deficit in order to keep the business.

3 As the error was the responsibility of the manager and travel consultant they could have made the gesture of compensating their employers, this would probably have been waived with a reminder to be more careful in future.

2: Stranded abroad with no cash

Reduce risks	Keep money in separate places
	Take small amounts of mixture – traveller's cheques, cash, credit card
	Keep record of traveller's cheques separate
	Keep small amounts in money belt
No money at all	Contact someone at home (reverse charges) and have money sent by Western Union (0800 833 833 – 24 hours). It can send money to banks and offices in 200 countries. Also British Consul, British Embassy or British High Commission may help in an emergency
Replacing traveller's cheques and credit cards	The cheques are self-insured, the receipts with serial number are required and the emergency contact number. They are usually replaced within 24 hours
	Replacement of credit cards also take about 24 hours. The emergency contact number will be required
Loss of passport	A replacement can be obtained from the nearest British Embassy, High Commission or Consulate. It must be reported to the police

Solutions to Exercise 12.1: Foreign currency

1 (a) £90 worth of Canadian dollars = CAN $225, (b) 35 divided by 3.40 = £10.29
2 (a) £400 worth of Australian dollars = Aus $1108, (b) 45 divided by 3.10 = £14.51
3 (a) £290 worth of US dollars = £400.20, (b) 120 divided by 1.94 = £61.85

Solutions to Where in the world?

The Vatican City

Chapter 13

Solutions to Exercises

Exercise 13.1

1 Answer calls promptly
2 Do not leave the caller on hold
3 Think about the greeting – not too long or too short

4 Control the tone, pace and volume of your voice
5 Do not use words that are ugly or hard to understand
6 Allow thinking and writing time
7 Aim to communicate simply and easily
8 Try to sound warm and friendly but not emotional

Exercise 13.3

(a) When are you travelling to Japan?
   How are you travelling to Japan?
(b) When did you last travel to Madeira?
   Why would you like to travel to Madeira?
(c) Who will be travelling with you?
   How many people are travelling in your party?
(d) Which mode of transport have you chosen?
   Why have you chosen a holiday by rail?

Solutions to Where in the world?

1 Lisbon
2 Thailand

Chapter 14

Solutions to Case studies

14.1 Mr Benson – Change of airport

You would need to establish that all this did happen as reported because there could be many events that would cause Mr Benson to miss his flight departing from Paris Orly Airport. The flight arriving into Charles de Gaulle could have been delayed for a variety of reasons (industrial disputes, weather conditions, technical problems, etc.). There are many reasons why Mr Benson could have been delayed travelling from one airport to another. Having established that none of these reasons did take place, on checking your record of the reservations, it is quite clear that the connecting time between the two flights was not sufficient. You are left standing with a very red face, and very nervous!

Being human, we all make mistakes. But this fact does not help Mr Benson. He wants know what you are going to do to put things right. In this particular case you can do nothing to alter the situation: it happened – Mr Benson missed part of the important meeting, and was also greatly inconvenienced. All you can do is offer some kind of compensation and ask him to give you another chance.

After the apologies, the travel agency would offer perhaps a complimentary weekend away for two, or a reduction on the next travel arrangements made for Mr Benson. You would need to assure the client that it would not happen again, and make perfectly sure that it does not. Double check every detail of the reservations you finalise. It is unlikely that you would ever make that same mistake again, you probably will never completely forget that nervous feeling!

Of course, your travel agency will not be able to offer compensation for every mistake that is made. However, when the fault is genuinely with the travel agency, and you wish to keep your client's business, the gesture must be made. Yes, we do have computers to pick up connecting times, but it has been known for data to slip through the safety net.

14.2 Mr Hart – no rail reservation

At this stage, Mr Hart is not concerned whether his secretary gave the incorrect date or whether you misheard the instructions. He needs to get to the conference in Edinburgh. Offer an alternative. The flight from London to Edinburgh takes one hour ten minutes. He will miss part of the conference, but it may still be worthwhile for him to attend. The refund from the rail reservation can be put towards the air fare, and adjustments can be discussed on his return. In future, even last-minute simple bookings should be confirmed in writing. The tickets would have the date for which they were booked printed on them, but, once again, this fact slipped through the net.

14.3 Miss Jones and the cheque

Check discreetly to find out whether she is on holiday or has in fact left the company! Wait until she returns and speak privately to her. It could just be a miscalculation when her salary was paid into her own bank account. Fingers crossed!

Other solutions

Unaccompanied 16-year-olds
Try the Youth Hostel Association Tel: 0870 870 8808 www.yha.org.uk
The Field Studies Council Tel: 01743 852100 www.field-studies-council.org
PGL Tel: 01989 767767 www.pgl.co.uk

Parents needing a holiday nanny
Try Tinies Childcare Tel: 020 7384 0322 www.tinies.co.uk
Some tour operators also feature this childcare option.

Solutions to Where in the world?

1 Cuba, Havana
2 Japan, Sapporo on Hokkaido, the Bullet Train

Glossary of terms

ABTA   Association of British Travel Agents

Agency account number   A reference number given to travel agents by a principal for easy identification

Balance of payment   The final amount of money due

Charter flight   Aircraft rented for a specific journey, can be shared by many tour operators

Check-in   Reporting time prior to departure

Client   The customer

Comprehensive insurance   A policy that embraces most eventualities

Confirmed   Positive – term used to indicate a travel or holiday booking is guaranteed

Deposit   An initial payment to secure a reservation

Discounted fares   Fares sold at a reduced price

Domestic flight   Flight within one country

En route   During the journey

Flight schedule   Published times of flight operation

Full board   Three meals per day

General Sales Agent   An agent representing a company in a country where the principal does not have a sales office. The General Sales Agent represents many companies and is paid by those companies for this service. This enables travel companies to have representatives throughout the world without actually having their own office.

Half board   Two meals a day, usually breakfast and dinner

IATA / UFTAA   International Air Transport Association and Universal Federation of Travel Agents' Association

Incentive tour   A travel arrangement given as a reward for an achievement

Inclusive tour   Travel arrangements that include several services, for example accommodation, flight, car rental and so on, sold at one price

International flight   Flight service operating between different countries

No show   Non-arrival, passenger does not turn up

Package holiday   Travel arrangements packaged and sold at one price

PAX Abbreviation for passengers

Producer Company that has a product to sell, also known as principal, for example hotel, airline, car rental company, shipping company and so on

Retailer The sales outlet. The travel agent is the retailer for travel goods

Round trip The term means travel from one point to another and return by any air route for which the same normal all year through one-way fare of the same class applies from the point of origin

Scheduled flight Flight that is published and will operate regardless of number of passengers. Usually the national airline

Spouse fare A discounted fare for a husband or wife travelling together

Third-party insurance Insurance against damage to someone else or their property

Validity Time limit minimum validity and maximum validity

Volume of traffic Amount of business, activity, people and so on

Wait-listed Waiting for the reservation to be confirmed

Wholesaler The tour operator, packaging the services together

Index